Costing Adult Attention Deficit Hyperactivity Disorder

The Rockwool Foundation Research Unit

The objective of the Rockwool Foundation Research Unit is to use its independent status to produce new, empirically based analyses related to the current problems faced by modern society, particularly within the areas of labour-market conditions (including the spread of undeclared work in Denmark and other North European countries) and the functions, stability, and legitimacy of the welfare state. The Rockwool Foundation takes it to be self-evident that a deep insight into the nature of a problem is a prerequisite for its solution.

With this primary objective of acquiring new knowledge about important social questions, the Research Unit has made a considerable impact since 1987 through a number of important research projects.

The Rockwool Foundation took the initiative to establish the Rockwool Foundation Research Unit in 1987. From the outset, the topics and the unit's research projects have been decided upon by the Board of the Foundation, which also grants the finance necessary to carry out the research. Once the topic, time frame, and budget of the project have been agreed upon, the research is carried out by the research unit, acting totally independently of the foundation. Since 2003 the research unit has been headed by Research Director and Professor Torben Tranæs, M.Sc., Ph.D. (Economics).

ROCKWOOL° FOUNDATION RESEARCH UNIT

Costing Adult Attention Deficit Hyperactivity Disorder

Impact on the Individual and Society

Cost Analysis Study Group for ADHD:
David Daley
Rasmus Højbjerg Jacobsen
Anne-Mette Lange
Anders Sørensen
Jeanette Walldorf

OXFORD
UNIVERSITY PRESS

OXFORD
UNIVERSITY PRESS

Great Clarendon Street, Oxford, OX2 6DP,
United Kingdom

Oxford University Press is a department of the University of Oxford.
It furthers the University's objective of excellence in research, scholarship,
and education by publishing worldwide. Oxford is a registered trade mark of
Oxford University Press in the UK and in certain other countries

© Rockwool Foundation Research Unit 2015

The moral rights of the authors have been asserted

First Edition published in 2015

Published in the United States of America by Oxford University Press
198 Madison Avenue, New York, NY 10016, United States of America

British Library Cataloguing in Publication Data
Data available

Library of Congress Control Number: 2015930101

ISBN 978-0-19-874555-6

The community stagnates without the impulse of the individual.
The impulse dies away without the sympathy of the community.

William James, American philosopher and psychologist
(1842–1910)

Foreword

The rapid increase over the past two decades in the number of both children and adults diagnosed with ADHD (Attention Deficit Hyperactivity Disorder) raises questions regarding the related costs. What are the costs to the individuals who suffer from ADHD and—more broadly—what are the costs of the disorder itself to society?

Since satisfactory scientific answers had not yet been provided to these important questions, the Rockwool Foundation decided in 2011 to grant funds to a project that would examine the subject in detail.

The purpose of this research, which is the central outcome from the grant, is to present the empirical results from the project, as described below in the Preface by the principal investigator, Professor Anders Sørensen.

The project has been carried out as a collaboration between the Rockwool Foundation Research Unit and a number of leading researchers in the field. The organization of the project, the participating researchers, and the aims of this book are described in more detail in the Preface by Anders Sørensen.

Over the course of the project I have witnessed sustained commitment, discipline, and academic excellence, and I wish to thank all the researchers involved most warmly.

As is the case with all the Rockwool Foundation Research Unit's projects, the research has been carried out with complete academic independence and free from the influence of any party, including the Rockwool Foundation itself, which simply provided the necessary resources for the project.

I would like to express my gratitude to the Rockwool Foundation and especially to Lars Nørby Johansen, Chairman of the Board, and President Elin Schmidt for their continued interest in the work of the Research Unit—including the preparation of this book.

Torben Tranæs
Research Director, Rockwool Foundation Research Unit
Copenhagen, January 2015

Preface

The rapid increase in the number of individuals diagnosed with ADHD (Attention Deficit Hyperactivity Disorder) among both children and adults over the past two decades raises questions regarding related costs. What are the costs to individuals with ADHD and—more broadly—what are the costs to society of the disorder? The purpose of this project is to answer these questions by estimating costs related to a long list of indicators associated with an individual: educational attainment, occupational status, income, family situation, criminal record, health, etc.

The existing literature on the costs of ADHD has many limitations. Although the evidence suggests that ADHD results in higher health-care and social costs, there are limitations in the design and sampling procedure of most of the studies that have examined the link between ADHD and health economics. The majority of studies have been conducted using American health-insurance databases, where belonging to a specific health insurer is indicative of socio-economic status. The aim of the present study is therefore to address the many methodological limitations in the current health-economics literature on ADHD by tapping into the unique Central Person Register (CPR) databases in Denmark. Thereby, the study will be based on rich and detailed Danish register data that cover the entire Danish population.

A key focus is to study the costs related to individuals with the condition who are not diagnosed and not treated. The study will identify important factors in an individual's life and investigate the extent to which individuals with undiagnosed ADHD in childhood fare differently to otherwise similar individuals without ADHD. The study, therefore, uses a retrospective evaluation of the private and social costs through life for individuals who receive a diagnosis of ADHD in adulthood. By using the CPR database, this retrospective analysis will allow an examination of the costs of ADHD while avoiding the contamination and bias of diagnosis and treatment for ADHD.

In this book the private and social cost estimates for ADHD are presented. The book also includes a summary of the findings in the study, a detailed description of ADHD, a description of the structure and organization of Danish mental-health services, a detailed description of the identification of treatment groups, the descriptive statistics for these groups when compared to the adult Danish population, as well as a description of the methodology and the econometric challenges of the project. Moreover, the estimated differences between individuals diagnosed with ADHD later in life and non-ADHD but otherwise similar individuals are presented.

The project is carried out by researchers affiliated to the Centre for Economic and Business Research (CEBR) at Copenhagen Business School. The study group consists of Professor David Daley, University of Nottingham, UK, clinical psychologist Anne-Mette Lange, Aarhus University Hospital, senior advisor Rasmus Højbjerg Jacobsen, scientific assistant Jeanette Walldorf, and Professor Anders Sørensen (principal investigator), Copenhagen Business School. We are grateful for the financial support of the Rockwool Foundation Research Unit.

Special thanks go to Torben Tranæs, Research Director and Professor, the Rockwool Foundation Research Unit, who tirelessly provided comments and asked questions. We would also like to thank Per Jørgensen, Medical Executive of Psychiatry and Social Affairs at the Region of Central Jutland, Jette Myglegaard, President of the Danish ADHD Association, and Camilla Lydiksen, Director of the Danish ADHD Association, for having read and commented on an earlier version of the manuscript. Finally, we would like to thank Philip Rosenbaum for efficient research assistance.

Anders Sørensen
Principal investigator

Contents

Part IV: The Costs of ADHD

List of Figures

List of Tables

1

Summary of Private and Social Costs of ADHD

The rapid increase in recent years in the number of children and adults diagnosed with ADHD (Attention Deficit Hyperactivity Disorder), raises a number of questions. It is unclear whether the increase is due to an increased public and professional recognition and awareness of ADHD as a debilitating human condition or to an actual increase in the incidence of individuals suffering from ADHD. Depending on the reasons behind the increase, and depending on whether effective treatments can be found, the future costs to society could be enormous. The study presented in this book estimates the private and social costs of ADHD.

The key focus of this book is to study the costs related to individuals with ADHD who have not been diagnosed and who have not received treatment. In this respect, the study makes a unique contribution to scientific knowledge by investigating the costs of untreated ADHD. The study investigates the extent to which individuals with undiagnosed ADHD in childhood fare differently to otherwise similar individuals without ADHD. A long list of important parameters in an individual's life (e.g. educational attainment, occupational status, income, family situation, criminal record, health) will be examined. The results of the study not only provide cost estimates of ADHD per se, but also create a point of reference which will be highly relevant for the evaluation of any future treatment for ADHD. In other words, it will be possible to measure the actual benefits of any treatment in the life of an individual with ADHD against the findings from the study.

Existing literature on the economic costs of ADHD suggests that ADHD results in higher health-care and social costs. Yet, so far, existing research contains considerable methodological limitations. For example, many studies have examined clinical cohorts of individuals diagnosed with ADHD (Hakkaart-van Roijen et al., 2007). Individuals who are currently receiving treatment for ADHD are more likely to exhibit higher health costs, but may not be representative of individuals with ADHD who are not in contact with clinical services (Leibson et al., 2001). In addition, treatment, and especially pharmacological treatment, should and does change the nature of health- and social-care utilization, leading to higher health costs in the short term but hopefully lower costs in the long run. The samples used in most economic cost evaluations of ADHD tend to be skewed, and unrepresentative of the wider population with ADHD. For example, the majority of studies have been conducted using American health-insurance databases, where belonging to a specific health insurer is indicative of socio-economic status, and the subsequent cost findings may not hold for other countries (Matza et al., 2005). Most health economics studies on ADHD have used insurance company claims data, which rarely contain accurate or detailed clinical information, thereby limiting the clinical validity of those studies (Hinnenthal, Perwien, and Sterling, 2005).

In order to address and overcome the limitations in the current health-economic literature on ADHD, the present study taps into the unique Danish Central Person Register (CPR) databases. The study uses a retrospective evaluation of the private and social costs through life for individuals who receive a diagnosis of ADHD in adulthood. The rationale behind the focus on adults diagnosed with ADHD in adulthood is really quite simple and should be understood in the context of the aim to investigate the cost of untreated ADHD. ADHD is a developmental disorder, and in order to receive a diagnosis of ADHD, the core symptoms of ADHD must be present from early childhood, according to diagnostic criteria. It is therefore possible to assume that individuals diagnosed in adulthood will have lived with undiagnosed and untreated ADHD throughout their childhood and adolescence. Thus, by using the CPR databases, this retrospective analysis will allow an examination of the costs of ADHD while avoiding the contamination and bias of diagnosis and treatment for ADHD. This will be an important contribution in itself, as well as the correct benchmark for an evaluation of the costs of individuals with ADHD who have received treatment. The study is based on data that cover the entire Danish population.

The presented study answers the research question 'What are the private and social costs of ADHD for individuals who have been diagnosed as adults?' To answer this question, the project:

i) identifies individuals who were diagnosed with ADHD later in life (i.e., after they turned 18 years of age), and explores their private and social costs;

ii) measures private and social costs on different dimensions, comparing the ADHD group with a number of different clinical and non-clinical control groups.

1.1 Attention Deficit Hyperactivity Disorder (ADHD)

ADHD is a developmental disorder characterized by developmentally inappropriate levels of hyperactivity, impulsivity, and inattention, according to the American Psychiatric Association's (APA) Diagnostic and Statistical Manual, fifth edition (DSM-5; American Psychiatric Association, 2013). In order to fulfil the diagnostic criteria, individuals must experience a minimum of six symptoms of inattention (e.g. failing to sustain attention in tasks or play activities, not listening when being spoken to directly), or six symptoms of hyperactivity/impulsivity (e.g. talking excessively, fidgeting with hands or feet). Symptoms must be persistent and interfere with functioning or development. For adults to fulfil the criteria of ADHD, symptoms must have been present since the age of 12. The age of symptom onset has been changed in the DSM-5 publication in 2013. Previously, the DSM criterion for the age of symptom onset was in early childhood by the age of 7 years.

In Europe, however, a different diagnostic classification system, the International Classification of Diseases (ICD-10; World Health Organization, 1992), is generally used, and the criterion for when symptoms must be present is still before the age of 7. The ICD-10 generally states more stringent diagnostic criteria for what is labelled Hyperkinetic Disorder. Regardless of the diagnostic manual used, however, the term ADHD is the commonly agreed everyday label used to describe disorders of inattention, hyperactivity, and impulsivity.

1.1.1 Prevalence and Developmental Course

ADHD is common, with a worldwide prevalence estimated at approximately 3–5 per cent (Polanczyk et al., 2007; 2014). Originally seen as a disorder of childhood, the lifelong prevalence of ADHD is now widely acknowledged. Symptoms and neuropsychological impairments associated with ADHD are evident in preschool children (Daley et al., 2009), and although symptoms may decline with age in some cases, ADHD symptoms and impairments can persist into adulthood (Geissler and Lesch, 2011). Prevalence rates in adult community samples are estimated at approximately 2.5 per cent (Simon et al., 2009). It is likely that a substantial number of young people accessing services for ADHD will require transition into adult services (Taylor et al., 2010). Consequently, adult ADHD services are now developing in many parts of Europe.

1.1.2 Aetiology

Despite being one of the most studied psychiatric disorders, the exact cause of ADHD is still unknown (Thapar et al., 2013). Potential risk factors can be

3

considered in terms of biological and environmental factors with emerging aetiological research focusing on potential interactions and correlations between inherited (genetic) and non-inherited (environmental) factors which may heighten risk for ADHD.

1.1.3 *Comorbidities and Functional Impairments*

Individuals with ADHD often present with a number of other psychiatric conditions and functional impairments which may become evident during clinical assessments. Whilst a discussion of all the possible presenting comorbid conditions and functioning deficits associated with ADHD is beyond the scope of this review, we touch upon some of the most common in the lives of individuals with ADHD.

1.1.4 *Academic Functioning*

Academic underachievement is a common feature of individuals with ADHD and is evident from preschool (DuPaul et al., 2001). ADHD is associated with poorer grades and lower scores on standardized tests of academic ability (Barry et al., 2002; Loe and Feldman, 2007). It has been suggested that symptoms of inattention and executive function deficits may play a larger role in academic functioning deficits than symptoms of hyperactivity or comorbid disruptive behaviour (Daley and Birchwood, 2010). Individuals with ADHD are more likely to require specialist academic support, repeat a school year, or leave school with few or no qualifications (Barkley et al., 2006).

1.1.5 *Disruptive Behaviour Disorders*

ADHD is highly comorbid with disruptive behaviour disorders including Oppositional Defiant Disorder (ODD) and Conduct Disorder (CD). As many as 50 per cent of children also display CD or ODD (Biederman et al., 1991; Faraone et al., 2003). Early intervention may be key with children displaying early signs of hyperactivity and disruptive behaviour, given the added complexity and more adverse long-term outcomes associated with comorbid behavioural problems (Connor et al., 2010).

1.1.6 *Substance Misuse*

ADHD is also associated with later substance misuse. Approximately one in four individuals with substance dependence will also have ADHD (van Emmerik-van Oortmerssen et al., 2012). It is unclear at this stage to what extent this association is accounted for by comorbid CD. Whilst it is likely that children with comorbid CD are at heightened risk for later substance misuse (Lee et al., 2011), the independent effect of ADHD symptoms on later substance misuse is also evident (Szobot et al., 2007).

In the remainder of this chapter, the main findings of the project are presented. The main findings are grouped in descriptive statistics for adult individuals with ADHD and the private and social costs of the ADHD group. The results demonstrate the considerable financial burden of ADHD on both the individual and the state, even when other relevant factors are controlled for. Finally, a number of recommendations based on the project's findings are presented.

1.2 Identification of Treatment Groups

In order to access information relevant to the social and private costs of ADHD in adults, the present study has accessed information on individuals diagnosed with ADHD through the Danish Psychiatric Central Register and the Danish Register of Medicinal Products Statistics. The Danish Psychiatric Central Register is an electronic register containing information on every psychiatric admission from 1969 onwards, with data on outpatient treatment and psychiatric accident and emergency department contacts included from 1995 (see Mors et al., 2011). The register contains individuals' unique Danish personal identification number (CPR number), which allows for register linkage with every other population-based register in Denmark. It is mandatory for all secondary sector hospital in- and outpatient mental-health services to register the above information in the Danish National Patient Register from which monthly updates are transferred onto the Danish Psychiatric Central Register. Psychiatrists in private practice and GPs are not required to register psychiatric patient data in the National Patient Register. Thus, the Register contains psychiatric data on patients referred to and diagnosed in secondary hospital-based in- and outpatient mental-health services only. Individuals referred to, assessed, and treated in primary and private-sector mental-health services, who are prescribed ADHD medications, but who are not formally diagnosed in the secondary mental-health sector, do not appear in the Danish Psychiatric Central Register.

The population of patients with ADHD identified through the Danish Psychiatric Central Register contains all individuals who received at least one of five specific ICD-10 Hyperkinetic (ADHD) diagnoses between 1995 and 2010 and who were between 18 and 50 years of age at the time of diagnosis. This results in a group of 5,331 individuals identified through the Danish Psychiatric Central Register.

The study also identifies individuals with ADHD from the Danish Register of Medicinal Products Statistics (RMPS), maintained by the Danish Medicines Agency. In this register, individual-level data on all prescription drugs sold in Danish community pharmacies has been recorded since 1994 (Kildemoes et al., 2011). Considering that ADHD is a condition which often does not require inpatient or highly specialized services at the secondary level of mental-health care provision, a considerable number of individuals in need of an assessment for ADHD are referred not to highly specialist hospital-based psychiatry units, but for an assessment in private psychiatric practice. Psychiatrists in private practice do not enter patients' diagnoses or data into the Danish registers. So in order for our analysis to capture this potentially large group of individuals with ADHD, the study accesses data from the Register of Medicinal Products Statistics. This register allows data on ADHD medication prescriptions at an individual level to be retrieved and linked with many other nationwide individual-level data sources (Kildemoes et al., 2011).

For the purpose of the present study, ADHD medications have been defined as the purchase of a drug containing methylphenidate, atomoxetine, or dex-amphetamine. Through the Register of Medicinal Products Statistics we have identified a group of individuals prescribed at least one of the three types of medicines in adulthood, between the ages of 18 and 50 from 1995 to 2010. 2010 was the most recent year of accessible, complete register data from Statistics Denmark at the time our analyses commenced. We have excluded individuals with specific psychiatric disorders (including dementia, narcolepsy, and pervasive developmental disorders) from this group because of their non-representativeness of ADHD per se. And we have excluded individuals above the age of 50 who received a prescription for the first time, due to the possibility of the prescription of ADHD medications for other conditions than ADHD. The study has therefore set a pragmatic upper-age-inclusion criterion at 50 years for first diagnosis or first prescription of ADHD medication for all individuals. A group of 13,662 individuals was specifically recruited from the Register of Medicinal Products. The two treatment groups are independent of each other such that there is no overlap in the populations. Individuals who have received an ADHD diagnosis in the secondary care hospital-based system are always included in the former treatment group and not in the latter. If an individual has received the diagnosis in a year before receiving medication for the first time, we register the diagnosis in the year it has been received. If an individual has purchased ADHD medication in a year before receiving the diagnosis, we register the diagnosis at the time of the first purchase of medication.

We combine the information about individuals diagnosed with ADHD from the Danish Psychiatric Central Register and the Register of Medicinal Products Statistics with information from a number of other registers available from

Statistics Denmark covering demographic background, educational attainment, the labour market, crimes committed, traffic accidents, and foster care.

1.3 Descriptive Statistics

Table 1.1 shows a number of statistics comparing individuals with ADHD diagnosed as adults to the members of the general population who have never been diagnosed with ADHD. In order to make the comparison more valid, we only use the adult population aged 18–65 as the comparison group. This is because the treatment groups are also limited to individuals aged 18–65, as explained above in Section 1.2.

The first section of Table 1.1 contains information about demographic background. Almost three-quarters of all individuals with ADHD who were diagnosed as adults are 40 years old or younger. This means that individuals with ADHD are on average younger than the general adult population, where only 35 per cent are 40 years old or younger. The share of males is almost 60 per cent among individuals with ADHD, but only 51 per cent among the general population. Finally, relatively fewer first- or second-generation immigrants have been diagnosed with ADHD.

The second section of Table 1.1 shows labour-market variables. The average wage income of individuals with ADHD diagnosed as adults is 26,000 euros,[1] when they are in employment, compared to the average work salary of 41,000 euros for individuals who do not have ADHD. When we look at total income (i.e., wage income and income from all other sources), this difference narrows slightly. Finally, only 33 per cent of individuals with ADHD are wage employed compared to 67 per cent among the general adult population.

The third section of Table 1.1 illustrates that just over half of individuals diagnosed with ADHD as adults have completed minimum education as their highest educational attainment. For the general population this share is only 38 per cent. Fewer than one in eight individuals with ADHD complete tertiary education, but almost one in four of the general population achieves this.

In the fourth section of Table 1.1 family-background variables are shown. As illustrated, individuals with ADHD diagnosed as adults have fewer children on average than members of the adult population who do not have ADHD. Yet this could be due to the fact that the ADHD group is younger. With respect to number of siblings, there are no large differences between the two groups, except that 34 per cent of individuals with ADHD have three siblings or more, while only 29 per cent of the general population does. Sixty-two per cent of

---

[1] Throughout this book, we use an exchange rate of 7.45 Danish kroner per euro.

Table 1.1. Selected descriptive statistics

	Adults with ADHD	General population (cut off at age 65)
Demographic background		
Percentage aged 18–25	28.5	14.2
Percentage aged 26–40	45.8	31.0
Percentage aged 40+	25.7	54.8
Percentage male	59.3	51.1
Percentage immigrants	5.8	15.8
Labour market		
Average annual wage income, EUR	26,130	41,458
Total annual income, EUR	28,383	43,078
Percentage wage employed	33.1	67.1
Education		
Percentage only minimum level	54.5	38.3
Percentage obtained third level	11.0	19.3
Family		
Number of children		
0	49.8	38.6
1	16.8	15.1
2	20.3	30.3
3+	13.1	16.1
Number of siblings		
0	6.1	7.3
1	32.4	35.6
2	27.8	28.4
3+	33.8	28.8
Stable childhood*	62.2	78.0
Percentage having been placed away from home	22.1	3.1
Average yearly parental income, EUR**	59,632	63,660
Share of parents with only minimum education	39.6	35.6
Health		
Average number of comorbid psychiatric diagnoses***	2.5	0.3
Percentage receiving ADHD medicine	95.9	–
Average spending on medicine, EUR	1304	209
Average number of primary-care services	30.8	16.5
Average number of secondary inpatient days	4.5	2.4
Crime and traffic		
Percentage with conviction or fine****	50.8	19.7
Percentage with conviction or fine under Road Traffic Act	13.5	11.4
Percentage having been in traffic accident*****	7.0	2.2
Age at diagnosis (percentage)		
18–20	16.0	–
21–25	18.9	–
26–30	16.0	–
31+	49.1	–

* If the individual's parents have been living together and the individual only has siblings with the same mother and father, or is an only child.
** Average yearly parental income until the 18th birthday of the individual with ADHD.
*** Psychiatric diagnoses per person.
**** Share of the individuals that have been convicted at least once.
***** Share of the individuals that have been in a traffic accident at least once.

individuals with ADHD come from a stable family background, compared to 78 per cent of the general population. Individuals with ADHD are much more likely to have experienced placement outside the home. Of adults in the ADHD group, 22 per cent have experienced placements outside the home at some stage in their lives, compared to only 3 per cent in the general population. Parents of individuals with ADHD earn slightly less and have on average a slightly lower education level than parents of individuals in the general population.

The fifth section of the table shows statistics related to health and health care. Individuals with ADHD diagnosed as adults have on average 2.5 psychiatric diagnoses (in addition to the ADHD diagnosis), whereas individuals from the general population have only 0.3 diagnoses on average. Also, expenses on prescription medicine, number of hospital inpatient days, and the number of primary health-care services received by individuals with ADHD are all significantly higher than for members of the general population.

Section six also shows that 51 per cent of individuals with ADHD have received a conviction or a fine, and fewer than one third of these involve road traffic fines. By implication, over two-thirds of convictions in the group of adults with ADHD involve more serious crimes such as property crimes or violent crimes. For the general population only slightly less than one-fifth have ever received a conviction or fine, and the majority of these are traffic fines.

The final part of Table 1.1 summarizes the age at diagnosis among the individuals with ADHD. Roughly half have been diagnosed before they turned 30, with more or less one in six being diagnosed in early adulthood aged 18–20.

1.4 Cost Calculation

The total private and social costs of ADHD have been calculated based on estimates of the difference in performance between individuals with ADHD and individuals from different control groups (see chapters 7 and 8 for description of selection procedures). One control group is based on the entire adult population whereas the other control group is based on siblings of the individuals with ADHD. It should be emphasized that basing a cost analysis of ADHD on a sibling-based analysis has never been carried out before.

The advantage of the sibling-based analysis is that siblings are similar with respect to many of the aspects that are difficult to observe; these aspects may influence characteristics concerning education and income, among others. For example, genetic differences and social-background factors during childhood and upbringing are similar across siblings. In this sense, we reduce the risk of unobserved differences between the treatment and control groups playing an important role in determining the differences between individuals with ADHD and individuals without. Thus, we attempt to explore possible biases that may influence the cost estimates to approximate the costs of ADHD as accurately as possible.

By *the private costs of ADHD* we refer to all costs sustained by individuals. This means that the private costs include the following areas: loss of work income, income replacement transfers, individual costs of being a victim of a crime, and private costs of prescription medicine.

The public costs of ADHD are all costs paid by the local or central government. This includes income transfers, cost of crime (police and correctional system), state education, cost of traffic accidents, cost of foster care, and preventive measures,[2] and cost of publicly provided health care including subsidies for prescription medicine.

It should be mentioned that some income transfers to ADHD individuals are not counted as public costs because they are redistributions between groups within the private sector. This is the case, for example, when unemployment benefits are financed through privately organized unemployment insurance, implying that such transfers represent redistributions across groups within the private sector. *The social costs of ADHD* are the total costs to society as a whole and are defined as the sum of the private and the public costs.

When calculating the costs of ADHD we use the cross-sectional method, which means that we use the data on individuals from a single year and calculate the cost for this specific year (in this case 2010, which is the latest year for which data are available). The costs we report are therefore to be interpreted as average yearly costs of ADHD.

The monetary cost measures used in the calculations come from a variety of different sources. Some of the estimated differences in outcomes are measured directly in monetary terms—wage income, for example. For other outcomes the estimated differences are measured in shares or in crude numbers. This is true for placements outside the home, for example, where the unit cost of placements away from home is calculated by dividing the total public costs to placements by the number of individuals placed away from home at the end of 2010.

---

[2] Preventive measures are social measures aimed at children or youths. These measures take place in the local environment and are aimed at avoiding having to take individuals away from family and environment. These measures include an institutionalized contact person and youth sanctions (where the young person is obliged to attend classes or be in his/her home at specific times).

The estimation of outcome differences between individuals with ADHD and their control group of non-ADHD individuals is an important part of the cost calculations. For example, it is important to know the difference in the share of individuals who are wage employed as well as the difference in wage income between the two groups in order to calculate the difference in wage income before tax. The estimation of such outcome differences is an important task for this project.

The cost measures presented below are estimates for *individuals diagnosed with ADHD later in life*. These measures will (most likely) deviate from the costs for the combined group of individuals diagnosed with ADHD later in life *and adults with ADHD not yet diagnosed* as there are many individuals with undiagnosed ADHD in the adult population (see Dalsgaard et al., 2013). We consider cost measures for the combined group of individuals to represent the 'true' cost of adult ADHD. The cost measures presented below will therefore deviate from the 'true' cost of adult ADHD. Before presenting the cost estimates, we discuss the consequence for the cost analysis of using ADHD diagnosed in adulthood. The *average cost* estimates presented below will probably exceed the average costs of the combined group of individuals, diagnosed or undiagnosed. This will be the case when individuals diagnosed with ADHD generally represent severe ADHD cases, whereas there is a significant number of undiagnosed individuals with (less severe) ADHD in the adult population at large. If this bias exists, the average cost estimates presented below will exceed the average costs of the entire group of adult individuals with (undiagnosed and untreated) ADHD.

Why do we assume that undiagnosed adults represent less severe cases of ADHD? One reason is that individuals with ADHD who present with considerable personal and social functional impairment are more likely to be referred to diagnostic and treatment mental health services, than less severe cases. Thus, our cost estimates cover individuals who are affected by ADHD in a way that causes considerable personal and social functional impairment. It should of course be stressed that we, by definition, cannot identify undiagnosed adults from the registers and make accurate predictions about the severity of their symptoms.

Moreover, aggregate cost estimates for individuals diagnosed with ADHD later in life will be lower than the aggregate costs for the entire group of adults with ADHD. The cost measures presented below will be underestimated when only a certain percentage of adults with ADHD are diagnosed. In this sense, we estimate the aggregate costs for the group of individuals with ADHD who have been diagnosed later in life and ignore the costs for adults with undiagnosed ADHD. Since we are focusing on ADHD in adults, the cost measures presented below also disregard costs of adults diagnosed as children.

Below, we report the private and social cost of ADHD compared to two different control groups. It should be remembered that the two control groups consist of:

i) the entire population (weighted to control for age and gender—as well as immigration status and regional residency in 2010 for individuals with ADHD)

ii) a control group we have selected from the siblings of individuals in the treatment group. Again, it should be emphasized that no cost analysis of ADHD based on a sibling-based control group has ever been carried out before. Also it should be highlighted that using sibling-based control groups constitutes an attractive methodological design as the sibling analysis is a way to handle unobserved heterogeneity within a shared environment (e.g., within the family and household).

Table 1.2 shows the individual costs of ADHD when compared to an average member of the Danish population controlled for gender and age—as well as immigration status and regional residency. The total private costs of ADHD are approximately 8,900 euros per individual, and the total public costs are approximately 15,800 euros per individual, leading to a total yearly social cost of ADHD of approximately 24,800 euros per individual when compared to an average member of the population.

The top panel of Table 1.2 outlines the private costs and shows that individuals with ADHD have a much lower disposable income on average, as the estimated loss is 7,900 euros per year. When adding the other private costs of a little over 1,000 euros, the total private cost of ADHD is found to be around 8,900 euros per individual.

Turning to the public costs in the bottom panel of Table 1.2 we can see that income replacement transfers and loss of income taxes count as a cost for the

Table 1.2. Cost difference between ADHD individuals and the general population, EUR per individual

Private costs	
Disposable income	−7,922
Other private costs	−1,009
Total private costs	**− 8,930**
Public costs	
Tax and transfers	−12,098
Educational expenses	56
Crime and traffic	−1,355
Public expenses on placements	−951
Medical expenses	−1,475
Total public costs	**−15,823**
TOTAL COSTS	**−24,753**

Note: Calculations are based on N = 18,993 identified individuals who were diagnosed with ADHD as adults.

public sector with these two areas alone leading to a public-sector loss of about 12,100 euros per individual. In addition to this, individuals with ADHD also present with larger public-sector expenses due to crime and traffic accidents of around 1,400 euros per individual and with higher health-care expenses of around 1,500 euros per individual when compared to an average member of the population.

The measured cost of ADHD of approximately 25,000 euros as an overall measure may appear quite interesting. Yet it says little about the cost of the disorder per se, as individuals who have been diagnosed with ADHD as adults differ from the general population with respect to many background characteristics.

Table 1.3 therefore shows the calculated individual private and social costs of ADHD when individuals diagnosed with ADHD are compared to a control group of their siblings who are not diagnosed with ADHD or have not been prescribed ADHD medication. By using this control group we are able to get a better estimate of the true costs of ADHD.

When compared to a control group of siblings without ADHD, the total yearly social costs are reduced to approximately 17,800 euros per individual, as illustrated in Table 1.3. The private costs are slightly lower at approximately 8,600 euros per individual, while the public costs are much lower at approximately 9,200 euros per individual.

Individuals diagnosed with ADHD as adults have a total yearly loss of disposable income of approximately 7,900 euros per individual—a loss of roughly 650 euros per month—when compared to their non-ADHD siblings. This is a significant amount when we notice that the average disposable income for individuals in Denmark was 2,200 euros per month in 2010 (Statistics Denmark, 2012). The remaining private costs are roughly 700 euros per year.

Table 1.3. Cost difference between ADHD individuals and the Sib-Demo group, EUR per individual

Private costs	
Disposable income	−7,923
Other private costs	−664
Total private costs	**−8,587**
Public costs	
Tax and transfers	−6,295
Educational expenses	89
Crime and traffic	−897
Public expenses on placements	−575
Medical expenses	−1,504
Total public costs	**−9,182**
TOTAL COSTS	**−17,769**

Note: Calculations are based on N = 18,993 identified individuals who were diagnosed with ADHD as adults.

We now turn to the public costs, where we observe a large change compared to Table 1.2. The main reason for this difference is that the estimated public costs in terms of loss of income tax revenue and extra expenses to income replacement transfers in Table 1.3 only amounts to about 6,300 euros compared to around 12,000 euros that was found when compared to the general population in Table 1.2. The main reason for this difference is that the control group of non-ADHD siblings on average are 'worse off' than the general population and therefore have a significantly smaller wage income and hence pay less income taxes. This shows the importance of using the sibling control group to control for family and genetic background.

To summarize, the total yearly loss to society in terms of lost production (measured by wage income) and costs related to health care etc. is almost 18,000 euros per individual compared to their non-ADHD siblings.

Finally, Table 1.4 shows the aggregate private and social costs when aggregating the individual numbers from Tables 1.2 and 1.3. When comparing to the general population the total social costs of ADHD for individuals diagnosed as adults were approximately 470 million euros in 2010. This figure consists of private costs of approximately 170 million euros and public costs of approximately 301 million euros. The right-hand column of Table 1.4 shows the aggregate costs of ADHD for individuals diagnosed as adults when compared to their non-ADHD siblings. In this case the estimate of the total social costs of ADHD is 337 million euros, with private costs of 163 million euros and public costs of 174 million euros.

The clear picture that emerges from the results presented in Tables 1.2–1.4 is that ADHD is associated with considerable private and social costs. As a comparison, the total social cost of arthritis was estimated at 900 million euros in a recent calculation, but arthritis is estimated to affect 17 per cent of the

Table 1.4. Aggregate social costs of ADHD diagnosed in adults, EUR millions

Private cost	Compared to general population	Compared to siblings
Disposable income	−150	−150
Other private costs	−19	−13
Total private cost	**−170**	**−163**
Public cost		
Tax and transfers	−230	−120
Educational expenses	1	2
Crime and traffic	−26	−17
Public expenses on placements	−18	−11
Medical expenses	−28	−29
Total public cost	**−301**	**−174**
TOTAL COSTS	**−470**	**−337**

Note: Calculations are based on N = 18,993 identified individuals who were diagnosed with ADHD as adults.

population, whereas the prevalence of ADHD is much lower (Johnsen et al., 2014; Polanczyk et al., 2007).

1.5 Generalizability Beyond Denmark

This study is based on analyses of data from identified groups of the Danish population with or without ADHD. It is therefore reasonable to question whether the results outlined in this book are specific to Denmark or whether it is indeed possible to generalize the results to other countries. In this section, we present a quantitative evaluation of the results obtained in the study and answer these important questions.

In Table 1.5 we present aggregate social costs for individuals with ADHD for a number of countries. The numbers are constructed using back-of-the-envelope calculations of total costs of ADHD. In addition to the Danish costs, we present results for Canada, France, the Netherlands, the US, and the UK. The calculations are carried out by simply taking the individual cost of ADHD obtained in this book and multiplying these by the prevalence rate of ADHD and by the country's population in the group between 18 and 50 years of age.

The aggregate costs presented in Table 1.5 vary for three reasons. First, the costs vary across countries due to different magnitudes of the adult population. Second, the costs vary across applied prevalence rates. Third, the costs vary across applied social costs of ADHD per individual.

Two observations from Table 1.5 should be commented upon. First, it is seen that our observed prevalence rate is lower than the estimated prevalence rate from other studies. The observed prevalence rate is as low as 0.8 per cent

Table 1.5. Aggregate social cost for ADHD individuals for different countries, EUR millions

		Canada	Denmark	France	Netherlands	United Kingdom	United States
Prevalence rate from:		Cost estimates from sibling-analysis					
Present study	0.8%	2,183	337	3,959	1,044	4,033	19,796
Simon et al. (2009)	2.5%	6,643	1,027	12,045	3,175	12,270	60,233
		Cost estimates from analysis using general population					
Present study	0.8%	3,041	470	5,515	1,454	5,618	27,577
Simon et al. (2009)	2.5%	9,254	1,431	16,780	4,424	17,093	83,909
Population (18–49 years)		14,953,601	2,311,645	27,114,916	7,148,383	27,621,979	135,592,181

Source: Based on cost estimates from Table 10.1 and Table 10.3; the prevalence rate found in this study from 18,993 individuals with ADHD diagnosed in adulthood—corresponding to 0.8%—and country-specific population in the age group 18–50 years. The latter data stem from US Census, international database. In addition to our own calculated prevalence rate, the rate from Simon et al. (2009) of 2.5% is applied.

compared to an estimated rate of 2.5 per cent from Simon et al. (2009). This means that costs are three times larger for the estimated prevalence rate compared to the observed prevalence rate. However, this aggregate cost is most likely overestimated since we have applied individual cost measures estimated for the diagnosed—probably most severe—ADHD cases. Even though this is the case, the calculation is useful for an evaluation of the generalizability beyond Denmark of the results. Second, it is seen that using the cost difference between ADHD individuals and the general population that we presented in Table 1.2 leads to higher costs than using the cost difference between ADHD individuals and their siblings presented in Table 1.3.

All in all, we find that aggregate costs are more than four times higher when using a control group based on estimated prevalence rates and individual costs from the general population, instead of using a control group based on observed prevalence rate and individual costs for siblings. This observation is important when evaluating the results established in this book. We turn to this issue next.

Most cost of illness studies in relation to ADHD have been based on children and adolescents. Only a few report costs for adults with ADHD. In a recent systematic review of US based cost studies of ADHD, Doshi et al. (2012) included nineteen studies. It was found that adult costs are significantly higher than childhood costs, since income/productivity losses are large for adults. They have calculated total costs on the basis of individual costs and have aggregated using estimated prevalence rates. Their reported adult costs do not distinguish between those diagnosed as children and those diagnosed as adults. Doshi et al. (2012) report productivity losses of between USD 87 billion and USD 138 billion out of total adult cost of between USD 105 billion and USD 194 billion. Using the estimated prevalence rate of Simon et al. (2009), we estimate a cost of almost 84 billion euros, as presented in Table 1.5. Using the average USD/EUR exchange rate of 1.27, this aggregate cost amounts to USD 107 billion, which is of the same magnitude as found in Doshi et al. (2012), though closer to the lower limit in the presented cost range.

Next, we attempt to answer the two questions about whether the results outlined in this book are specific to Denmark or whether it is indeed possible to generalize the results to other countries in a qualitative manner. To do this, we provide a brief overview of the Danish welfare system, highlighting some of the most important features of Danish society that may deviate from other countries.

Denmark is a small, high-income country that has a long tradition of social welfare (Olejaz et al., 2012). Legislation on health care and education, for example, provides residents with the right to equal access to health care and education. Financing for public services is derived through state incomes from a number of different sources including personal income tax payable on wages and almost all other forms of income (Olejaz et al., 2012). Danish welfare legislation is based on the principle that all residents are guaranteed rights and support in the event of unemployment, sickness, or dependency. Social-security benefits and social services are available to residents in need, regardless of their attachment to the labour market. Areas such as health and education have traditionally received high priority in Denmark.

The above description of the welfare state gives a few examples of how Denmark differs from other countries on public expenditure. This may lead to the obvious conclusion that the measures of outcomes in the present study cannot easily be generalized to other countries, as the outcomes used are clearly different compared to other countries. This is a fair point. The present analysis has indeed evaluated a vast range of social and private outcomes for adults with ADHD in the same study, including health, education, income transfers, crime, prison services, and so on. The range of outcomes assessed is in itself unprecedented in the current economic literature on ADHD. Yet this broad range of outcomes clearly also complicates comparisons of overall findings with other countries, as health-care systems, prison systems, education systems, and what defines them vary considerably.

It is beyond the scope of this book to provide a comprehensive comparison of social and private outcomes between countries. And while it is not the aim to present an extensive review of the complexities involved in comparing such outcomes, this discussion does warrant a brief summary of the main challenges involved in generalizing the present findings to other countries.

We are confident that the rigorous approach that we have applied to the very detailed data available from the Danish National Registers has provided results that apply not only in a Danish context but also internationally. To some degree this has been documented in Table 1.5. In addition to this, the use of sibling data to create cost differences helps to control for many differences between the Danish systems of health, social care, education, employment, and social services and those of other countries.

We argue that the remaining differences between Denmark and other countries will not lead to higher social costs. However, there will most likely be a different allocation of costs to the private and public cost categories. In the following section we discuss these differences:

- **Labour market**: The Danish labour market is characterized by relatively high earnings at the bottom of the income distribution and a relatively compressed wage distribution, such that the difference between top earners and bottom earners is smaller in Denmark compared to most other Western countries. In relation to the labour-market performance of individuals with ADHD, it may be harder to gain entry into the labour market, since very few low-wage jobs exist. If individuals with an ADHD diagnosis have lower productivity than other individuals (with the same formal qualifications), then that may lead to difficulties in finding ordinary employment in a labour market with inflexible wage rates. In combination with the generous welfare-state income transfers, the most likely implication for our study is that the difference in employment rates between ADHD individuals and the various control groups may be larger in Denmark than what would be expected in other countries. These Danish labour-market characteristics may well imply a lower employment rate of individuals with ADHD which will result in higher costs of ADHD.

• **Education:** In Denmark, education is free and, on top of this, educational support is the highest in the world. Hence, even though the educational attainment of individuals with ADHD is poor, it may be even poorer in countries where students have to pay tuition fees and take out loans to finance their studies. In addition to this, Denmark has a well-developed apprenticeship system embedded in the state education system. This may well result in a better level of education of adults with ADHD and thereby lower total costs of ADHD.

• **Income transfers:** One important difference between Denmark and other countries is that income transfers from the state to individuals are relatively generous. This may well imply that the Danish state has to cover a larger share of total social costs compared to other countries. The flip side is, of course, that individuals with ADHD have to cover a lower cost share. As a consequence, the private costs of ADHD may well be higher in other countries, whereas the public costs may be lower.

Even though the Danish welfare state in many respects is different from other countries, we have applied our findings for social costs of ADHD per individual to other countries, such as the UK and the US. We presented the quantitative findings in Table 1.5 and we have presented a qualitative approach by discussing generalizability beyond Denmark. We find aggregate ADHD costs for the US of the same magnitude as those found in a study for the US with robust cost estimates (Doshi et al., 2012) when using our Danish cost estimates for the US in back-of-the-envelope calculations. Consequently, we believe that our cost estimates for Denmark—especially total social costs per individual—can be used for calculating conservative estimates of aggregate social costs of ADHD for other countries.

1.6 Findings, Current Literature, and Key Recommendations

The clear picture emerging from this study is that ADHD is associated with considerable private and social costs. From an 'invest to save' perspective, recommendations that might mitigate the early impact of ADHD on academic attainment, family well-being, and early career productivity are made. From this perspective, the purpose of early investment would be to help reduce the long-term impact of ADHD, but also reduce costs to the individual as well as the state. These recommendations are set out in the following sections.

1.6.1 *Employment, Income, and Tax Contributions*

FINDINGS
- There is a considerable negative impact of ADHD on employment, income, and therefore tax contributions. Compared to adults in the general population, adults with ADHD experience much lower levels of employment, considerably lower levels of wage income, and therefore make less tax contributions.

- Adults with ADHD are therefore on average in receipt of much greater levels of income support from the Danish Government than adults in the general population.

CURRENT LITERATURE
- Adults with ADHD, as a group, experience impairment in all aspects related to employment, from the initial job search, to the interview, and then in employment (Adamou et al., 2013).

RECOMMENDATIONS
- The occupational functioning of adults with ADHD should be explored. There is a need for an informed understanding of possible barriers to employment for adults with ADHD, but also of the mediating factors that may lead to successful employment.

- The best ways to address the vocational needs of individuals with ADHD to increase employability and improve occupational achievement should be investigated, in order to facilitate the development of effective employment schemes.

1.6.2 *Educational Attainment*

FINDINGS
- There is considerable impact of ADHD on educational attainment, both in terms of the highest level of education achieved and the grades achieved for core subjects, when compared against the average Danish citizen.

- The striking differences in educational attainment remain even when demographic and parental variables are controlled for.

- In reality, the very negative impact of ADHD on academic attainment means that the majority of individuals with ADHD are going to be consigned to low incomes for their entire lifetime.

CURRENT LITERATURE

- Most children with ADHD do not enter school with the core skills necessary to their education. They lack the concentration skills necessary to engage successfully in lessons, and have levels of impulsivity and hyperactivity that make managing the child in the classroom difficult (Daley 2006; Tarver, Daley, and Sayal, 2014).
- School-related difficulties in the primary school years include disruptive classroom behaviour and academic underperformance, including poor scores on standardized tests of achievement (Frazier et al., 2007). These difficulties continue into adulthood and have been demonstrated in both estimates of academic achievement and also actual exam performance (Birchwood and Daley, 2012).

RECOMMENDATIONS

- Ways to facilitate and ensure school readiness are important to secure a positive developmental pathway for children with early symptoms of ADHD.
- The investigation and development of effective inclusion practices and interventions in schools for children with moderate to severe ADHD should be initiated.

1.6.3 *Crime and Driving*

FINDINGS

- Adults with ADHD commit more crimes and driving offences than the Danish average, and also commit more crimes and driving offences than their sibling controls.
- Individuals with ADHD are also more likely to be the victims of crime than adults in the general population.

CURRENT LITERATURE

- A recent Danish study (Dalsgaard et al., 2013) which followed a cohort of children who received a diagnosis of ADHD reported that 47 per cent of the sample had received a criminal conviction in adulthood.
- Adults with ADHD are more likely to have traffic accidents (Vaa, 2003; Jerome et al., 2006). These risks are then compounded by the fact that adults with ADHD drive more frequently than adults without ADHD, which means that their poor driving skills represent a greater road-safety threat (Vaa, 2013).

RECOMMENDATIONS

- There should be an exploration of the best ways to identify and treat ADHD symptoms in the prison population and in young offenders to reduce crime in order to prevent the cycle of re-offending and the high costs attributed to the judicial and prison systems.

- Adults with ADHD should be made more aware of the potential impact of their ADHD symptoms on driving performance in order to reduce traffic offences.

1.6.4 *Health-care Utilization*

FINDINGS

- Adults with ADHD use more health-care services than the Danish average, and also use more health-care services than their sibling controls.

CURRENT LITERATURE

- Some of these differences can be attributed to assessment and treatments related to their ADHD (Doshi et al., 2012), and from accidents that result from inattention and impulsivity (Lange et al., 2014); other health-care usage may arise from common health-care problems associated with ADHD, as well as other mental-health difficulties that may arise as a result of ADHD.

RECOMMENDATIONS

- The relationship between ADHD and increased health-care utilization is not fully understood and warrants further research. Research should inform the development of management approaches to improve health-care outcomes for individuals with ADHD and reduce the burden of care (see also Kawatkar et al., 2014).

- The role of impulsivity and inattention in the aetiology of other serious psychiatric difficulties (e.g. adolescent self-harm) is not understood. It may be useful to investigate how the alleviation of core ADHD symptoms may improve co-occurring psychiatric conditions of ADHD in order to improve health-care outcomes and reduce the burden of care.

1.6.5 *Impact on the Family*

FINDINGS

- There are considerable expenditures on preventive measures and respite/foster care for adults with ADHD compared to both the Danish average and their sibling controls.

CURRENT LITERATURE

- ADHD is a complex neurodevelopmental disorder with a social context. It is associated with social disadvantage (Russell et al., 2014; Nigg and Craver, 2014). Children with ADHD have an impact on their parents and families, and vice versa. Adverse familial environments and parenting practices are commonly observed in families of children with ADHD (Hinshaw, 2002; Johnston and Mash, 2001). Parents of children with ADHD experience more parenting stress—and severity of ADHD symptoms is associated with parenting stress (Theule et al., 2013).

RECOMMENDATION

- The best ways to support families of children and young people with ADHD should be identified in order to support family stability and help reduce expenditure on preventive and respite/foster-care costs.

1.6.6 *Comorbidity*

FINDINGS

- There is a considerable degree of comorbidity associated with a diagnosis of ADHD.
- Substance abuse was found to be a common co-occurring condition in adults with ADHD. At the same time, negative life events (e.g. offending, unemployment, low educational attainment, family break-up) were considerably more prominent for adults with ADHD.

CURRENT LITERATURE

- Approximately 70–80 per cent of adult patients with ADHD have at least one comorbid disorder (Kessler et al., 2006).
- Individuals with ADHD suffer significantly more often from other psychiatric disorders and are furthermore impaired in several areas of psychosocial functioning (Sobanski, 2006).

RECOMMENDATIONS

- The best ways to identify and manage ADHD in the context of substance-abuse disorders should be investigated to ensure that effective treatment approaches are available for this group of individuals. The benefits of recently published guidelines for the diagnosis and treatment of ADHD in adults with substance-abuse disorders can be explored (Matthys et al., 2014).
- Ways to increase access to mental-health care for children and adolescents with or at risk of ADHD should be investigated to help prevent the development of associated negative conditions and life events for individuals with ADHD.

1.7 Structure of this book

In the following chapters, we present the analysis. The book is organized in four parts. In the first part, we discuss the nature of ADHD, the structure of the Danish health-care system, and how it is organized to provide assessment and treatment services for individuals with ADHD. In the second part, groups of adult individuals diagnosed with ADHD are defined and compared with one another and with the general population in a number of areas: educational attainment, occupational status, income, family situation, criminal record, health, etc. The third part presents an empirical analysis that estimates differences in performance measures between the group of individuals with ADHD and members of the non-ADHD group who are otherwise similar. In the fourth part, the cost calculations for ADHD are presented and the findings are discussed in national and international perspectives. Each single part begins with an introduction so that readers may skip any part without loss of comprehension and move directly to chapters of high interest.

Part I
Attention Deficit Hyperactivity Disorder

In the first section of this book we discuss the nature of ADHD, the structure of the Danish health-care system, and how it is organized to provide assessment and treatment services for individuals with ADHD.

Attention Deficit Hyperactivity Disorder (ADHD) is a developmental disorder characterized by developmentally inappropriate levels of hyperactivity, impulsivity, and inattention. ADHD is common, with a worldwide prevalence estimated at approximately 5 per cent. Although originally seen as a disorder of childhood, the persistence of ADHD into adulthood is now widely acknowledged. ADHD is often comorbid with a number of other psychiatric conditions, and functional impairments often become evident during clinical assessments. ADHD is associated with a considerable burden to the individual and society in terms of increased health costs, poor academic achievement, lower income levels, higher crime rates, and higher risk of car accidents.

Mental-health services for individuals with ADHD in Denmark are predominantly financed and operated by the public sector and organized within primary- and secondary-sector levels of care. The assessment and diagnosis of ADHD in adults in Denmark is carried out by a psychiatrist or a neurologist in private practice or by a psychiatrist in regional adult psychiatry. Individuals with the most severe and complex psychiatric conditions, including complex comorbid psychiatric disorders, are referred to regional hospital-based inpatient or outpatient psychiatry. Individuals with less severe conditions are referred to a psychiatrist in private practice.

The International Classification of Diseases (the ICD-10) is used for classifying mental-health disorders, including ADHD, in the Danish health-care system. The current study uses information from adults with ADHD prescribed ADHD medication in the primary sector and from adults diagnosed with ADHD in the secondary mental-health sector in Denmark. The Danish Psychiatric Central Register and the Danish Register of Medicinal Products Statistics are used to identify individuals with ADHD in this study.

We combine the information about individuals diagnosed with ADHD from the Danish Psychiatric Central Register and the Register of Medicinal Products Statistics with information from a number of other registers available from Statistics Denmark covering demographic background, educational attainment, the labour market, crimes committed, traffic accidents, and foster care.

2

Attention Deficit Hyperactivity Disorder

Attention Deficit Hyperactivity Disorder (ADHD) is a highly prevalent and heterogeneous developmental disorder, meaning that the problems that children with ADHD have and the underlying causes of their behaviour can be very different. It is characterized by age-inappropriate levels of inattention and/or hyperactivity and impulsivity (DSM-5; American Psychiatric Association, 2013). Essentially, children with ADHD have levels of attention, concentration, and activity of children much younger than them. If we were to examine very young children, then most two-year-old children would meet the criteria for ADHD. However, nearly all of those children would have enhanced their concentration, and reduced their impulsive behaviour by age four.

ADHD is typically associated with impairment across several domains of functioning (Nijmeijer et al., 2008), and children with ADHD typically have difficulty with their family at home and in the classroom as well as when playing with peers. At home, children with ADHD usually have a poor short-term memory (remembering things they are asked to do immediately). They have a very active brain, which means that they like to be kept busy, they hate waiting, and therefore they will do anything to avoid being bored (Tarver, Daley, and Sayal, 2014). They talk and fidget when they are supposed to be sitting quietly, and they interrupt when people are talking. In the classroom, ADHD children often become a focus for classroom disruption: they usually blurt out answers to questions rather than waiting until the teacher asks them for the answer; they find it difficult to listen to the teacher, and therefore often miss instructions and announcements; they usually find interfering or pestering other children an excellent way of avoiding boredom (Daley, 2006). When playing with peers, ADHD children struggle to wait their turn, rarely attend to important rule changes in games, and give up on the game very easily if they don't get what they want, making them less than ideal playmates.

2.1 Classification and Symptom Structure

What is now known as ADHD has been the subject of many name changes over the years, from *hyperkinetic syndrome* to *attention deficit disorder* (*ADD*) to *ADD with hyperactivity* (American Psychiatric Association, 1994) to *Hyperkinetic Disorder* (World Health Organization, 1992); as research into the disorder advances, the working definitions subsequently change. The most widely used diagnostic tools are the American Psychiatric Association's Diagnostic and Statistical Manual (DSM), whose most recent edition (DSM-5; American Psychiatric Association, 2013) cites the disorder named Attention Deficit Hyperactivity Disorder (ADHD) and the World Health Organization's International Classification of Disease (ICD), whose 11th version (World Health Organization, 1992) cites the disorder Hyperkinetic Disorder. Both diagnostic tools recognize three subtypes of the disorder:

a) predominantly inattentive type
b) predominantly hyperactive type
c) combined type.

A diagnosis of ADHD combined type in childhood (DSM-5; American Psychiatric Association, 2013)—the most common diagnosis—requires a minimum of six out of nine inattentive symptoms, and a minimum of six out of nine hyperactive/impulsive symptoms. Symptoms must be present in two or more settings (for example, at school and at home), and must significantly impair everyday functioning (American Psychiatric Association, 1994). Symptoms of inattention include daydreaming, distractibility, and disorganization; symptoms of hyperactivity include restlessness and fidgeting; while symptoms of impulsivity include impatience and inability to refrain from acting (American Psychiatric Association, 2013).

It is widely accepted that ADHD consists of two key difficulties, which are inattention and hyperactive–impulsive behaviour (American Psychiatric Association, 2013). However some researchers have questioned the validity of this claim. The DSM structure was devised using large childhood samples, and therefore concerns have been aired over the validity of diagnosing pre-schoolers and adults using a structure derived from children (Span, Earleywine, and Strybel, 2002). Subsequently, the same two-factor structure has been replicated in adult samples (DuPaul et al., 2001). However, Span, Earleywine, and Strybel (2002) concluded that a three-factor structure with separate factors for inattention, hyperactivity, and impulsivity best described adult ADHD symptoms. In a college-student study, Glutting, Youngstrom, and Watkins (2005) found that the factor structure changed according to where symptom reports came from: analysis using parental reports demonstrated the DSM-iv two-factor structure; however self-report symptoms showed a three-factor solution, in line with the work of Span, Earleywine, and Strybel (2002).

2.2 Prevalence and Developmental Span

It is estimated that ADHD affects about 4 per cent of children in the UK (Daley, 2006) and at least 5 per cent of children worldwide (Faraone et al., 2003; Polanczyk et al., 2007), with approximately 40 per cent of children with ADHD continuing to meet diagnostic criteria in adulthood (Fischer et al., 1993). There have been many criticisms of the studies that have examined the prevalence of ADHD, as different studies report widely different prevalence rates. It is clear that both the method of measuring ADHD and also the particular respondent influence the calculation of the prevalence: for example, mothers tend to report lower levels of ADHD symptoms than fathers do (Davé et al., 2008). Culture is also important: Sonuga-Barke et al. (1993) suggest that teachers' ratings of ADHD symptoms in children vary according to the child's ethnicity. Their work suggests that teacher ratings of Asian children are biased, and that Asian children have to display fewer ADHD symptoms in the classroom than British children to be rated by their teacher as problematic.

At one time the commonly held viewpoint was that ADHD existed in school-age children only (Willoughby, 2003). However, research has shown that ADHD has an early, preschool onset (Lavigne et al., 1996). Despite the similarities between preschool ADHD and school-aged ADHD, little is known about what constitutes impairment during the preschool years, although school readiness should be what clinicians focus on (DuPaul, Weyandt, and Janusis, 2011). Even less is known about the relationship between risk for ADHD and later expression of ADHD. For example, for some children positive transition into school may reduce the risk of developing ADHD, while for others negative transition may exacerbate the risk of developing ADHD (Sonuga-Barke et al., 2005). ADHD has also been shown to persist through adolescence (Wolraich et al., 2005) and into adulthood (Barkley et al., 2002). In general, symptoms of ADHD—especially symptoms of hyperactivity diminish over time as the child develops. However, our understanding of ADHD in adulthood is mostly based on the vast amount of research conducted on childhood ADHD. Less research has been conducted on the disorder in adulthood, and definitions of adult ADHD include numerous aspects of mental functioning and behaviour that are not usually examined in children such as mood swings, irritability, stress intolerance, anger, and risk taking and play down central features of childhood ADHD such as hyperactivity (Moncrieff and Timimi, 2010). The methods for assessing

ADHD in adulthood are also controversial, as until the DSM-5 they were based on childhood measures (Tarver, Daley, and Sayal, 2014).

2.3 ADHD in the Preschool Years

A notable increase over recent years in the number of preschool children coming to clinical attention with ADHD symptoms and being prescribed medication for their ADHD symptoms (Zito et al., 2000) has driven researchers to examine ADHD in the preschool period (Daley et al., 2009). Findings from this research suggest that children with preschool ADHD symptoms share many of the characteristics associated with their school-aged counterparts. Typically, preschool children with ADHD present with the same symptom structure (Gadow and Nolan, 2002); they experience similar associated impairment, comorbidity, and developmental risk (Lahey et al., 1998); and they have similar neuropsychological deficits (Sonuga-Barke, Dalen, and Remington, 2003). Several studies have examined the longitudinal stability of preschool ADHD (Speltz et al., 1999), and results generally confirm that children characterized as hyperactive during the preschool years continue to manifest problems with impulsive behaviour, aggression, and social adjustment in primary school. Pierce, Ewing, and Campbell (1999) found that symptoms of ADHD identified in preschool boys predicted continuing problems in middle childhood. Consistent with these findings, Lahey et al. (2004) found that children who met full diagnostic criteria during their first assessment were likely to continue to meet diagnostic criteria for ADHD over the next three years.

Preschool children at risk of ADHD are often given the label 'hyperactive'. Hyperactivity is a dimensional term, and reflects the fact that every child demonstrates some inattention, impulsivity, and hyperactive behaviours. In the preschool period we are most interested in children who exhibit extremely high levels of hyperactivity. This dimensional concept differs from the categorical concept of ADHD, i.e., that a clinical subgroup of children have such extreme scores for inattention, impulsivity, and hyperactive behaviour that they are different from the rest of the population and warrant a clinical label. The difference between hyperactivity and ADHD is mostly related to what we call 'impairment'. Having high levels of symptoms does not mean that the child has ADHD. The child has to have very high levels of symptoms, those symptoms need to have been present for at least six months, and the presence of symptoms needs to create other difficulties for the child. Within an ADHD context, impairment is usually interference with school work (or school readiness in the preschool years, such as being able to sit and listen to a story, and take turns sharing toys). Impairment can also be seen in children's peer relationships, where ADHD symptoms may prevent children from making friends or engaging in the same activities as their friends. Similar levels of impairment have been found when children have been recruited from community samples without a formal diagnosis (Sonuga-Barke et al., 1994) and in children recruited from clinics or hospitals (DuPaul et al., 2001). Preschool children at risk of ADHD represent children with extreme scores for hyperactivity (Daley and Thompson, 2007), but that does not necessarily mean that they will all go on to develop ADHD.

2.4 ADHD in Adulthood

While originally conceived of as a disorder of childhood and adolescence, recent evidence suggests that there is scientific merit and clinical value in examining ADHD in adulthood (Daley, 2006; Tarver et al., 2014). ADHD symptoms have been shown to persist into later life with up to 40 per cent of childhood cases continuing to meet full criteria in the adult years (Fischer et al., 1993). Adult ADHD appears to share many characteristics of the childhood disorder. Like their childhood counterparts, adults with ADHD display impairment in the interpersonal, vocational, and cognitive domains. adults with ADHD find that their difficulties with impulsivity and inattention make it harder to stay in a romantic relationship and keep their job and tend to ensure that they make unwise decisions. The memory problems associated with ADHD also make it more difficult for them to plan their lives (Dinn, Robbins, and Harris, 2001). In general, adults with ADHD tend to choose jobs and careers that suit their specific difficulties. You are therefore less likely to find ADHD individuals sitting in front of computer screens all day, and they would make less than optimal air-traffic controllers. Instead, they tend to choose jobs that involve working outside, do not require sustained concentration, and involve a lot of movement and activity (e.g., construction work, agriculture, delivery work). Some individuals are able to capitalize on their difficulties and use them to their advantage. For example, in theory an individual with ADHD could make a good trader on the stock market, as their impulsive nature would allow them to make the sort of rapid decisions that the job requires.

The adult and childhood disorders also appear to share a common neuropathology, which means that the same components of the brain that have been shown to control ADHD in childhood are also responsible for the control of ADHD in adulthood (Hesslinger et al., 2001). Adults with ADHD also demonstrate a similar response to drug treatment for ADHD to children with the disorder (Sachdev, 1999), which underlines the similarities between ADHD in childhood and ADHD in adulthood. Differences in the rates of ADHD in adulthood found by some longitudinal studies, however, raise questions about the validity of the disorder in adults. Faraone (2000) claims that discrepancies in rates of ADHD in longitudinal studies can be explained by two other important factors: (i) psychiatric comorbidity and the way it is diagnosed, and (ii) the lack of developmentally appropriate ADHD symptoms in adulthood. The DSM-4, which is one common method for diagnosing ADHD, relies on hierarchical diagnosis, where disorders higher up the hierarchy are allowed a wider range of symptoms and more associated problems than those lower down. Faraone (2000) claims that reliance on hierarchical diagnoses can distort the diagnosis of ADHD in adulthood. He quotes an example from Mannuzza et al. (1993) who found very low levels of ADHD in a longitudinal study of adults who had been diagnosed with ADHD in childhood. The Mannuzza study applied a hierarchical rule, which excluded children whose primary referral had been conduct problems and aggression, even though they also had ADHD. However, as aggressive children with ADHD are more likely to have a more persistent disorder than non-aggressive children, the low rate of ADHD at follow-up in adulthood in the Mannuzza study reflected the study's hierarchical diagnosis, which excluded many possible cases, thus distorting the prevalence rate.

Despite the different expectations for children and adults, it is only in the recent DSM-5 (American Psychiatric Association, 2013) that diagnostic criteria for ADHD in adulthood have been devised. The new criteria adjust for the developmental nature of ADHD, which may mean that more adults meet criteria for ADHD in adulthood in the future, as up until now adults have had to meet the childhood criteria in order to get a diagnosis in adulthood. ADHD in adulthood is more likely to present as irritability, mood swings, and risk-taking behaviour, yet the symptoms used to diagnose ADHD in adults do not as yet emphasize these problems very well.

2.5 Comorbidity

It is widely accepted that ADHD is a comorbid disorder, although what is actually meant by this is far from clear. Gillberg et al. (2004) point out that comorbidity can mean a common underlying disease origin (aetiology), which leads to two or more different disorders, or that one disorder leads to another, or even that two unrelated disorders co-occur. The term comorbid also implies that their entities are morbid conditions, i.e., diseases. In fact, the vast majority of comorbidities with ADHD represent functional impairments and symptoms, which are not rooted in specific diseases (Gillberg et al., 2004). It therefore seems more prudent and more helpful to discuss associated problems with ADHD rather than comorbidity.

ADHD appears to be associated with a wide variety of other psychiatric problems. Notable associations exist with Oppositional Defiant Disorder (ODD), Conduct Disorder (CD), depression, and anxiety. About 50–60 per cent of children with ADHD meet criteria for ODD, even in the preschool period (Kadesjo et al., 2001). A neuropsychological study has demonstrated that ADHD children without associated conduct and aggression problems demonstrated greater levels of impairment than ADHD with associated conduct and aggression (Banaschewski et al., 2003). Busch et al. (2002) reported that ADHD children in primary-care settings were significantly more likely than non-ADHD clinical controls to demonstrate mood disorders such as depression (57 per cent), multiple anxiety disorders (31 per cent), and substance-use disorders (11.5 per cent). However, in the British Child Mental Health Survey (Ford, Goodman, and Meltzer, 2003) anxiety was not associated with ADHD when adjustment was made for the presence of a third disorder. In adult cases, comorbid conditions include mood disorders, antisocial behaviour disorders, and substance-use disorders.

2.5.1 *Associated Impairments*

In addition to associations with other psychiatric disorders, children with ADHD are also more likely than their non-ADHD counterparts to experience a substantial array of developmental, social, and health risks. These include:

Motor coordination: Studies using balance assessment, tests of fine motor gestures, and electronic or paper-and-pencil mazes often find children with ADHD to be less coordinated in these actions (Mariani and Barkley, 1997). As a group, as many as 60 per cent of children with ADHD—compared to up to 35 per cent of normal children—may have poor motor coordination or developmental coordination disorder (Kadesjo et al., 2001). The association between ADHD and poor motor coordination is most probably linked to a common but as yet unclear neurological problem.

Reduced intelligence: Clinic-referred children with ADHD often have lower scores on intelligence tests than control groups, particularly in verbal intelligence (McGee, Williams, and Feehan, 1992). These differences range from 7 to 10 standard score points. Studies using both community samples and clinical samples (Peterson et al., 2001; Sonuga-Barke, Houlberg, and Hall, 1994) have also found negative associations between ADHD and intelligence. The reason for lower levels of IQ in children with ADHD is less clear. Obviously, being inattentive means that children with ADHD are less likely to learn from what is going on around them. This may explain the particularly low levels of verbal IQ, as children with ADHD may find it harder to listen, remember, and therefore learn new words that are being used by people around them. Being inattentive may also mean that children with ADHD are less likely to observe and learn from the actions of other children and adults. Children with ADHD find it very difficult to concentrate and focus on an IQ test, and often just give the first answer that comes into their head, rather than taking the time to work out the answer. (See the discussion on delay aversion in Section 2.7 for why they might do this.)

Impaired academic functioning: The vast majority of clinic-referred children with ADHD have difficulty with school performance, often doing much worse at school than other children with the same level of IQ and ability. ADHD children frequently score lower than normal controls on standardized achievement tests (Hinshaw, 2007). These differences are likely to be found even in preschool children with ADHD (Barkley et al., 2002), suggesting that the disorder may influence school readiness. Preschoolers who express ADHD symptoms are likely to experience difficulties with pre-academic skills such as knowing their numbers, colours, and shapes (Mariani and Barkley, 1997) and social functioning (Spira and Fischel, 2005). ADHD children often struggle with schoolwork (Barry, Lyman, and Klinger, 2002) and social interaction (Nijmeijer et al., 2008). Adolescents with ADHD are also likely to experience academic attainment difficulties (Frazier et al., 2007; Daley and Birchwood, 2010) and social problems (Greene et al., 1997).

The research reviewed so far supports the notion that ADHD individuals experience academic problems. However, are these academic problems the result of factors directly related to ADHD (symptoms, underlying processes) or are they the result of factors that are indirectly related to ADHD? ADHD is a highly comorbid disorder—i.e., individuals with ADHD are likely to experience many other associated problems and have other diagnoses. Because of the close association between ADHD and Conduct Disorder (CD) (antisocial tendency), there has been a body of research investigating the outcomes of individuals with a comorbid ADHD and conduct disorder (ADHD+CD) diagnosis. This research suggests that ADHD+CD individuals experience both future academic and offending problems. However, it is their ADHD behaviours that predict future academic problems, and their CD behaviours that predict future criminal behaviour. Frick et al. (1991) investigated children with a diagnosis of ADHD and CD and found that CD was only related to academic problems because of its close ties with ADHD; ADHD was the significant predictor of academic performance. After controlling for comorbidity rates between ADHD and CD, Farrington, Loeber, and Van Kammen (1990) found that childhood CD was a strong significant predictor of later criminal offending, whereas childhood ADHD was only weakly related to offending. This suggests that conduct problems in children with ADHD do not explain their educational disadvantage.

Fergusson, Horwood, and Lynskey (1993) looked at the relationship between ADHD and CD behaviours at ages 6, 8, and 10 and later academic performance and juvenile offending at age 13. They found that early CD behaviours were a precursor for future juvenile offending, but were not linked to later school performance when the association between CD and ADHD behaviours was removed. They also found that early ADHD behaviours were related to future school performance, but not to juvenile offending problems (again, when the association between the two was taken into account). Rapport, Scanlan, and Denney (1999) support the work of Fergusson et al.; they found strong links between ADHD and later scholastic achievement, and only found links between CD and scholastic achievement by virtue of CD's correlation with ADHD. The ADHD/CD literature therefore suggests that the ADHD individual's academic struggle cannot be put down to associated conduct problems. This means that other explanations are required for the association between ADHD and academic disadvantage.

However, could IQ be the root of the academic disadvantage? Research has shown that negative associations exist between ADHD and intelligence (McGee, Williams, and Feehan, 1992; Sonuga-Barke et al., 1994), and—although the link between IQ and achievement is an age-old debate—evidence suggests that psychometric intelligence predicts future achievement (Watkins, Lei, and Canivez, 2007). However, studies that demonstrate the link between ADHD and academic underachievement have controlled for differences in intelligence within the sample (Diamantopoulou et al., 2007), or matched experimental and control groups for IQ level (Barry, Lyman, and Klinger, 2002), suggesting that ADHD individuals perform academically at a lower level than would be predicted by their IQ. Whilst ADHD individuals have been shown to score lower than controls on IQ tests, this may not be the primary cause of their impaired academic performance.

Social problems: Children with ADHD face serious social problems to the extent that some researchers are surprised that they are not included in the criteria for the disorder. Clark et al. (1988) in an observational study reported much higher levels of aggression, less joint play, and fewer verbal responses from ADHD children when they played with a non-ADHD child, compared to two non-ADHD children playing together. Children with ADHD are often rejected by their peers and have fewer friends than their non-ADHD peers (Hinshaw and Melnick, 1995). There are many possible explanations for why ADHD children have few friends. The most likely explanation is that they are difficult to play with, as they find it hard to attend to the subtle changes in the rules of games, they don't wait their turn, and they react very negatively to having to wait and to losing, all of which makes them less than ideal playmates. As a result ADHD children tend to choose other ADHD children as playmates which mean they frequently lack children within their friendship circles who can be models for attention, concentration, and positive behaviours.

Susceptibility to accidents: Studies have identified that up to 57 per cent of children with ADHD are said to be accident-prone by parents, relative to 11 per cent or fewer of control children (Barkley, 2002). ADHD children are more likely than their non-ADHD peers to have to visit accident and emergency units, even during the preschool period. Knowledge about safety does not appear to be lower in these children, implying that interventions aimed at increasing knowledge about safety may have little impact (Mori and Peterson, 1995). The higher accident rate is more probably the result of impulsivity and a lack of forethought (not thinking before you act), both of which would allow a child with ADHD to jump off a high wall without thinking about the fact that they might break their arm or leg. It is also worth remembering that ADHD children are also more likely to lack motor coordination, and so a greater tendency to be clumsy may also explain higher accident rates in ADHD.

Sleep problems: Studies report an association between ADHD and sleep disturbances (Gruber, Sadeh, and Raviv, 2000; Wilens, Biederman, and Spencer 1994). Corkum et al. (1999) found that sleep problems occurred twice as often in ADHD than in control children. The main issues are more behavioural problems at bedtime, taking a longer time to fall asleep, instability of sleep duration, tiredness at wakening, and frequent night waking. Parents of children with ADHD report that their children require significantly less sleep than their non-ADHD siblings, that they sleep much later than would be expected for their developmental age, but also that they wake earlier. Again, the association between ADHD and sleep difficulties is likely to be due to shared neurological processes in the brain.

2.6 What causes ADHD?

Everyone seems to have a theory as to what causes ADHD and most people are wrong! In this section we shall examine the evidence base for a range of explanations as to what causes ADHD. We shall then delve a little deeper, not only to discover the underlying causes of ADHD, but also in an attempt to explain why children with ADHD engage in inattentive, impulsive, and hyperactive behaviours rather than being quiet and focused.

2.6.1 Genetics

ADHD is a highly heritable disorder (Thapar et al., 1999). The genetics of ADHD have been demonstrated in many family, twin, and adoption studies. Parents and siblings of children with ADHD have been found to have a two- to eight-fold increased risk for ADHD (Biederman, 2005). In a review of several twin studies, Biederman (2005) calculated a mean heritability rate (an estimate of genetic risk where 1 would equal 100 per cent) of 0.77, suggesting that it is highly likely that the twin of an ADHD child will also have the disorder. Relatives of adopted ADHD children have been shown to have lower rates of ADHD than biological relatives of non-adopted ADHD children, and similar rates to the relatives of non-ADHD children (Sprich et al., 2000).

The genetics of ADHD are very complex. ADHD is not a single-gene disorder—unlike Huntington's disease, which is a progressive neurodegenerative disorder and a good example of an autosomal dominant single-gene disease. Most individuals with a single copy of the mutant Huntington gene (HTT) will develop Huntington's disease later in their life. The genetic risk associated with ADHD, on the other hand, appears to be related to many different bits of genetic code scattered across lots of different genes, and it must be conceded that we probably still don't fully understand the genetics of ADHD. Typically, molecular genetic studies have established an association with a single dopamine transporter gene (Cook et al., 1995), specifically implicating the 7-repeat allele of the human dopamine receptor D4 gene (Faraone et al., 2001; Brookes et al., 2006). However, other genes have also been implicated, including SNAP-25 (synaptosomal associated protein gene), DBH (dopamine beta-hydroxylase gene), and DRD-5 (dopamine receptor genes). But the influence of each gene on its own on ADHD is very small. (Faraone et al., 2005). This suggests that the real genetic influence of ADHD is probably a complex set of gene by gene interactions, which may differ across individuals and which may prove very difficult to untangle. Genetic inheritance also seems more likely to pass down the male line, with studies finding a bias towards inheritance of ADHD-risk genes from fathers rather than from mothers. When this fact is considered in combination with the fact that males are more like to receive a diagnosis of ADHD in childhood than females, it appears that greater consideration should be given to fathers of children with ADHD.

Other biological risk factors include maternal smoking during pregnancy and obstetric complications. The link between mothers smoking during pregnancy and their children being more at risk of developing ADHD is the result of the way that nicotine influences the various neurotransmitter systems in the body. For example, prenatal nicotine treatment has been shown to produce reductions in norepinephrine (Seidler et al., 1992), while drug treatments that act on and enhance the norepinephrine system have been shown to be effective at treating ADHD (Michelson et al., 2001). Obstetric complications including foetal postmaturity, low birth weight, and foetal distress are all thought to impact on the basal ganglia, which is particularly sensitive to these adverse events, but is also implicated with ADHD (Sprich-Buckminster et al., 1993; Banerjee, Middleton, and Faraone, 2007).

2.6.2 *The Environment*

While the genetic influences on ADHD have been widely reported (Thapar et al., 2007), it is vital not to underestimate the importance of the environment in general and the social environment in particular. Even processes that are predominantly influenced by genetics can be moderated by environment. For example, how tall we are is mostly determined by our genes. If you are tall then it is very likely that you have a tall parent and/or grandparent. Even so, during the 20th century the population has become much taller as a result of better nutrition, which is an environmental influence. Therefore, even though heritability estimates for ADHD are between 0.7 and 0.8, that does not rule out a very large and powerful role for environmental processes.

The power of the social environment has been clearly demonstrated by several studies that have examined the causal role that early adverse experience associated with institutional deprivation plays in determining developmental outcome. Findings consistently highlight the elevated rates of inattention/overactivity among children raised in deprived institutional care, both in the short term and in the longer term into early adolescence (Stevens et al., 2008). One possible connection between early deprivation and ADHD symptoms may be via stress reactivity. There is a growing interest in the way in which individuals with ADHD respond to stress. Some children with ADHD have displayed an atypical cortisol response to stress, in which their cortisol levels decrease following a stressor. These responses are primarily governed by part of the brain called the hypothalamic-pituitary-adrenal (HPA) axis. One possibility is that regulation of the HPA axis involves an underfunctioning behavioural inhibition system that results in poor response inhibition, one of the central deficits of ADHD. Adverse familial environments and parenting practices are commonly observed in families of children with ADHD (Seipp and Johnston, 2005; Johnston and Mash, 2001). However, the extent to which such parenting practices are causal factors in ADHD, or rather responsive to negative child behaviour remains unclear. Longitudinal evidence exploring the temporal relationship between parenting and ADHD is beginning to emerge, but thus far has produced relatively mixed findings (Lifford, Harold, and Thapar, 2008; Keown, 2012). It is most likely that the relationship between parenting and child behaviour is bi-directional, and parents respond to genetically determined negative child behaviour in a way that serves to maintain or exacerbate the child's behaviour (Johnston and Jassy, 2007). Encouraging parents to engage in supportive and proactive parenting could therefore interrupt risk pathways (Sonuga-Barke et al., 2005). Additionally, parenting may also be an important factor contributing to other areas of functioning that are commonly suboptimal in ADHD, including oppositional behaviour and academic, social, and cognitive functioning (Deault, 2010; Hughes and Ensor, 2009).

The high heritability rates of ADHD make it possible that a number of parents attending clinics may have ADHD themselves and their symptoms are likely to impact on their parenting skills. Parental ADHD is associated with the use of more adverse disciplinary practices and higher levels of family chaos (Johnston et al., 2012). Parental ADHD may only come to light when parents present to services with their children and they may consequently require referral to specialized adult ADHD services (National Institute for Clinical Excellence, 2008).

While ADHD is highly heritable, a key environmental risk factor is parenting: chaotic parenting is likely to bring about ADHD in genetically predisposed individuals (Johnston and Mash, 2001). Further support for the importance of parenting comes from intervention studies (see Section 2.8), where improvements in ADHD symptoms have come about when parents are taught alternative parenting skills (Sonuga-Barke et al., 2001; Jones et al., 2007).

Considerable evidence exists to support the view that parents engage in differential parenting, and have different emotional relationships with their ADHD and non-ADHD children (Daley, Sonuga-Barke, and Thompson, 2003). Emotional relationships that are high in warmth and low in criticism and hostility have been shown to have a protective function that interacts with genetic risk to reduce the likelihood of the child developing ADHD (Sonuga-Barke et al., 2008). Cartwright et al. (2011) have also shown that while the criticism and hostility that parents express towards their ADHD child can be mostly explained by the child's conduct problems, warmth appears to be uniquely related to the child's ADHD. Other family-environment risk factors have been identified, including chronic family conflict, decreased family cohesion, and exposure to parental psychopathology, particularly ADHD.

The potent role that environment plays in the establishment and maintenance of ADHD highlights the need for studies exploring ADHD to consider the most stringent form of control, which might be able to control for some if not all of these environmental processes. Siblings would offer the best form of control for such environmental factors.

2.6.3 *Diet*

While most individuals in the general population would select diet as one of the major causes of ADHD, there is very little scientific evidence to support this notion. Although research studies from the 1980s did suggest a link between diet and ADHD (Feingold, 1982), more recent research has failed to establish any real connection between the two. Sugar consumption is anecdotally linked in parents' minds to ADHD, but there is no scientific evidence to link sugar consumption in children and ADHD behaviour. In fact, Krummel et al. (1996) reviewed all twelve studies that had examined the relationship between sugar consumption and ADHD and concluded that sugar ingestion does not lead to any untoward behaviour in children with Attention Deficit Hyperactivity Disorder or in control children. However, the influence of artificial food additives and colours on ADHD is more complicated. Bateman et al. (2004) demonstrated that artificial food additives and colours were associated with higher ratings of hyperactive behaviour in preschool children who took part in a double blind placebo controlled trial. McCann et al. (2007) replicated these findings in preschool children and also extended their study to older children and obtained similar results. However, all these studies used children in the general population who did not have ADHD, and McCann et al. (2007) conclude that the adverse influence of additives and colours are seen not only in children with extreme hyperactivity (i.e., ADHD) but can also be seen in the general population regardless of the child's level of hyperactivity. These findings suggest that food additives and colours do not cause ADHD, but actually make all children more hyperactive.

Other environmental risk factors include excessive television viewing, which has been linked to small but non-significant associations with ADHD, and exposure to toxins such as lead and mercury. However, many children exposed to these toxins do not develop ADHD, and most ADHD children do not test positive for exposure to toxins (Banerjee, Middleton, and Faraone, 2007).

2.7 Neuropsychology of ADHD

Studies examining the neuropsychology of ADHD provide an opportunity to understand the relationship between underlying biological processes and symptoms of ADHD. For many years it was accepted that ADHD symptoms were the result of cognitive dysregulation (Nigg, 2001). The ADHD child's behaviour resulted from insufficient forethought, planning, and control (Schachar et al., 2000). Evidence to support this viewpoint came from many studies using neuropsychological tests that demonstrated that ADHD children performed less well on these tests than did matched controls (Inoue et al., 1998). ADHD children asked to match familiar figures demonstrated more impulsive responding and higher error rates than did matched controls (Sonuga-Barke et al., 1994). A summary of ADHD as a disorder of cognitive dysregulation suggested that the relationship between biology and behaviour in ADHD was mediated by inhibitory dysfunction (Sonuga-Barke, 2002). In contrast to the dominant view, Sonuga-Barke et al. (1994) offered an alternative view of ADHD, not as a disorder of cognitive dysregulation, but as a motivational style. This viewed ADHD as a functional response by the child, aimed at avoiding delay. This alternative viewpoint of ADHD was demonstrated by Sonuga-Barke et al. (1994), who showed that most of the neuropsychological evidence to support the notion that ADHD is a result of cognitive dysregulation, was confounded by delay. To demonstrate this, Sonuga-Barke et al. (1994) got ADHD and matched non-ADHD control children to participate in the matching familiar figures test, a computer-based task where children have to match a picture of an ordinary object with one of six variants. Sonuga-Barke et al. (1994) found the same results as previous studies. ADHD children made more impulsive responses and more errors. However, they also pointed out that all these studies involved trial constraints where as soon as one trial ended the next began, which meant that results were confounded with delay. In order words, ADHD children made more impulsive responses because it allowed them to complete the task more quickly and therefore escape delay. When Sonuga-Barke, Houlberg, and Hall (1994) re-ran their study under time constraint (for a fixed period of time where early or impulsive responses had no influence on delay), ADHD children performed no differently from controls.

Results of these studies led to the development of the delay-aversion hypothesis (Sonuga-Barke et al., 1996), which characterized the influence of delay on behaviour dependent upon whether children have control over their environment or not. When children are in control of their environment they can choose to minimize delay by acting impulsively, e.g. by skipping the queue at the end of the slide. When children are not in control of their environment, or at least where they are expected to behave in certain ways or face sanctions, they would choose to distract themselves from the passing of time. For example, in a classroom context, during literacy lessons the children could achieve this either by daydreaming (inattention) or by fidgeting (hyperactivity).

Traditionally, these two different accounts of ADHD have both sought to explain the disorder independently. However, a study by Solanto et al. (2001) compared the measurement of both of these hypotheses in a head-to-head study. Results of this study showed that measures used to test each hypothesis were uncorrelated, demonstrating that they measured different components of the ADHD construct. Both sets of measures were correlated with ADHD, and when combined were highly diagnostic, correctly distinguishing 87.5 per cent of cases from non-cases (i.e. classifying ADHD children from non-ADHD children).

These results suggested that both accounts appeared to help to explain ADHD, but that neither explanation was the 'single theory of ADHD' for which both theoretical camps had been searching. Based on these findings, Sonuga-Barke (2002) proposed his dual-pathway model of ADHD. This model proposed two possible routes between biology and ADHD behaviour: one via cognitive dysregulation and the other via motivational style. Clinically, the dual-pathway model suggests that there may be merit in targeting different subtypes with specific treatments, as well as allowing the development of novel interventions, perhaps aimed at desensitizing delay (Sonuga-Barke, 2002). Sonuga-Barke (2004) has suggested ways in which a greater understanding of the influence of delay aversion on the development of ADHD could be used to develop alternative interventions. His suggestions include the use of delay fading, a technique to systematically reorganize the child's delay experience, as a means of increasing tolerance for delay, and reducing ADHD symptoms.

2.7.1 *Other Neuropsychological Theories*

While cognitive dysregulation and delay aversion are the dominant neuropsychological theories of ADHD, other neuropsychological explanations also exist and may be highly relevant for some ADHD children.

Timing discrimination: There is some evidence to suggest that individuals with ADHD have difficulties with time discrimination, and it might be that an altered sense of time might be associated with many of the difficulties that individuals with ADHD have, especially impulsiveness. Smith et al. (2002) examined time-discrimination tasks in ADHD and non-ADHD control children. In this study, children with and without ADHD were presented with two circles on a screen and had to estimate which of the two were presented for the longest interval of time. The study found that ADHD children found it very difficult to distinguish between brief intervals of time which differ by only a few hundred milliseconds. Rubia et al. (2007) also found evidence for time-discrimination difficulties in ADHD and reported large differences between ADHD and non-ADHD children on a similar task to that used by Smith et al. (2002), and suggest that time-discrimination difficulties may be more central to ADHD than previously thought. However, it is not yet clear how time discrimination might actually impact on ADHD children's symptoms, or even on their experience of time. To date, the research evidence has focused on examining small time-estimation intervals of milliseconds and seconds, rather than longer intervals of time. If time discrimination is implicated in ADHD, then it might be that ADHD children are less good at judging the passing of time, and so if a parent asks the child to 'wait a minute'—as parents often do—the ADHD child might have more difficulty in working out how long that actually was.

Working memory: While we have focused in general on cognitive dysregulation as an explanation for ADHD symptoms, one component of this dysregulation—working memory—might be especially important.

Martinussen et al. (2005) conducted a meta-analysis of findings examining working-memory deficits in children with ADHD. Their results suggest that working-memory processes are impaired in children with ADHD. These working-memory deficits may help to explain the academic difficulties that children with ADHD experience, as well as the many reports from parents of how their children with ADHD are so forgetful (Daley, 2006).

2.8 Treatment for ADHD

Interventions for ADHD are a relatively controversial topic, and dominated by the results of two large American studies, the Multi-Modal Treatment Study of ADHD (MTA Group, 1999) and the Preschool ADHD Treatment Study (PATS) (Kollins et al., 2006). The controversy surrounds whether or not it is appropriate to medicate children with ADHD. On the one hand, medication appears to yield significant improvements in symptoms (Konrad et al., 2005). However, a number of concerns have been raised regarding the use of psycho-stimulant medication for children with ADHD, especially younger children.

These range from ethical objections to utilizing medication to modify children's behaviour (Perring, 1997) to concerns about the lack of evidence for the long-term effectiveness of stimulant medication (Pelham, Wheeler, and Chronis, 1998). Side effects of stimulant medication have also been a cause of concern. Research has indicated that preschool children seem to be at increased risk of developing short-term side effects (Ghuman et al., 2001). There is also a lack of research evidence regarding the long-term effects of stimulant medication on preschool children's physical and neurological development (Sonuga-Barke et al., 2003).

2.8.1 *How Does Medication for ADHD Work?*

When most parents of children with ADHD are told that the most common drug therapy for ADHD is stimulant medication, they tend to laugh nervously and point out that their child is already overstimulated, and what they need is a drug to calm them down. The reality is that the most common and effective drug therapy for ADHD is a drug called methylphenidate (whose brand names include Ritalin, Equasym, and Concerta). This drug is an amphetamine, and therefore a stimulant. While we do not fully understand why methylphenidate works for individuals with ADHD, the most common explanation is that ADHD is in part the result of a dopamine imbalance in the brain.

Methylphenidate is a norepinephrine and dopamine reuptake inhibitor, which means that it increases the level of the dopamine neurotransmitter in the brain by partially blocking the dopamine transporter (DAT) that removes dopamine from the synapses. You may remember from our discussion of the genetics of ADHD that the dopamine transporter gene was one of the important genes associated with the heritability of ADHD. The other commonly used drug is called atomoxetine (brand name Strattera). This is a selective norepinephrine reuptake inhibitor that targets norepinephrine only, but is a non-stimulant drug.

2.8.2 *Evidence for Drug Treatments*

The MTA study set out to compare the efficacy of medication management, psychosocial intervention, and combined intervention (medication and psychosocial intervention) against routine community care. Results of the MTA study suggested that medical management alone was found to be significantly more effective for the core symptoms of ADHD compared with psychosocial treatment alone and routine community care (MTA Group, 1999). In addition, psychosocial intervention did not significantly improve outcomes when combined with medical treatment. The results of this study influenced recommendations made in the British National Institute of Clinical Excellence report (National Institute for Clinical Excellence, 2000) on interventions for ADHD, which recommended medication as the front-line intervention to be followed by psychosocial intervention, if necessary. However, later analysis using different outcome measures of ADHD symptoms indicated the superiority of combined intervention over medical management alone in the long term (Swanson et al., 2001), while subgroup analysis suggests large effects for psychosocial intervention in certain groups and settings (Swanson et al., 2002). However, the relevance of the MTA study results to intervention in clinical settings remains unclear. The study compared a drug intervention tailored to each child's needs using a sophisticated titration protocol to a psychosocial intervention much less tailored to children's needs (Greene and Ablon, 2001). The psychosocial intervention used could never be replicated clinically, as it involved a multitude of individual sessions for the child, summer camps, additional classroom help, support for the child's teacher, and group and individual sessions for the child's parents (Greene and Ablon, 2001). More important is the fact that no theoretical rationale for the content of the behavioural intervention has ever been published. It seems to have been developed from little bits of interventions developed by individuals involved in the study, all mixed up together. While never formally tested, it is possible that elements of the intervention were also counterproductive (Morrell and Murray, 2003), as what was taught directly to parents may not have supported what teachers were told to do in the classroom, for example.

The MTA did not include preschool children. The lack of a rigorous trial on pharmacological intervention for preschool children with ADHD was the rationale for PATS (Kollins et al., 2006). This was a multicentre, randomized, placebo-controlled trial designed to evaluate the five-week efficacy and forty-week safety of methylphenidate in preschool children with ADHD. The protocol involved eight phases, one of which was parent training. Children aged 3–5.5 years (n=303) were recruited if they met the criteria for a primary DSM-iv diagnosis, including impairment for nine months, based on parent and teacher ratings and expert clinical opinion. A total of 279 parents entered the parent-training phase, which involved a group training package consisting of manual-driven, weekly two-hour group sessions delivered by trained clinicians over ten weeks (Cunningham, Bremner, and Boyle, 1995). The trainers were supported by weekly telephone calls. Only 7 per cent of children demonstrated a significant improvement in this phase, although an additional 7 per cent showed otherwise satisfactory improvement. A further 12 per cent were not entered into the medication phases in accordance with parental wishes, and a smaller number were lost to follow-up. The poor rate of response to parent training in this study may have been an artefact of the intervention, which was less tailored to ADHD symptoms than other evidence-based interventions reviewed later in this chapter. The remaining children with continued impairment after the parent-training phase were entered into the medication phases. The criteria for monitoring side effects were rigorous; 11 per cent of participants dropped out because of medication side effects at some point in the trial. Parents provided consent at each stage, which may also have encouraged drop-out. The side effects were similar to those found in older children, with the most common being decreased appetite, emotional outbursts, difficulty falling asleep, and weight loss (Wigal et al., 2006). There was also an overall slowing of growth, although the children were heavier than expected at baseline based on population levels (Swanson et al., 2006). The effect size observed for medication was lower than in the MTA (which investigated older children), based on both parent and teacher ratings. Overall, the results suggest that medication may be useful for some preschool children, but that it should be used with caution. Furthermore, the sample size was too small to attest effectively to the safety of methylphenidate with preschool children (Wigal et al., 2006). Purely pharmacological interventions for ADHD preschoolers are therefore less than desirable due to (i) lack of evidence for short-term or long-term effectiveness (Greenhill et al., 2006), (ii) concerns about side effects (Wigal et al., 2006), and (iii) ethical objections to the use of medication to modify child behaviour (Perring, 1997). This highlights the need to offer effective psychosocial interventions for preschool ADHD.

2.8.3 *Psychosocial Interventions*

As an alternative to drug therapy, psychosocial treatment with parent training (PT) is considered a suitable first-level treatment for young children presenting with signs of ADHD (Conners et al., 2001). Due to some evidence of the efficacy of these interventions with school-age children with ADHD (e.g. Anastopoulos et al., 1993; Pollard, Ward, and Barkley, 1984), an increasing number of empirical studies have, over the last two decades, evaluated the outcomes of PT intervention for preschool age children with ADHD, and such interventions appear to be notably successful for this age group (Erhardt and Baker, 1990; Chronis, Jones, and Raggi, 2006; Hartman, Stage, and Webster-Stratton, 2003). Following PT intervention, improvements have been found in parent–child interaction (Pisterman et al., 1989), in compliance and on-task behaviour (Sonuga-Barke et al., 2001), and in parent-reported ADHD symptoms and child behaviour problems (Sonuga-Barke et al., 2001; Bor, Sanders, and Markie-Dadds, 2002; Jones et al., 2007; Jones et al., 2008). However, a recent meta-analysis (Sonuga-Barke et al., 2013) has questioned the evidence base for behavioural interventions for ADHD, finding evidence that behavioural interventions were rated as effective when outcomes were rated by parents who received the intervention but non-significant when estimates were taken by blind raters or other individuals such as teachers who were not involved in the receipt of intervention. A second meta-analysis (Daley et al., 2014) expanded on the work of Sonuga-Barke et al. (2013) and showed that behavioural interventions did improve parenting practices with evidence to confirm this found for both parents who took part in the intervention as well as blind raters.

2.9 Summary and Conclusion

Our conclusions at the end of this introduction to ADHD are that the disorder is both complex and fascinating; that ADHD is a disorder with multiple probable causes, most of which interact with each other, so that no two individuals with ADHD are likely to have developed the disorder for exactly the same set of reasons; that ADHD is a lifetime disorder, recognizable from very early in the preschool period, and remains a problem for some individuals through into adulthood; that it rarely occurs on its own, and is associated with a wide range of other problems; that both genetics and environment are very important in increasing the likelihood that an individual will develop ADHD; and, more importantly, that the role of neuropsychological deficits such as inhibitory control, delay aversion, working-memory deficits, etc., help us to understand the links between what happens in the ADHD brain and ADHD behaviours. Many treatments are available for ADHD; drug treatments are effective mostly for older children, but are less effective and have greater side effects for young children. The influence of age and treatment will be explored in greater detail when we examine the costs of ADHD later in the book.

3

The Structure and Organization of Danish Mental-Health Services

This chapter outlines and explains the structure and organization of Danish mental-health assessment and treatment services. Services are broadly organized within two public-health sectors, i.e. primary-care services and secondary-care hospital-based services. In order to understand Danish diagnostic practices and thus the diagnostic registrations made in the Danish registers, which are central to this study, the chapter provides descriptions of mental-health referral pathways, and provides examples of the development in diagnostic practices over the last decade. Finally, the formal diagnostic registration practice in the Danish hospital-based psychiatry system is described.

3.1 Health-Care Services in Denmark

Danish health-care services are predominantly financed and operated by the public sector. The political responsibility for health-care tasks is placed in the country's five regions as well as, to some degree, the ninety-eight municipalities in Denmark. For the purpose of this overview, we distinguish between primary-care services provided through local health-care systems in the municipalities and secondary-care services provided through regional health-care systems. This distinction is illustrated in Figure 3.1.

In Denmark there are five regions responsible for the provision of health care. These are the Capital Region of Denmark, the Zealand Region, the Region of Southern Denmark, the Central Denmark Region, and the North Denmark Region. The population of the regions ranges from approximately 600,000 in the North Denmark Region to approximately 1,630,000 in the Capital Region of Denmark. In terms of surface area, the Capital Region of Denmark is the smallest, covering 2561 square kilometres and the Central Denmark Region the largest, covering 13,142 square kilometres (Danish Regions, 2011). Health

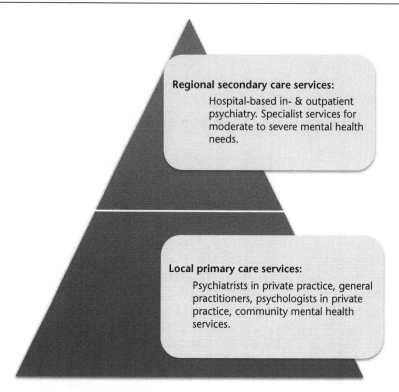

Figure 3.1. Primary and secondary levels of Danish mental-health services

services are organized within primary- and secondary-sector levels of care. The five regions are governed by an overall interest organization: Danish Regions. The overall mission of Danish Regions is to safeguard regional government interests within areas such as health care, including mental-health care, hospitals, and special education, and to negotiate the annual financial frames of the regions with the national government (Danish Regions, 2011).

Denmark is divided into ninety-eight municipalities, which also attend to a number of tasks especially in the primary, local health-care service. In terms of mental-health care, the following sections describe the organization and nature of mental-health assessment and treatment services at the primary-sector and the secondary-sector levels of service provision, respectively.

3.2 Primary-Sector Mental-Health Services

3.2.1 *Psychiatrists in Private Practice*

A total of 124 full-time 'adult psychiatry practice units' and sixteen full-time 'child and adolescent psychiatry practice units' have been established by the

Danish Regions and are available for psychiatrists in private practice in Denmark by way of application. These services constitute a public service, and patients are seen free of charge and can be referred by their general practitioner (GP) to a psychiatrist in private practice who holds an agreement with the Danish Regions. The number of psychiatrists occupying these private-practice units established by the Danish Regions varies considerably in terms of inhabitants and across regions. Thus, for example, there is one adult psychiatrist in private practice per 24,023 inhabitants in the Capital Region, while the North Region has one adult psychiatrist per 57,697 inhabitants. When it comes to private psychiatry units established by the Danish Regions in child and adolescent psychiatry, there is one child and adolescent psychiatrist per 233,336 inhabitants in the Capital Region of Denmark, while the North Region has one child and adolescent psychiatrist per 576,942 inhabitants. In addition to adult and child and adolescent psychiatrists who hold formal private-practice unit agreements with the Danish Regions, a number of child and adolescent and adult psychiatrists have set up their own private practices throughout the country, where payment is private (or through private health insurance) (Psykiatriudvalget, 2013).

3.2.2 *Private Adult Psychiatry Services*

Services provided in the 124 full-time adult psychiatry private-practice units established by the Danish Regions consist of diagnostic assessment, pharmacological treatment, and various forms of psychological therapy. Adult psychiatrists in these settings also work in collaboration with social services in the assessment of patients' social and workforce functioning and prepare medical sickness certificates for individuals when appropriate.

A recent report analysing the capacity of Danish psychiatry (Deloitte, 2012) states that 56,562 patients were seen in adult private-practice units under the agreement with the Danish Regions in 2009, whereas this figure had risen slightly to 57,706 in 2011, showing a 2 per cent increase. The number of new referrals was relatively stable, whereas the number of later appointments had slightly increased. There are no reports of adults seen by psychiatrists in private practice who do not hold agreements with the Danish Regions.

There are few systematic registrations of the diagnoses of patients seen by psychiatrists in private practice. In a study carried out between 1996 and 2006, thirty-seven adult psychiatrists in private practice registered diagnoses on 35,205 patients in total (Munk-Jørgensen and Andersen, 2009). The study showed the following diagnostic distribution: 41 per cent of patients were diagnosed with an affective disorder, 30–35 per cent were diagnosed with an anxiety or stress-related disorder, and 10 per cent received a diagnosis of personality disorder. Similarly, a group of fourteen psychiatrists in private practice (Monitoreringsgruppen, 2013) have registered patient data between 1 November 2008 and 1 March 2012. Of the 4,235 patients included in the data, 41 per cent had diagnoses of affective disorders (mainly unipolar depression), 28 per cent had diagnoses of anxiety or stress-related conditions, 8 per cent had diagnoses of personality disorders, 14 per cent had diagnoses of ADHD, and 3 per cent had diagnoses of psychosis (Psykiatriudvalget, 2013). The assessment and treatment of ADHD in private adult psychiatric practice may, on the basis of these limited figures, be on the rise.

3.2.3 *Private Child and Adolescent Psychiatry Practice*

Services provided in the sixteen full-time child and adolescent psychiatry private-practice units established by the Danish Regions consist of diagnostic assessment and evaluation of the social or environmental factors that may exacerbate and worsen a child's condition and mental health. Treatment services can include psycho-education, pharmacological treatment, and a variety of psychological therapies and interventions, as well as consultations to the child's network (e.g. school).

A report published in 2012 outlines that 3760 patients were seen in private child and adolescent psychiatry units under the agreement with the Danish Regions in 2009, whereas this figure had risen to 4049 patients in 2011, showing a 7 per cent increase. The number of new referrals was relatively stable, whereas the number of later appointments had slightly increased (Deloitte, 2012). There are no reports of children seen by psychiatrists in private practice who do not hold agreements with the Danish Regions.

There are no systematic registrations of diagnoses for patients seen in private child and adolescent psychiatry practice. However, child and adolescent psychiatrists report that a growing number of children are being referred for private assessment and treatment (Psykiatriudvalget, 2013).

3.2.4 *Psychologists in Private Practice*

There are a number of psychologists in private practice in all five regions to whom patients between the ages of 18 and 37 with specific mental-health problems (i.e., mild to moderate depression and mild to moderate anxiety) can be referred for psychological treatment subsidized by the regional health authority following referral by their GP (Sundhedsstyrelsen, 2012). Psychological treatment for ADHD is not subsidized by the regional health authority, and GPs do not routinely refer patients to a psychologist for the treatment of ADHD per se. Formal diagnostics are not carried out by psychologists, and there are no systematic registrations of the diagnoses of patients seen by psychologists in private practice.

3.2.5 *Mental-Health Services in the Community*

In Denmark, mental-health treatment is also provided by primary-care community services set up in local councils or municipalities. Each region consists of a number of municipalities, equivalent to local councils.

By law, regions sign formalized health-care agreements with each individual council within the region to manage the ongoing care of chronic mental-health conditions and associated difficulties, and/or the coordination of mental-health care between the primary and secondary sector (Madsen, 2007). Services for people with mental-health disorders in the community range from the practical support from social services key workers to mental-health counselling provided by social workers. However, mental-health service provision in the community varies considerably between each council. Specific areas of mental-health service provision are agreed by law and councils cannot set service levels below the limits outlined in these laws (e.g. the Social Service Law and the Health Service Law; Madsen, 2007). Yet the extent and degree of specific levels of mental-health care remain dependent upon individual council budgets and priorities.

3.3 Secondary-Sector Mental-Health Services

The five Danish regions are responsible for mental-health diagnostic, assessment, and treatment services for all age groups. Hospital-based mental-health services constitute secondary-sector services. Services are broadly divided into adult psychiatry services and child and adolescent psychiatry services respectively, also reflecting the two different medical specialties in psychiatry.

3.3.1 *Secondary-Sector Adult Psychiatry Services*

Adult psychiatry (18+) assessment, diagnosis, and treatment are carried out through different services, including stationary and outpatient assessment and treatment services at psychiatric hospitals, centres, and inpatient wards. Services also include psychiatric accident and emergency departments, district psychiatry, investigative psychosis teams, and other travelling teams. A growing number of adults with mental-health disorders are seen in secondary-sector adult psychiatry services, and a growing number of these are seen in outpatient adult psychiatry, with recent figures indicating that three-quarters of patients are seen as outpatients (Psykiatriudvalget, 2013). Table 3.1 shows key figures for the number of individuals seen in secondary-sector adult psychiatry services. As can be seen, the number of days spent in stationary services is falling, whereas the number of patient discharges is increasing, indicating that inpatient admissions are increasingly shorter.

Table 3.1. Development in Danish secondary-sector psychiatry services (adults)

	2007	2008	2009	2010	2011
Patients	86,464	87,460	91,742	93,216	95,571
Days as inpatient	1,081,391	1,063,368	1,160,083	1,021,300	950,448
Discharges	38,153	38,769	38,675	39,399	40,168
Outpatient visits	732,950	718,694	788,436	808,756	842,711

Source: Psykiatriudvalget, 2013: Bilagsrapport 2. Table 8.9: 109; reproduced with permission.

Danish psychiatry services have seen a reduction in inpatient services—a general trend seen in Western psychiatry services over the past decades. However, whereas the number of inpatient beds has decreased, the number of admissions has increased, but shortened. Danish inpatient adult psychiatry services today consist of psychiatric accident and emergency services, acute services, general psychiatry wards, and specialized wards. Usually these services see individuals with severe or complicated mental-health disorders, e.g. schizophrenia, severe affective disorders, severe personality disorders, severe eating disorders, and individuals with suicidal impulses (Psykiatriudvalget, 2013).

3.3.2 Secondary-Sector Child and Adolescent Mental-Health Services

Child and adolescent mental-health (ages 0–18) assessment, diagnosis, and treatment services include general and specialist stationary and outpatient services, usually located at child and adolescent psychiatric units and hospitals. Services also include specialist regional day and inpatient institutions for children and adolescents with complex and/or severe mental-health disorders.

The number of children seen in secondary outpatient child and adolescent psychiatry services has increased considerably in recent years. The increase in children seen in outpatient services totals 172 per cent in the period 2001–11. The number of days spent as an inpatient is declining (Table 3.2).

There is currently some regional variation for the age bands seen in child and adolescent psychiatry, with most regions taking referrals of children and adolescents between the ages of 0 and 17 years (inclusive), but the Region of Southern Denmark taking referrals of children and adolescents up to the age of 19 (inclusive). Child and adolescent psychiatry departments are, however, able to continue offering services to a young adult up to the age of 21 if the individual is actively seen in services at the age of 18. Any comparisons between regions and departments should take these variations into account.

Table 3.2. Development in child and adolescent psychiatry activity

	2007	2008	2009	2010	2011
Patients	14,608	16,503	18,788	21,050	22,788
Days as inpatient	64,120	62,308	60,948	60,778	53,067
Discharges	1,393	1,619	1,466	1,450	1,427
Outpatient visits	95,703	98,686	102,436	113,765	125,400

Source: Psykiatriudvalget, 2013: Bilagsrapport 2. Table 8.4: 110; reproduced with permission.

3.3.3 *Diagnostic System for Classifying Mental-Health Disorders in the Danish Health System*

There are currently two widely established systems for classifying mental disorders: the International Classification of Diseases (ICD-10) produced by the World Health Organization (World Health Organization, 1992) and the Diagnostic and Statistical Manual of Mental Disorders (DSM-5) produced by the American Psychiatric Association (American Psychiatric Association, 2013). Both list categories of disorders thought to be distinct types, and have deliberately converged their codes in recent revisions so that the manuals are often broadly comparable, although significant differences remain. ADHD (Attention Deficit Hyperactivity Disorder) is the diagnostic label used in the American DSM-5 system, whereas Hyperkinetic Disorder is the ICD-10 equivalent. ADHD is thought to be the commonly used term in the scientific literature, by patient organizations, and in everyday language.

In the Danish health system, in line with most European countries, the ICD-10 is used for categorizing mental-health disorders. Both classification systems operate lists of cardinal behavioural features that a person must meet in order to fulfil the diagnostic criteria for Hyperkinetic Disorder (ICD-10) or ADHD (DSM-5) respectively.

The list of behaviours is essentially the same in both. However, the DSM-5 list of items allows for the existence of subtypes of ADHD depending on the balance of symptoms of inattention and hyperactivity/impulsiveness. The ICD-10 criteria for the diagnosis of Hyperkinetic Disorder, on the other hand, are a combined set of criteria from a list of distinct symptoms of inattention, hyperactivity, and impulsivity. In essence, the ICD-10 criteria require that an individual meets distinct deficits on all three core symptoms of inattention, hyperactivity, and impulsivity in order to meet the criteria of Hyperkinetic Disorder (i.e., six inattention symptoms, three of the hyperactivity symptoms, and one of the impulsivity symptoms). The age of symptom onset is before the age of 7 years.

For ADHD (DSM-5), essentially, the same axes are used, i.e. inattention and hyperactivity/impulsivity. However, deficits need only be present on one axis and not both inattention and hyperactivity as in ICD-10. Furthermore, the recent DSM-5 revision has increased the symptom threshold for age of onset to before the age of 12 years. ADHD (DSM-5) therefore defines a milder and broader category than the Hyperkinetic Disorder classified in the ICD-10.

Psychiatric nosology and confusion aside, ADHD is the everyday generic term used to describe one of the most common childhood psychiatric disorders, and is the term used throughout this book.

3.3.4 *Patient Groups in Danish Psychiatry*

To illustrate the diagnostic patient groups typically seen in Danish secondary care (hospital-based psychiatry), the two tables below show patients distributed on diagnostic groups in 2011 and indicate how frequently each ICD-10 diagnosis occurred. Table 3.3 illustrates diagnostic groups in adult psychiatry

Table 3.3. Distribution of psychiatric diagnoses in secondary-sector adult psychiatry, 2011

2011 Adult ICD-10 Diagnosis category	Inpatients		Outpatients		Psychiatric Accident and Emergency	
	number	percentage	number	percentage	number	percentage
DF00–DF09: Organic, including symptomatic, mental disorders	1,502	5%	11,212	13%	639	2%
DF10–DF19: Mental and behavioural disorders due to psychoactive substance use	4,144	14%	2,199	3%	4,775	16%
DF20–DF29: Schizophrenia, schizotypal, and delusional disorders	7,320	25%	18,824	22%	5,326	18%
DF30–DF39: Mood (affective) disorders	7,144	25%	20,103	24%	7,015	24%
DF40–DF49: Neurotic, stress-related, and somatoform disorders	4,984	17%	13,705	16%	3,300	11%
DF50–DF59: Behavioural syndromes associated with physiological disturbances and physical factors	143	0%	1747	2%	191	1%
DF60-DF69: Disorders of adult personality and behaviour	1,644	6%	7,109	8%	1,275	4%
DF70–DF79: Mental retardation	164	1%	2,021	2%	176	1%
DF80–DF89: Disorders of psychological development	129	0%	722	1%	170	1%
DF90–DF98: Behavioural and emotional disorders with onset usually occurring in childhood and adolescence	328	1%	2,774	3%	478	2%
DF99: Unspecified mental disorder	236	1%	1235	1%	2696	9%
Other diagnosis	1110	4%	3573	4%	3238	11%
Total	**28,848**	**100%**	**85,224**	**100%**	**29,279**	**100%**

Source: Psykiatriudvalget, 2013: Bilagsrapport 2: 113; reproduced with permission.

Table 3.4. Distribution of psychiatric diagnoses in secondary-sector child and adolescent psychiatry, 2011

2011 Child and adolescent	Inpatients		Outpatients	
ICD-10 diagnostic category	number	percentage	number	percentage
DF00–DF09: Organic, including symptomatic, mental disorders	20	2%	33	0%
DF10–DF19: Mental and behavioural disorders due to psychoactive substance use	36	3%	199	1%
DF20–DF29: Schizophrenia, schizotypal, and delusional disorders	225	17%	729	3%
DF30–DF39: Mood (affective) disorders	210	16%	1,344	6%
DF40–DF49: Neurotic, stress-related, and somatoform disorders	246	19%	2,571	11%
DF50–DF59: Behavioural syndromes associated with physiological disturbances and physical factors	144	11%	1,574	7%
DF60–DF69: Disorders of adult personality and behaviour	51	4%	397	2%
DF70–DF79: Mental retardation	16	1%	608	3%
DF80–DF89: Disorders of psychological development	111	9%	4,144	17%
DF90–DF98: Behavioural and emotional disorders with onset usually occurring in childhood and adolescence	164	13%	11,057	47%
DF99: Unspecified mental disorder	5	0%	43	0%
Other diagnosis	68	5%	1,025	4%
Total	**1,296**	**100%**	**23,724**	**100%**

Source: Psykiatriudvalget, 2013: Bilagsrapport 2: 115. Reproduced with permission.

and Table 3.4 illustrates the distribution of diagnostic groups for child and adolescent psychiatry.

As the tables indicate, ADHD and ADHD differential diagnoses (F90–F98) constitute a considerable percentage of referrals in child psychiatry (13 per cent of inpatients, 47 per cent of outpatients), whereas the number of individuals with ADHD diagnoses in adult psychiatry services constitutes a noticeably smaller proportion (1 per cent of inpatients, 3 per cent of outpatients). Thus, the diagnosis of ADHD in adults does not represent a large number of total ICD-10 diagnoses made in adult psychiatry, secondary-sector mental-health services in Denmark. This finding is in line with those reported in the international literature, where ADHD in adults has only recently been recognized in mental-health services (Kooij et al., 2010).

3.4 Referral Routes for Individuals with Mental-Health Problems

3.4.1 *Adults*

The assessment and diagnosis of ADHD in adults in Denmark is carried out by a psychiatrist or a neurologist in private practice or by a psychiatrist in regional adult psychiatry. The referral is made by a GP. The GP can refer a patient to regional psychiatry or to a psychiatrist in private practice. Patients with the most severe and complex psychiatric conditions are referred to regional hospital or district psychiatry departments (Psykiatriudvalget, 2013). Patients with less severe conditions are referred to a psychiatrist in private practice (Psykiatriudvalget, 2013).

However, waiting lists to see an adult psychiatrist in private practice can be long. The average waiting time for non-acute patients is twenty-eight weeks (sundhed.dk, 26 October 2012), and, as mentioned previously, the availability of private psychiatry varies significantly from region to region. This means that a GP may find it necessary to refer a patient with a less severe, but nevertheless impairing, condition to regional hospital or district psychiatry.

3.4.2 *Children*

The assessment and diagnosis of ADHD in children and young people in Denmark is a specialist task and are carried out by a child and adolescent psychiatrist or a neurologist. Educational psychologists, GPs, school doctors, paediatric departments, and social services can refer children to regional child and adolescent psychiatry departments for assessment and treatment, and GPs can also refer to a child and adolescent psychiatrist in private practice. According to practice guidelines, it is recommended that children with moderate to severe ADHD symptoms are referred to regional child and adolescent psychiatry, whereas children with milder symptoms and no comorbid symptoms can be referred to specialists in private practice (Sundhedsstyrelsen, 2013).

Waiting lists to regional child and adolescent psychiatry departments have historically been very long. Only a few years ago, it was not uncommon for children to wait up to two years to be seen in regional child and adolescent psychiatry departments. Recent government legislation has brought waiting lists down and children and young people now have a right to be seen within two months of referral (Ministeriet for Sundhed og Forebyggelse, 2012).

Children diagnosed before this new legislation are likely to have experienced a considerable time on the waiting list before they were seen and their diagnosis was registered. Again, waiting times will have varied considerably from region to region.

3.5 Treatment of ADHD in Denmark

3.5.1 *Adults*

Formal guidelines for the diagnosis and management of adults with ADHD in Denmark have only very recently been published by the Danish Department of Health (Sundhedsstyrelsen, 2015). However, guidelines concerning the pharmacological treatment of adults with ADHD have been in place since 2008 (Sundhedsstyrelsen, 2008). All of the guidelines above highlight that the ADHD diagnosis in adults should be made by an adult psychiatrist or a child and adolescent psychiatrist prior to the prescription of stimulants.

Pharmacological treatment of ADHD in adults is widely used. Stimulant medication (methylphenidate) and non-stimulant medication (atomoxetine) are the most commonly prescribed drugs for ADHD in adults (Thomsen, 2011). However, it is only recently that atomoxetine and certain products containing methylphenidate have been approved by the Danish Department of Health for the initiation of pharmacological treatment of ADHD in adults (Sundhedsstyrelsen, 2015). Multimodal treatment (i.e. a combination of pharmacological and psychosocial intervention) is recommended (Thomsen, 2011; Arngrim et al., 2013; Sundhedsstyrelsen, 2015). There are no studies of actual clinical ADHD treatment practices for adults in Denmark within secondary or primary mental-health services. Thus, it is not known to what extent treatment guidelines are implemented.

3.5.2 Children

Danish guidelines for the diagnosis and management of ADHD in children and young people were published in 2008 by the Danish Society for Child and Adolescent Psychiatry (Børne- og Ungdomspsykiatrisk Selskab i Danmark, 2008) and have only very recently be replaced by formal guidelines set out by the Danish Department of Health (Sundhedsstyrelsen, 2014). Pharmacological treatment is the first-line treatment for ADHD in children between the ages of 6 and 18. The Danish guidelines cite the guidelines developed by the Danish Health and Medicines Authority, and state that stimulant medication in the treatment of ADHD in children and young people between the ages of 6 and 18 years may only be initiated following assessment by a child and adolescent psychiatrist or by a paediatrician or neurologist with specialist knowledge of ADHD.

The Danish guidelines state that medication should not stand alone in the treatment of ADHD. Multimodal treatment is recommended in the treatment of ADHD in children between the ages of 6 and 18 years with moderate to severe symptoms, including pharmacological treatment, psycho-education, and school and parent support. The new guidelines state that it is appropriate to initiate non-pharmacological treatment for children with a lesser degree of functional impairment. However, the guidelines do not define formal criteria for determining degree of functional impairment for this heterogeneous group of children with ADHD between the ages of 6 and 18.

For preschool children with ADHD under the age of 6, the Danish guidelines have traditionally been very sparse. In essence, previous guidelines stated that diagnosis and treatment of ADHD in preschool children is more difficult and less valid and that extra caution should be demonstrated (Børne- og Ungdomspsykiatrisk Selskab i Danmark, 2008). The newly published guidelines by the Danish Department of Health (Sundhedsstyrelsen, 2014) concern children and young people between the ages of 6 and 18, and do not include guidelines for the assessment and treatment of young children below the age of 6. The Danish Department of Health has, however, not approved stimulant medication in the treatment of children below the age of 6, and prescriptions for young children are made off label.

There are no studies of actual clinical treatment practices for ADHD in children and young people in Denmark. Thus, it is not known to what extent clinical guidelines of ADHD assessment and treatment are implemented in hospital-based or community-based mental-health services.

3.5.3 Registration of Mental-Health Disorders in Denmark in the Psychiatric Central Register

Denmark has exceptional opportunities to perform register-based research, and the CPR number given to all Danish permanent residents makes it possible to link information at the individual level from several registers for investigation of various research questions (see Thygesen and Ersbøll, 2014). The Psychiatric Central Register is an electronic register containing information on every psychiatric admission from 1969 onwards. It became an integrated part of the Danish National Patient Register in 1995. Psychiatric data from the National Patient Register is now passed on to the Psychiatric Central Register at the centre for Psychiatric Research every month (see Mors et al., 2011).

The Psychiatric Central Register contains, beyond CPR numbers, the following data: type of referral, dates and mode of admission, discharge, start and end of any outpatient treatment, psychiatric accident and emergency visits, all diagnoses, place of treatment with identification of the specific department, and municipality of residence (Mors et al., 2011).

It is mandatory for all secondary-sector hospital inpatient and outpatient mental-health services to register the above information in the National Patient Register. Psychiatrists in private practice and GPs are not required to register psychiatric patient data in the National Patient Register. Thus, the register contains psychiatric data on patients referred to secondary hospital inpatient and outpatient mental-health services only.

As outlined previously, patients referred to secondary-sector mental-health services may represent a group of individuals with more severe and complex symptoms and impairment. In contrast, patients with milder symptoms and impairment may be referred to psychiatrists in private practice. This assumption is made upon directions outlined in referral guidelines only, as there are very few systematic registrations of any kind, including psychiatric diagnoses of patients seen in private practice (Psykiatriudvalget, 2013). Diagnoses of individuals diagnosed in primary-care private psychiatry practice are not registered in the Danish Psychiatric Central Register.

3.5.4 *Validity and Reliability of Psychiatric Diagnoses in the Danish Registers*

The most fundamental scientific criticism of psychiatric diagnoses concerns their validity and reliability. Simply stated, this refers to whether psychiatric diagnoses are actually real conditions in people in the real world that can be consistently identified by their diagnostic criteria. Systematic validation studies of clinical diagnoses in the Danish case registers against research diagnoses do not exist (Mors et al., 2011). Validation of some diagnoses (e.g. schizophrenia) has been carried out with good results (see Mors et al., 2011), but, to date, a validation of Danish case-register diagnosis for ADHD has not been performed.

Clinical diagnoses vary considerably across psychiatric practices, which has implications for the reliability of the clinical diagnoses in the Danish registers. Whilst diagnostic manuals, such as the ICD-10, provide a description of the diagnostic criteria required to meet a certain diagnosis, it is widely acknowledged that there is large inconsistency in the application of those criteria by clinicians. Standardized diagnostic assessments and measurements in Danish psychiatry have been the exception rather than the rule. In clinical psychiatric practice, the clinical diagnostic measure consists of the observation of the individual psychiatrist, which in turn is dependent upon his or her training, knowledge, experience, bias towards certain diagnoses, and sensitivity to the patient's experience and life circumstances (Parnas, Mors, and Kragh-Sørensen, 2009). Thus, in reality, psychiatric diagnoses can vary extensively between individual psychiatrists and consequently between individual hospital departments, hospitals, and regions. This is true for all clinical primary and comorbid secondary psychiatric diagnoses made in routine clinical practice. Similarly, the variation in the extent to which clinicians diagnose psychiatric comorbid conditions is also considerable.

The problems relating to the reliability and validity of psychiatric diagnoses are not specific to Danish psychiatric practice or to the diagnoses entered in the Danish registers. They are universal problems in clinical psychiatric practice, and their implications can be generalized to all research using routine clinical diagnoses in the scientific literature (Aboraya et al., 2006).

3.5.5 *The Danish National Prescription Registry*

As has been outlined in this chapter so far, not all individuals with ADHD in Denmark are referred to, diagnosed, or treated in secondary-care hospital-based psychiatry services—services which are highly specialized and intended for complex mental-health problems and needs. Individuals who are referred for specialist assessment for ADHD, but who may not be severely functionally impaired, or who present with complex comorbid mental-health conditions, may, according to Danish guidelines, be referred to private psychiatry practice, which provides general psychiatry services. However, psychiatrists in private practice in Denmark do not register patient data in the Danish Psychiatric Central Register. Unfortunately, from the perspective of registry studies, this means that individuals diagnosed with ADHD in private psychiatry practice cannot be identified by their ADHD diagnosis in the Danish registers.

Considering that ADHD is a condition which often does not require inpatient or highly specialized services at the secondary level of mental-health care provision, a considerable number of individuals in need of an assessment for ADHD will be referred by their GP for an assessment in private psychiatry practice. To gain access in our analysis to this, in theory, large group of individuals with ADHD, the study accesses data in a different Danish register, the Register of Medicinal Products Statistics (RMPS), maintained by the Danish Medicines Agency. In this register, individual-level data on all prescription drugs sold in Danish community pharmacies has been recorded since 1994. From an international perspective, the RMPS is unique, providing individual-level information on dispensed prescriptions for an entire nation since 1994 (Kildemoes et al., 2011). In terms of the validity and coverage of data in this register, reimbursement-driven record keeping, with automated bar-code-based data entry provides data of high quality, including detailed information on the dispensed drug (Kildemoes et al., 2011: 38).

Thus, using this register, data on ADHD medication prescriptions at an individual level can be retrieved and linked with many other nationwide individual-level data sources (Kildemoes et al., 2011). For the purpose of the present study, ADHD medication has been defined as the purchase of a drug containing methylphenidate (ATC-code: N06BA04), atomoxetine (ATC-code: N06BA09), or dexamphetamine (ATC-code N06BA02).

3.5.6 *ADHD: Diagnostic and Pharmacological Treatment Trends in Denmark*

The past decade has seen a marked rise in the number of individuals diagnosed with ADHD. In 2001, 1206 cases were registered in Denmark, and in 2010 and 2011 there were 9495 and 10,662 cases respectively. In 2002, 96 per cent of cases were children. In 2011, more than 75 per cent of cases diagnosed with ADHD were children (Psykiatriudvalget, 2013).

ADHD is the most frequently registered psychiatric diagnosis in children and young people. A recent analysis shows wide variation in children and young people diagnosed with ADHD between regions (Psykiatriudvalget, 2013). Consistently, between 2005 and 2011, fewest ADHD cases were diagnosed in the North Denmark Region. Between 2005 and 2009, ADHD was consistently diagnosed most in the Central Denmark Region. And in 2010 and 2011, ADHD was diagnosed most in the Zealand Region. The difference between the highest and lowest number of cases per 1,000 inhabitants rises during the six-year period, except in 2010. In 2005 the difference was 2.1 children/young people per 1000 inhabitants, whereas this figure had risen to 5.3 children/young people in 2011 (Psykiatriudvalget, 2013). The regional differences are more likely to be the result of different diagnostic practices than the result of an actual difference in the incidence of ADHD in different regions (Psykiatriudvalget, 2013).

The overall rise in the number of children, young people, and adults diagnosed with ADHD has also seen a marked increase in stimulant prescription rates. Over the past ten years the number of individuals receiving pharmacological treatment for ADHD has risen from 2901 individuals in 2002 to 35,554 individuals in 2011 (Statens Serum Institut, 2012). ADHD is a new diagnosis for adults. In 2001, there were hardly any registered ADHD diagnoses in adults. In 2009, more than 11,000 adults were prescribed methylphenidate off label (Psykiatriudvalget, 2013).

Part II
Adults with ADHD

MAIN CONTENT: The main purpose of the second part of this book is to define groups of adult individuals diagnosed with ADHD and to compare these groups with one another and with the general population in a number of areas.

Part II will provide a number of interpretations along the descriptive statistics. However, it will not contain any estimation results. The estimation results are presented in Part III.

METHOD: We use several data registers that are available from Statistics Denmark to define two groups of individuals with ADHD and to measure their performance. These registers contain detailed information about the entire Danish population over an extended period of time and make it possible to follow individuals before and after ADHD diagnosis. The year 2010 is the latest fully updated year for all the registers used in this book, and 2010 is thus the year of focus.

MAIN RESULTS: In Chapter 4, we construct two groups of individuals who were diagnosed with ADHD as adults. One group consists of individuals diagnosed with ADHD in the secondary health sector; we call individuals in this group diagnosed adults (DA). The other group consists of individuals who are receiving either first-, second-, or third-line medication to treat ADHD and are not being treated for other diseases for which this medication could be prescribed. These individuals have been diagnosed in the primary health sector, and we call individuals belonging to this group prescribed adults (PA).

The DA group consists of 5,331 individuals, and the PA group consists of 13,662 individuals.

In addition to our formal register-based definition of individuals with ADHD, the two chapters in this part of the book also contain a large body of descriptive statistics. The main points arising from these statistics are as follows:

- In most of the statistics individuals in the DA group are more impaired by ADHD than individuals in the PA group. Individuals in the PA group are placed between individuals in the DA group and the general population.

- With respect to demographics, the two groups of individuals with ADHD have a younger age distribution than the general population and contain a larger share of males. However, the two groups have smaller shares of first- and second-generation immigrants than the rest of the population.

- Both groups of individuals with ADHD have on average more psychiatric diagnoses than the general population, but individuals in the DA group have far more comorbid diagnoses than individuals in the PA group. A large share of comorbid diagnoses are substance-abuse-related disorders.

- Parents of individuals with ADHD are younger and earn less than parents of the average person in the rest of the population, and members of the two ADHD groups are much more likely to have an unstable family background than members of the general population.

- Individuals who have ADHD on average have less education, are more likely to be out of the labour force, and earn significantly less than members of the general population. In fact, less than 30 per cent of the DA group were wage earners in November 2009, and these wage earners earned a lower hourly wage than the rest of the population.

- Persons with ADHD are more likely to engage in criminal activity, and, when they do, these crimes are on average more serious than crimes committed by other individuals. Individuals with ADHD are also more likely to be victims of crimes and in particular of violent crimes.

- Individuals with ADHD are more likely to be involved in traffic accidents than members of the general population, and the accidents that such individuals are involved in are more likely to result in injury. A larger share of traffic accidents involving persons with ADHD are alcohol-related compared with traffic accidents involving other individuals.

- Individuals diagnosed with ADHD have a three- to four-fold increased likelihood of being placed away from home at some point during their childhood compared to a member of the general population, and the children of persons with ADHD are also more likely to have received preventive measures[1] or to be placed away from home.

- Individuals with ADHD, on average, use both the primary and the secondary health-care sector more than the average individual from the general population, and the average medicine costs for individuals with ADHD exceed those for members of the general public.

---

[1] Preventive measures include, among other things, stays providing respite care for parents etc., personal advisers, trainee stay, maintenance of a permanent contact person or personal adviser for young people over 18 years, appointment of a welfare officer for the young person, and appointment of a permanent contact person for the young person.

4

Identification of Treatment Groups

The main purpose of this chapter is to identify and characterize the two groups of individuals who are referred to as 'treatment groups' in the following chapters. These two groups consist of individuals who have been diagnosed with ADHD as adults and will serve as the basis for comparison with a number of other groups in later chapters in order to determine the private and social costs of ADHD.

The primary reason for working with two different patient groups is that ADHD may be diagnosed in two different parts of the Danish health system—both in private specialized psychiatry practice and in secondary-sector hospital-based psychiatry (as described in Chapter 3). It might be argued that we should pool together all individuals into one group instead of working with two groups; however, this chapter and the following chapter will demonstrate that these two groups are different with respect to a number of socioeconomic characteristics, and we thus prefer to keep them distinct from one another. Furthermore, the referral pathways for the two groups are very different. Less severely impacted individuals are not referred into secondary-care psychiatry, but are seen in private psychiatry practice in the primary sector.

In addition to defining the two treatment groups, this and the following chapter present background information about the two treatment groups. This chapter focuses on presenting demographic and medical information for the groups, whereas Chapter 5 presents data on family background, labour-market performance, educational attainment, criminal history and traffic accidents, childhood performance, parenthood, and health.

Before turning to the precise definitions of the two treatment groups, we offer a detailed explanation on the applied data sets.

4.1 Data Sources

The data sets used originate from administrative registers maintained primarily by Statistics Denmark. These registers contain detailed information about the Danish population but preserve individuals' anonymity.

Any person registered as of April 1968 in the Danish civil register receives a personal identification number. This includes persons who (i) are born in Denmark of a mother already registered in the civil register, (ii) have their birth or baptism registered in the Danish electronic church book, or (iii) reside legally in Denmark for three months or more. Furthermore, any person who is required to pay tax in Denmark also receives a personal identification number.[1] Statistics Denmark receives individual-level information from the civil register linked to each personal identification number on a daily basis.

In this way Statistics Denmark provides information about the entire Danish population. The statistics are updated with births to all women with residence in Denmark and all deaths of people with residence in Denmark, regardless of whether the birth or death happens outside Denmark.

Based on personal identification numbers, it is possible to link every person to all of the different registers maintained by Statistics Denmark.

Obtaining authorization to access the required data set for this study involves a number of approvals:

- Statistics Denmark has to authorize the overall access to their hosted register data. Only Danish research environments are granted authorization. Foreign researchers can, however, get access to register data through an affiliation to a Danish authorized environment. Access is given to anonymized micro data, i.e. data at an individual level. Access takes place via the researcher's own computer over the Internet through remote access to data servers hosted by Statistics Denmark.

- Data from other sources can also be linked to data from Statistics Denmark, e.g. data from other administrative registers. Data from external sources requires approval from the Danish Data Protection Agency. Hence, for the data set applied in this study, approval has been obtained for the Danish Psychiatric Central Register and the Register of Medicinal Product Statistics.

- Moreover, approvals from National Health Surveillance and Research have also been given to obtain access to the Danish Psychiatric Central Register and Register of Medicinal Product Statistics. These approvals are needed because National Health Surveillance and Research are the register owners.

---

[1] Danish citizens who are living abroad do not have an active personal identification number.

66

The following is a short description of the data sources used in this and the following chapters.

4.1.1 *The Danish National Patient Register*

Every time a person is in contact with the Danish secondary-sector-based hospital system—for example, to receive a medical examination or treatment—such information is recorded in the National Patient Register. Information recorded relates to hospital admissions, outpatient visits, and accident and emergency department visits. In addition, the National Patient Register includes information on the hospital and departments involved, hospitalization and discharge dates, discharge diagnoses, and any surgeries performed. For more detailed descriptions, see Lynge et al. (2011).

The National Patient Registry available for researchers only includes observations from secondary hospital-based psychiatry services in the years 2006 and 2007. Therefore we also need the Psychiatric Central Register to identify individuals diagnosed with ADHD going back to 1995 and after 2007.

4.1.2 *The Danish Psychiatric Central Register and the Register of Medicinal Product Statistics*

The Danish Psychiatric Central Register contains information about all admissions to all Danish secondary-sector hospital-based psychiatry. Individual records include date of admission, diagnoses, date of discharge, and reason for admission, including whether the person was admitted voluntarily. The records in the Psychiatric Central Register cover the period from 1967 onwards and thus cover hospital admissions for almost all of the current Danish population. For more detailed description, see Chapter 3 or Mors et al. (2011).

Statistics Denmark provides access to a special database constructed to supply data to epidemiological projects (the Register of Medicinal Product Statistics). This database contains records for all sales of prescription medication in Denmark, with individual records that show the recipient, type of drug, price paid, etc. The extracted data sets consist entirely of personal data. The data set does not contain information on non-prescription medications because only prescription medication is subject to individual subsidies (Kildemoes et al., 2011).

4.1.3 *Student Register*

The Student Register records the educational programmes in which individuals have been enrolled. The register is updated annually with reports from educational institutions. Terminations in enrolment, whether a student drops out or graduates with a diploma, are recorded. The register covers student enrolment in educational institutions from elementary school (grade 8) to graduate studies at the university level and includes students from programmes that are publicly regulated by the Ministry of Education or other ministries that regulate education. Finally, the register also contains information regarding students' grades in high school. For more detailed description see <http://dst.dk/en/Statistik/dokumentation/declarations/the-student-registre.aspx>.

Based on this register, Statistics Denmark also provides a data set with individual-level information about highest attained educational level, the Danish Education Register (Jensen and Rasmussen, 2011).

4.1.4 *The Danish Central Crime Register*

Statistics on criminal activities are part of the Danish Central Crime Register. This register contains reports on criminal activity, which includes information on reported crimes, victims, criminal arrests, verdicts, and incarcerations. These statistics are person-based case statistics that indicate the number of violations of criminal law, traffic law, and/or special legislation attributed to an individual. The statistics include imprisonments, fines, indictments or failed indictments, and acquittals. The statistics do not include fines below 200 euros for violations of traffic law or other laws. The statistics are compiled annually (see <http://www.dst.dk/en/Statistik/emner/kriminalitet.aspx>).

4.1.5 *Traffic Accident Register*

Statistics on traffic accidents include reports on all accidents with personal injury known by the police. The statistics include, among other things, information about injury (persons killed, injured, or uninjured) and alcohol exposure. The statistics are compiled annually (see <http://www.dst.dk/en/Statistik/emner/trafikulykker.aspx>).

4.1.6 *Integrated Database for Labour Market Research (IDA)*

Data from the Integrated Database for Labour Market Research (IDA) link people and businesses. In IDA, individuals are described in terms of information about the company at which they are employed, and companies are described on the basis of information about their employees.

There are more than 250 variables in the database, including a variety of background variables describing the population. It is possible to follow both individuals and companies over time.

As far as possible, variables are coded the same way all year so that information can be compared throughout the year. The IDA provides information on the entire Danish population (5.5 million individuals in 2010) and all businesses with employees (approximately 230,000 firms). For more details, see <http://dst.dk/en/Statistik/dokumentation/declarations/register-based-labour-force-statistics-register-based-labour-force-statistics.aspx>.

4.1.7 Income Statistics Register

The purpose of the income register is to provide information about income, taxes, and deductions. The statistics include total income (net and gross), taxable income, tax, etc. For more information, see Baadsgaard and Quitzau (2011).

4.1.8 The National Sickness Benefit Register

This register consists of every sickness-benefit transfer made throughout the year in focus. The register records information on the kind of benefit and the period of absence due to sickness. For more details, see <http://www.dst.dk/da/Statistik/dokumentation/Times/sygedagpenge.aspx>.

4.2 Treatment Groups

Having introduced the main data sources, we turn to the precise definitions of the two treatment groups. The remainder of the chapter is divided into three parts. First, we present the group of individuals with ADHD who were diagnosed in the secondary health sector; then, we present the group of individuals with ADHD who were diagnosed in the primary health sector; finally, we make a few comparisons between and within the two groups.

With respect to the above-mentioned data sources, the latest available full year with updated information is 2010. Therefore, we define the two treatment groups based on data from no later than 2010.

4.2.1 Individuals with ADHD Diagnosed in the Secondary Sector

This group of patients consists of individuals referred to and diagnosed within secondary health-care psychiatry services in Denmark.

We refer to this group as the diagnosed adults (DA) group.

We define individuals as having ADHD if they have at least one of the following ICD-10 diagnoses:

- disturbance of activity and attention (F90.0)
- hyperkinetic conduct disorder (F90.1)

- other hyperkinetic disorders (F90.8)
- hyperkinetic disorder, unspecified (F90.9)
- other specified behavioural and emotional disorders with onset usually occurring in childhood and adolescence (F98.8).

The population of patients with ADHD thus contains all individuals who received at least one of the above-listed diagnoses between 1995 and 2010 and who were at least 18 years old at the time of their diagnosis. Concurrently, we exclude individuals from our analysis who were more than 50 years old at the time of their diagnosis in order to harmonize the inclusion criterion for age in both treatment groups (explained below). The group consists of 5,331 individuals.

Table 4.1 shows the distribution of adults who have received an ADHD diagnosis in the secondary health sector. This group includes 9,457 individuals, of whom 5,331 were diagnosed as adults (older than 18 years of age), whereas the remaining individuals were diagnosed when they were younger than 18 years of age. Approximately 70 per cent have an F90.0 diagnosis (disturbance of activity and attention), and approximately 15 per cent have an F90.9 diagnosis (hyperkinetic disorder, unspecified).

Comparing the distribution in columns 2 and 4 in Table 4.1, it is clear that a relatively larger share of those with an F98.8 diagnosis (other specified behavioural and emotional disorders with onset typically occurring in childhood and adolescence) were not diagnosed as adults.

However, including information from registrations of ADHD diagnoses made in the secondary hospital-based psychiatry only is likely to lead to a narrow definition of patients with ADHD. As explained in Chapter 3, in Denmark not all patients with symptoms of ADHD are referred to secondary hospital-based psychiatry services. Some may consult or be referred to a psychiatrist in private practice. Over the last 5–6 years, the number of ADHD diagnoses has increased considerably, and a relatively large share of persons are likely to have been diagnosed outside the secondary-sector hospital-based

Table 4.1. ADHD diagnosis of individuals who were older than 18 years of age in 2010

	Diagnosed adults		ADHD, total	
Disturbance of activity and attention (F90.0)	3,909	73.33%	6,183	65.38%
Hyperkinetic conduct disorder (F90.1)	390	7.32%	1,022	10.81%
Other hypekinetic disorders (F90.8)	64	1.20%	103	1.09%
Hyperkinetic disorder, unspecified (F90.9)	786	14.74%	1,155	12.21%
Other specified behavioral and emotional disorders with onset usually occurring in childhood and adolscence (F98.8)	182	3.41%	994	10.51%
Total	5,331	100.00%	9,457	100.00%

psychiatry system, partly because their impairment may not have been severe enough to warrant a hospital-based referral, but has been considered manageable within private psychiatry services. To secure inclusion of these individuals, we turn to the definition of our second treatment group in this study.

4.2.2 Individuals with ADHD Diagnosed in the Primary Sector

Our second treatment group of individuals with ADHD is identified on the basis of the individuals' medication use. As psychiatric disorders diagnosed in the private psychiatric practice are not registered in the Danish registers, we identify individuals with ADHD using the Register of Medicinal Product Statistics. From this database, we have identified a group of individuals who have been prescribed the first-, second-, or third-line treatment medicines methylphenidate, atomoxetine, or dexamphetamine, respectively, in adulthood (not before the age of 18 years) from 1995 to 2010. We have excluded individuals with certain psychiatric disorders from this group because of the non-representativeness of ADHD.

We refer to this group as the prescribed adults (PA) group.

More specifically, PA individuals are defined as those adults who received one or more of the following three medicines between 1995 and 2010 (numbers in parentheses are ATC codes):

- methylphenidate (N06BA04)
- atomoxetine (N06BA09)
- dexamphetamine (N06BA02).

Our hypothesis is that this group consists of individuals with less severe conditions because they have been treated not at hospitals but in the primary health-care sector. The three medications are also used for disorders other than ADHD. In particular, they are sometimes used in the treatment of individuals with narcolepsy and experimentally in dementia. Therefore, we have excluded individuals with either of these diagnoses from the group.[2] Moreover, those individuals who are in the group defined in the previous section are excluded from the PA group because they were diagnosed in the secondary health sector and therefore belong to the DA group.

As was the case with the group of individuals with ADHD defined above, the present group of individuals is also limited to include only those who began

---

[2] The precise ICD-10 diagnoses that were excluded are F00 (dementia in Alzheimer's disease), F01 (vascular dementia), F02 (dementia in other diseases classified elsewhere), F03 (unspecified dementia), G47.4 (narcolepsy and cataplexy), F70–F79 (excl. F78) (mental retardation), and F84–F89 (excl. F84.5) (pervasive developmental disorders).

Table 4.2. ADHD medicine use among individuals who were older than 18 years of age in 2010 (excl. DA)

	Prescribed adults		ADHD, total	
Methylphenidate (N06BA04)	12,774	93.50%	14,347	93.50%
Atomoxetine (N06BA09)	843	6.17%	913	5.95%
Dexamphetamine (N06BA02)	45	0.33%	84	0.55%
Total	13,662	100.00%	15,344	100.00%

their treatment after they turned 18 years of age. Finally, individuals more than 50 years old when they began their treatment are also excluded, due to the possibility that stimulant medication has been used in the treatment of dementia, for example.

The group consists of 13,662 individuals.

Table 4.2 shows the medicines received by PA individuals. A large share (almost 95 per cent) of these individuals received the first-line treatment methylphenidate rather than the second- or third-line treatments.

We present a detailed comparison of the two ADHD groups below and in the following chapter.

4.3 Comparison of the Two ADHD Groups

In this section, we compare the two groups defined above with respect to a number of characteristics. First, we look at the year of diagnosis, which is presented in Table 4.3.

The increase in ADHD diagnoses in recent years is reflected in both treatment groups. For both ADHD groups, more than 85 per cent of the diagnoses were made in 2006 and later. However, it seems clear from comparing the two panels that the increase in the number of diagnoses is even more rapid for those recently diagnosed in the secondary sector because more than 90 per cent began their treatment in 2006 or later.

Table 4.4 presents the age of the individuals when the diagnosis was registered. The table shows that almost half of the PA and more than half of the DA were younger than 30 years of age at the time of their diagnosis. In fact, more than 45 per cent of the DA were 25 years or younger when they received the diagnosis.

In the appendix to this chapter, Table 4.A.1 shows the age distribution in 2010 of the individuals in the two ADHD groups compared with that of the general population. As would be expected from Table 4.4, individuals in the two ADHD groups are much younger than individuals in the rest of the population, on average. In fact, a third of the DA and almost a quarter of the PA were between

Table 4.3. Year of diagnosis

	Diagnosed adults		Prescribed adults	
1995–1999	68	1.28%	687	5.03%
2000–2005	425	7.97%	1,247	9.13%
2006	457	8.57%	660	4.83%
2007	659	12.36%	1,196	8.75%
2008	1,057	19.83%	2,076	15.20%
2009	1,272	23.86%	3,565	26.09%
2010	1,393	26.13%	4,231	30.97%
Total	5,331	100%	13,662	100%

Table 4.4. Age when diagnosed

	Diagnosed adults		Prescribed adults	
18–20	1,260	23.64%	1,771	12.96%
21–25	1,245	23.35%	2,344	17.16%
26–30	945	17.73%	2,096	15.34%
31–35	753	14.12%	2,325	17.02%
36–40	583	10.94%	2,053	15.03%
41–45	363	6.81%	1,793	13.12%
46–50	182	3.41%	1,280	9.37%
Total	5331	100.00%	13,662	100.00%

Table 4.5. Gender

	Diagnosed adults		Prescribed adults		Population	
Female	1,919	36.00%	5,811	42.53%	1,954,593	48.92%
Male	3,412	64.00%	7,851	57.47%	2,041,253	51.08%
Total	5,331	100.00%	13,662	100.00%	3,995,846	100.00%

18 and 25 years of age in 2010, whereas only 14 per cent of individuals in the general population were between 18 and 25 years of age in 2010.[3]

Table 4.5 shows the gender distribution of the two groups compared with that of the general population. Approximately two-thirds of the DA individuals are males, whereas only 57 per cent of the PA individuals are males. The table thus confirms what has previously been found elsewhere: namely, that more males than females are diagnosed with ADHD.

A somewhat surprising picture arises from an analysis of the geographic distribution of individuals with ADHD across Denmark, as shown in Table 4.6. The table shows that the Central Region is highly overrepresented among the

---

[3] In the comparisons, individuals older than 65 years of age were excluded because no individuals who were diagnosed with ADHD were older than 65 years of age in 2010.

Table 4.6. Geographic region

	Diagnosed adults		Prescribed adults		Population	
North Denmark	273	5.21%	1,310	10.07%	316,824	9.24%
Central Denmark	2,408	45.99%	4,580	35.22%	971,684	28.34%
Southern Denmark	820	15.66%	1,339	10.30%	557,857	16.27%
Capital Region of Denmark	1,093	20.87%	3,578	27.52%	1,039,887	30.33%
Zealand	642	12.26%	2,196	16.89%	542,654	15.83%
Total	5,236	100.00%	13,003	100.00%	3,428,906	100.00%

Table 4.7. Immigration status

	Diagnosed adults		Prescribed adults		Population	
Native	5,084	95.37%	12,800	93.70%	3,310,406	84.20%
Immigrant	189	3.55%	748	5.48%	579,854	14.75%
Second-generation immigrant	58	1.09%	113	0.83%	41,430	1.05%
Total	5,331	100.00%	13,661	100.00%	3,931,690	100.00%

DA and PA groups with 46 per cent and 35 per cent of the cases, respectively, whereas this region contains only 28 per cent of the population. The main reason for this skewed distribution is not that individuals in certain regions are more likely to have ADHD, but more probably the result of difference in diagnostic practice across regions. (See also Chapter 3 for discussion of regional variation in diagnostic practices.)

The final table in this first part of the demographic comparison is Table 4.7, which shows individuals' immigration status.

Although more than 15 per cent of the general adult population in Denmark are either immigrants or second-generation immigrants, this is true for less than 5 per cent of the individuals in the DA group and less than 6 per cent of those in the PA group. Immigrant groups are thus substantially underrepresented in the ADHD groups.

4.3.1 Comorbidity

We now turn to the medical comorbidity of the two groups. In particular, we focus on the mental health of individuals with ADHD compared with that of the general population.

Table 4.8 shows the number of psychiatric diagnoses per individual grouped by the classification system in the ICD-10. The table compares the average number of psychiatric diagnoses for the two ADHD groups with that of the remaining population.

A number of points should be made regarding the information presented in Table 4.8. First, the average number of diagnoses is clearly highest for DA.

Table 4.8. Number of psychiatric diagnoses

(F00–F99)	Diagnosed adults		Prescribed adults		Population	
Organic, including symptomatic, mental disorders (F00–F09)	218 **0.04**	0.95%	346 **0.03**	1.44%	20,618 **0.01**	1.75%
Mental and behavioural disorders due to psychoactive substance use (F10–F19)	5,494 **1.03**	23.87%	7,009 **0.51**	29.13%	349,758 **0.09**	29.71%
Schizophrenia, schizotypal, and delusional disorders (F20–F29)	1,457 **0.27**	6.33%	1,800 **0.13**	7.48%	116,809 **0.03**	9.92%
Mood [affective] disorders (F30–F39)	2,608 **0.49**	11.33%	4,439 **0.32**	18.45%	238,808 **0.06**	20.28%
Neurotic, stress-related, and somatoform disorders (F40–F48)	3,203 **0.60**	13.92%	4,952 **0.36**	20.58%	271,779 **0.07**	23.09%
Behavioural syndromes associated with physiological disturbances and physical factors (F50–F59)	254 **0.05**	1.10%	527 **0.04**	2.19%	32,896 **0.01**	2.79%
Disorders of adult personality and behaviour (F60–F69)	2,117 **0.40**	9.20%	2,995 **0.22**	12.45%	76,362 **0.02**	6.49%
Mental retardation (F70–F79)	152 **0.03**	0.66%	154 **0.01**	0.64%	6,102 **0.00**	0.52%
Disorders of psychological development (F80–F89)	260 **0.05**	1.13%	315 **0.02**	1.31%	7,937 **0.00**	0.67%
Behavioural and emotional disorders with onset usually occurring in childhood and adolescence (F90–F98)	6,535 **1.23**	28.40%	548 **0.04**	2.28%	19,037 **0.00**	1.62%
Unspecified mental disorder (F99–F99)	714 **0.13**	3.10%	975 **0.07**	4.05%	37,176 **0.01**	3.16%
Total	23,012	100.00%	24,060	100.00%	1,177,282	100.00%
Ratio (Diagnosis per patient)	**4.32**		**1.76**		**0.29**	

Individuals in the DA group have an average of 4.3 different psychiatric diagnoses compared with an average of 1.8 diagnoses for the PA and 0.3 diagnoses for the rest of the population. In fact, when looking at each of the groups separately, the DA group clearly has more diagnoses than the two other groups. This is perhaps not surprising, as the DA group has been seen in secondary-sector hospital-based psychiatry services, which is the sector where registration of psychiatric diagnoses is mandatory. Moreover, individuals referred to secondary-sector hospital-based psychiatry services (DA) would be considered more functionally impaired, with complex mental-health problems (i.e. increased comorbidity), than individuals referred to and managed in primary-care private psychiatry practice.

Second, the number of diagnoses of 'mental and behavioural disorders due to psychoactive substance use' and 'behavioural and emotional disorders with onset typically occurring in childhood and adolescence' is particularly large for the DA group. It is hardly surprising that the number of diagnoses in the latter classification is higher for this group, because these diagnoses form the basis of our definition of the individuals in this treatment group (cf. Table 4.1). This suggests that a relatively large share of individuals in the DA group have problems with substance abuse. We examine this in more detail below.

Third, although the number of diagnoses is much smaller for PA than for DA, the average number of diagnoses for PA remains significantly higher than that for the rest of the population. For example, members of the general population have 0.09 diagnoses in 'mental and behavioural disorders due to psychoactive substance use' on average, whereas the similar number for the PA group is 0.51.

To further understand the nature of the substance abuse among individuals with ADHD in more detail, we look at the diagnoses of 'mental and behavioural disorders due to psychoactive substance use' among the groups in Table 4.9.

Roughly half of the diagnoses of mental disorders due to psychoactive substance use are due to alcohol use (F10), with 0.43 such diagnoses, on average, for the DA group and 0.26 such diagnoses, on average, for the PA group. However, cannabis use (F12) and multiple drug use (F19) also seem to be common among those identified as having ADHD.

Table 4.9 thus confirms that substance abuse is more widespread among individuals with ADHD—this is true for both groups of individuals with ADHD, albeit to a much larger extent for DA. As shown in Table 4.8, it is also clear that more individuals with ADHD have diagnoses of mental and behavioural disorders than those in the general population, even for those diagnosed in the primary sector.

In the appendix to this chapter, we present tables similar to Table 4.9 for other psychiatric disorders comorbid with ADHD. The overall picture derived from Tables 4.8 and 4.9 is confirmed by these tables: the number of diagnoses is highest for individuals in the DA group; the number of diagnoses for individuals in the PA group is much smaller but still larger than that of the general population.

A final table in the appendix shows the medical use of centrally acting sympathomimetic drugs (the group of medicines to which the ADHD medicines belong). Not surprisingly the medicines used for ADHD treatment are highly represented in the statistics with 4,269 DA and 13,155 PA receiving methylphenidate, 1,135 DA and 1,907 PA receiving atomoxetine, and 18 DA and 89 PA receiving dexamphetamine. The only other medicine with a significant number of users is modafinil, with 180 in DA and 832 in PA. This drug is registered for the treatment of severe sleepiness/narcolepsy, but prescribed by some psychiatrists to individuals in the treatment of ADHD (see Arngrim et al., 2013).

Table 4.9. Diagnoses of 'mental and behavioural disorders due to psychoactive substance use'

(F10–F19)	Diagnosed adults		Prescribed adults		Population	
Mental and behavioural disorders due to use of alcohol (F10)	2,306 **0.43**	41.97%	3,511 **0.26**	50.09%	262,074 **0.07**	74.93%
Mental and behavioural disorders due to use of opioids (F11)	320 **0.06**	5.82%	443 **0.03**	6.32%	11,872 **0.00**	3.39%
Mental and behavioural disorders due to use of cannabinoids (F12)	735 **0.14**	13.38%	786 **0.06**	11.21%	14,179 **0.00**	4.05%
Mental and behavioural disorders due to use of sedatives or hypnotics (F13)	147 **0.03**	2.68%	210 **0.02**	3.00%	7,285 **0.00**	2.08%
Mental and behavioural disorders due to use of cocaine (F14)	183 **0.03**	3.33%	183 **0.01**	2.61%	2,923 **0.00**	0.84%
Mental and behavioural disorders due to use of other stimulants, including caffeine (F15)	276 **0.05**	5.02%	280 **0.02**	3.99%	3,576 **0.00**	1.02%
Mental and behavioural disorders due to use of hallucinogens (F16)	30 **0.01**	0.55%	35 **0.00**	0.50%	624 **0.00**	0.18%
Mental and behavioural disorders due to use of tobacco (F17)	194 **0.04**	3.53%	257 **0.02**	3.67%	27,273 **0.01**	7.80%
Mental and behavioural disorders due to use of volatile solvents (F18)	5 **0.00**	0.09%	11 **0.00**	0.16%	486 **0.00**	0.14%
Mental and behavioural disorders due to multiple drug use and use of other psychoactive substances (F19)	1298 **0.24**	23.63%	1293 **0.09**	18.45%	19,466 **0.00**	5.57%
Total	5,494	100.00%	7,009	100.00%	349,758	100.00%
Ratio (Diagnosis per patient)	**1.03**		**0.51**		**0.09**	

4.4 Summary

In this chapter we have defined two groups of individuals with ADHD, on whom we shall focus throughout the remainder of this book. One group consists of individuals diagnosed with ADHD in the secondary health sector (DA), whereas the other group consists of individuals who receive either first-, second- or third-line medication as treatment for ADHD and are not being treated for other specific psychiatric disorders that are treated with the same medication (PA).

Furthermore, we have presented descriptive statistics comparing the two groups with one another and with the general population. These statistics show that the two groups of patients with ADHD are young—approximately half are younger than 30 years of age in 2010. Males and native Danes are overrepresented compared to the general population. And more individuals are diagnosed or treated for ADHD in Central Denmark. Moreover, individuals with ADHD have a higher risk of having a comorbid psychiatric diagnosis than individuals in the rest of the population, and this is particularly true for individuals in the DA group. The main comorbid diagnoses are disorders related to substance abuse.

Appendix to Chapter 4: Supplementary Tables

In order to avoid any violations of the anonymity rules of Statistics Denmark some cells in tables in the appendix have been removed.

Table 4.A.1. Age in 2010

	Diagnosed adults		Prescribed adults		Population	
18–20	622	11.67%	1,067	7.81%	212,777	5.32%
21–25	1,414	26.52%	2,305	16.87%	353,368	8.84%
26–30	1,001	18.78%	2,031	14.87%	372,404	9.32%
31–40	1,543	28.94%	4,118	30.14%	867,250	21.70%
41–50	688	12.91%	3,301	24.16%	928,873	23.25%
51–60	63	1.18%	744	5.45%	817,640	20.46%
61–65	0	0.00%	96	0.70%	443,534	11.10%
Total	5,331	100.00%	13,662	100.00%	3,995,846	100.00%

Table 4.A.2. Selected diagnoses with 'schizophrenia, schizotypal, and delusional disorders'

(F20–F29)	Diagnosed adults		Prescribed adults		Population	
Schizophrenia (F20)	576	39.53%	847	47.06%	55,676	47.66%
	0.11		0.06		0.01	
Schizotypal disorder (F21)	128	8.79%	196	10.89%	9,321	7.98%
	0.02		0.01		0.00	
Persistent delusional disorders (F22)	175	12.01%	171	9.50%	13,823	11.83%
	0.03		0.01		0.00	
Acute and transient psychotic disorders (F23)	356	24.43%	367	20.39%	23,586	20.19%
	0.07		0.03		0.01	
Schizoaffective disorders (F25)	77	5.28%	86	4.78%	7,819	6.69%
	0.01		0.01		0.00	
Unspecified non-organic psychosis (F29)	110	7.55%	109	6.06%	4,947	4.24%
	0.02		0.01		0.00	
Total	1,457	100.00%	1,800	100.00%	116,809	100.00%
Ratio (Diagnosis per patient)	0.27		0.13		0.03	

Table 4.A.3. Diagnoses with 'mood [affective] disorders'

(F30–F39)	Diagnosed adults		Prescribed adults		Population	
Manic episode (F30)	28	1.07%	30	0.68%	3,882	1.63%
	0.01		**0.00**		**0.00**	
Bipolar affective disorder (F31)	406	15.57%	625	14.08%	37,057	15.52%
	0.08		**0.05**		**0.01**	
Depressive episode (F32)	1,200	46.01%	2,015	45.39%	114,578	47.98%
	0.23		**0.15**		**0.03**	
Recurrent depressive disorder (F33)	823	31.56%	1,504	33.88%	73,043	30.59%
	0.15		**0.11**		**0.02**	
Persistent mood [affective] disorders (F34)	84	3.22%	176	3.96%	6,563	2.75%
	0.02		**0.01**		**0.00**	
Other mood [affective] disorders (F38)	19	0.73%	34	0.77%	1,239	0.52%
	0.00		**0.00**		**0.00**	
Unspecified mood [affective] disorder (F39)	48	1.84%	55	1.24%	2,446	1.02%
	0.01		**0.00**		**0.00**	
Total	2,608	100.00%	4,439	100.00%	238,808	100.00%
Ratio (Diagnosis per patient)	**0.49**		**0.32**		**0.06**	

Table 4.A.4. Diagnoses with 'neurotic, stress-related, and somatoform disorders'

(F40–F48)	Diagnosed adults		Prescribed adults		Population	
Phobic anxiety disorders (F40)	154	4.81%	270	5.45%	14,977	5.51%
	0.03		**0.02**		**0.00**	
Other anxiety disorders (F41)	524	16.36%	947	19.12%	51,743	19.04%
	0.10		**0.07**		**0.01**	
Obsessive-compulsive disorder (F42)	123	3.84%	209	4.22%	9,411	3.46%
	0.02		**0.02**		**0.00**	
Reaction to severe stress, and adjustment disorders (F43)	2,257	70.47%	3,269	66.01%	175,369	64.53%
	0.42		**0.24**		**0.04**	
Dissociative (conversion) disorder (F44)	31	0.97%	46	0.93%	3,067	1.13%
	0.01		**0.00**		**0.00**	
Somatoform disorders (F45)	58	1.81%	105	2.12%	10,784	3.97%
	0.01		**0.01**		**0.00**	
Other neurotic disorders (F48)	56	1.75%	106	2.14%	6,428	2.37%
	0.01		**0.01**		**0.00**	
Total	3,203	100.00%	4,952	100.00%	271,779	100.00%
Ratio (Diagnosis per patient)	**0.60**		**0.36**		**0.07**	

Table 4.A.5. Selected diagnoses with 'disorders of adult personality and behaviour'

(F60–F69)	Diagnosed adults		Prescribed adults		Population	
Specific personality disorders (F60)	1,797 **0.34**	84.88%	2,580 **0.19**	86.14%	63,725 **0.02**	83.45%
Mixed and other personality disorders (F61)	188 **0.04**	8.88%	263 **0.02**	8.78%	6,485 **0.00**	8.49%
Enduring personality changes, not attributable to brain damage and disease (F62)	23 **0.00**	1.09%	41 **0.00**	1.37%	1,758 **0.00**	2.30%
Habit impulse disorders (F63)	11 **0.00**	0.52%	16 **0.00**	0.53%	658 **0.00**	0.86%
Gender identity disorders (F64)	9 **0.00**	0.43%	14 **0.00**	0.47%	944 **0.00**	1.24%
Other disorders of adult personality and behaviour (F68)	11 **0.00**	0.52%	13 **0.00**	0.43%	888 **0.00**	1.16%
Unspecified disorder of adult personality and behaviour (F69)	70 **0.01**	3.31%	55 **0.00**	1.84%	1,056 **0.00**	1.38%
Total	2,117	100.00%	2,995	100.00%	76,362	100.00%
Ratio (Diagnosis per patient)	**0.40**		**0.22**		**0.02**	

Table 4.A.6. Diagnoses with 'behavioural and emotional disorders with onset usually occurring in childhood and adolescence'

(F90–F98)	Diagnosed adults		Prescribed adults		Population	
Disturbance of activity and attention (F90)	5,785 **1.09**	88.52%	0 **0.00**	0.00%	3,893 **0.00**	20.45%
Conduct disorders (F91)	189 **0.04**	2.89%	139 **0.01**	25.36%	2,299 **0.00**	12.08%
Mixed disorders of conduct and emotions (F92)	96 **0.02**	1.47%	124 **0.01**	22.63%	2,590 **0.00**	13.61%
Emotional disorders with onset specific to childhood (F93)	38 **0.01**	0.58%	39 **0.00**	7.12%	2,196 **0.00**	11.54%
Disorders of social functioning with onset specific to childhood and adolescence (F94)	45 **0.01**	0.69%	55 **0.00**	10.04%	1,660 **0.00**	8.72%
Tic disorders (F95)	65 **0.01**	0.99%	83 **0.01**	15.15%	1,887 **0.00**	9.91%
Other behavioural and emotional disorders with onset usually occurring in childhood and adolescence (F98)	317 **0.06**	4.85%	108 **0.01**	19.71%	4,512 **0.00**	23.70%
Total	6,535	100.00%	548	100.00%	19,037	100.00%
Ratio (Diagnosis per patient)	**1.23**		**0.04**		**0.00**	

Table 4.A.7. Diagnoses with 'hyperkinetic disorders' and 'other behavioural and emotional disorders with onset usually occurring in childhood and adolescence'

(F90.0–F90.9 + F98.0–F98.9)	Diagnosed adults		Prescribed adults		Population	
Hyperkinetic disorders (F90)	27	0.44%			34	0.41%
	0.01				**0.00**	
Disturbance of activity and attention (F90.0)	4,116	67.45%			2,450	29.45%
	0.77				**0.00**	
Hyperkinetic conduct disorder (F90.1)	509	8.34%			810	9.74%
	0.10				**0.00**	
Other hyperkinetic disorders (F90.8)	86	1.41%			51	0.61%
	0.02				**0.00**	
Hyperkinetic disorder, unspecified (F90.9)	1,047	17.16%			548	6.59%
	0.20				**0.00**	
Non-organic enuresis (F98.0)	11	0.18%	7	6.54%	688	8.27%
	0.00		**0.00**		**0.00**	
Non-organic encopresis (F98.1)	18	0.29%	14	13.08%	904	10.87%
	0.00		**0.00**		**0.00**	
Other specified behavioural and emotional disorders with onset usually occurring in childhood and adolescence (F98.8)	214	3.51%	0	0.00%	898	10.79%
	0.04		**0.00**		**0.00**	
Unspecified behavioural and emotional disorders with onset usually occurring in childhood and adolescence (F98.9)	72	1.18%	81	75.70%	1,544	18.56%
	0.01		**0.01**		**0.00**	
Total	6,102	100.00%	107	100.00%	8,319	100.00%
Ratio (Diagnosis per patient)	**1.14**		**0.01**		**0.00**	

Table 4.A.8. Medication—centrally acting sympathomimetics

(N06BA)	Diagnosed adults		Prescribed adults		Population	
Amphetamine (N06BA01)	5	0.09%	23	0.14%	172	1.72%
	0.00		**0.00**		**0.00**	
Dexamfetamine (N06BA02)	18	0.32%	89	0.56%	139	1.39%
	0.00		**0.01**		**0.00**	
Methylphenidate (N06BA04)	4,269	76.14%	13,155	82.19%	6,117	61.15%
	0.80		**0.96**		**0.00**	
Modafinil (N06BA07)	180	3.21%	832	5.20%	2782	27.81%
	0.03		**0.06**		**0.00**	
Atomoxetine (N06BA09)	1,135	20.24%	1907	11.91%	793	7.93%
	0.21		**0.14**		**0.00**	
Total	5,607	100.00%	16,006	100.00%	10,003	100.00%
Ratio (Medication per patient)	**1.05**		**1.17**		**0.00**	

5

Descriptive Statistics for ADHD Individuals

The purpose of this chapter is to continue the characterization of the two groups of individuals with ADHD that were identified in Chapter 4. The areas covered in this chapter concern family background, labour-market success (including wage earnings and educational attainment), criminal history and traffic accidents, childhood performance, parenthood, and health measures.

Where possible, we compare the values within the different areas to similar values for the general population. Thus, the graphs and tables in this chapter aim to provide an overview of how individuals with ADHD fare in day-to-day life compared with the rest of the population.

5.1 Family Background

In this section we present tables on the family background of the ADHD groups defined in Chapter 4. ADHD is a hereditary disorder; if a person has ADHD, it is likely that one or both of his/her parents also has the disorder. Thus, we should expect the background variables to reflect this fact. The number of individuals in this section does not exactly match the numbers in the ADHD groups or in the general population because it was not possible to find information about some individuals' parents. This is particularly true for immigrants and people at the upper end of the age distribution. The DA group presented in this chapter is reduced by less than two per cent whereas the PA group is reduced by six per cent.

First, we present the number of siblings of individuals with ADHD in Table 5.1. The table clearly shows that individuals with ADHD are more likely than individuals in the general population to come from families with more siblings. More than 30 per cent of individuals in the DA have three or more siblings, whereas only 20 per cent of the general population have three or more siblings. The PA group is placed between the two other groups but closer to the DA group.

Table 5.1. Number of siblings

	Diagnosed adults		Prescribed adults		Population	
0	317	6.06%	936	7.30%	293,727	10.67%
1	1,695	32.40%	4,561	35.55%	1,067,745	38.79%
2	1,453	27.78%	3,638	28.36%	790,373	28.71%
3+	1,766	33.76%	3,694	28.79%	600,975	21.83%
Total	5,231	100.00%	12,829	100.00%	2,752,820	100.00%

Table 5.2. Stability of family background

	Diagnosed adults		Prescribed adults		Population	
Unstable	2,250	43.01%	4,585	35.74%	606,203	22.02%
Stable	2,981	56.99%	8,244	64.26%	2,146,617	77.98%
Total	5,231	100%	12,829	100%	2,752,820	100.00%

To examine the stability of the family background of the individuals with ADHD, we have constructed a stability indicator variable with the following property: if the individual comes from a family with information on both parents available in the registers from Statistics Denmark and has only been living together with siblings with the same mother and father (or is an only child), we define the family background as stable. If this is not the case, we define the family background as unstable. Table 5.2 shows the distribution of the stability indicator for the two ADHD groups and for the rest of the population.

The table clearly shows that individuals with ADHD are less likely than the rest of the population to have a stable family background. Only 57 per cent of individuals in the DA group have a stable family background according to our definition, whereas the number of individuals in the PA group with a stable family background is 64 per cent. However, in the general population, 78 per cent of individuals have a stable family background.

Turning to another indicator for unstable family background, we now examine the ages of the mothers and fathers of individuals with ADHD. Figure 5.1 depicts the cumulative distributions for parental ages at first childbirth.

Figures showing the cumulative distribution are used in the following way: on the horizontal axis, select an age (for instance, 25); then, follow this number upwards and read the level of the different curves. In the top panel of Figure 5.1 (for fathers), the age of 25 years meets the dotted curve for the general population at approximately 0.3, while it meets the dashed and solid curves of the two ADHD groups at approximately 0.5. The number 0.3 on the dotted curve signifies that 30 per cent of individuals in the general population have a father who was 25 years or younger at the time of first childbirth. Similarly, the number 0.5 on the dashed and solid curves indicates that 50 per cent of individuals with ADHD have a father who was 25 years or younger at the

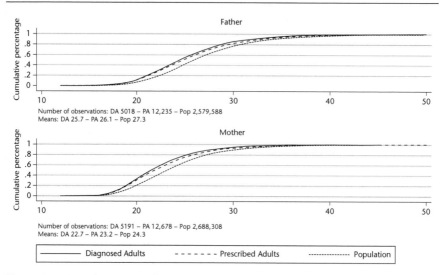

Figure 5.1. Age of parents at first childbirth

Source: Statistics Denmark and own calculations.

time of first childbirth. Below, we present more figures that show cumulative distributions; these figures are read in a similar fashion to that described above.

Going back to Figure 5.1, we can see that the parents of individuals with ADHD are, in fact, on average somewhat younger than the parents of the rest of the population—the dotted curve for the population is to the right of the dashed and solid curves. Thus, individuals with ADHD are more likely to come from a family with younger parents than individuals from the rest of the population.

As an indicator of parents' labour-market performance, we now look at their income throughout the years of their ADHD child's childhood. Figure 5.2 thus shows the cumulative distribution of parents' annual average income over the first eighteen years of the child's life, deflated to the 2000 level using the Danish consumer price index.

The figure clearly shows that the income of the parents of individuals with ADHD is much less than that of parents of other individuals—again the dotted curve is to the right.

However, as shown above, the parents of individuals with ADHD are also younger, on average, than individuals in the rest of the population, so their lower income may simply be a result of their younger age. To investigate whether this is the case, we also look at the education level of the parents.

In Figure 5.3, the distribution of the education level of parents is shown. The figure shows that the average education level of parents of individuals with

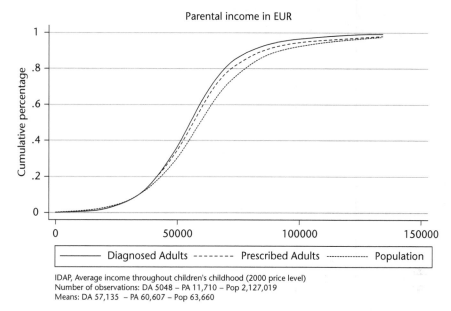

IDAP, Average income throughout children's childhood (2000 price level)
Number of observations: DA 5048 – PA 11,710 – Pop 2,127,019
Means: DA 57,135 – PA 60,607 – Pop 63,660

Figure 5.2. Parental yearly average income in the childhood of the individual with ADHD (deflated with CPI)

Source: Statistics Denmark and own calculations.

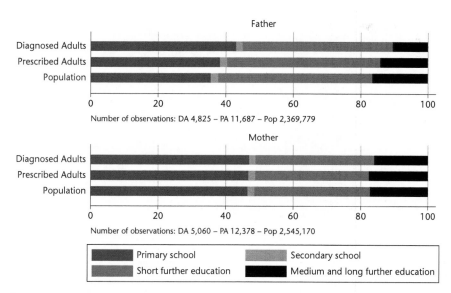

Figure 5.3. Parents' level of education

Source: Statistics Denmark and own calculations.

ADHD is lower than the average education level of parents of individuals in the rest of the population. Whereas there is only a small difference for mothers' education levels across the three groups, it is clear that the education level of fathers differs substantially among the groups. Moreover, a larger share of fathers of individuals with ADHD have completed only primary school compared with the fathers of individuals from the rest of the population.

5.2 Labour Market

We next examine to what extent the two groups of individuals with ADHD in our study are able to obtain employment or an education.

First, we look at the educational attainment of the individuals with ADHD, which is shown in Figure 5.4. This figure indicates that individuals with ADHD have a much lower education level than the general population. Two-thirds of those in the DA group have completed primary school only, compared with 50 per cent of those in the PA group and 38 per cent of the general population. At the other end of the education spectrum, only 6 per cent of the DA group have completed tertiary education, whereas this is true for 13 per cent of the PA group and 29 per cent of the general population.

Chapter 4 demonstrated that the ADHD groups, on average, are much younger than the general population, which may, in part, explain the lower

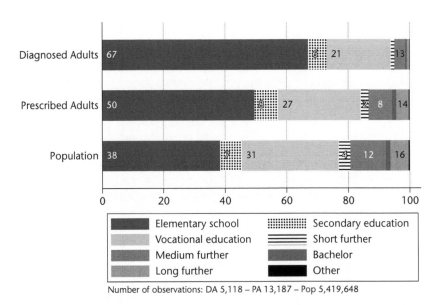

Number of observations: DA 5,118 – PA 13,187 – Pop 5,419,648

Figure 5.4. Educational attainment

Source: Statistics Denmark and own calculations.

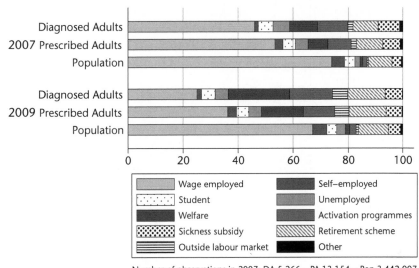

Number of observations in 2007: DA 5,266 – PA 13,154 – Pop 3,442,007
Number of observations in 2009: DA 5,253 – PA 13,056 – Pop 3,453,892

Figure 5.5. Occupational status
Source: Statistics Denmark and own calculations.

educational level of the ADHD groups: a relatively large share of individuals with ADHD belong to age groups that are school age. To investigate this, Figure 5.5 shows the distribution of the two ADHD groups and the general population according to occupational status.

Figure 5.5 shows the distribution of the groups according to occupational status in both 2007 and 2009 to explore whether the groups may have been affected differently by the substantial business-cycle setback following the 2008 financial crisis.

The overall conclusion from Figure 5.5 is that a much smaller share of both ADHD groups are in wage employment, compared to the general population. In fact, only around 40 per cent of the DA group were wage earners in 2007, and this share fell to less than 30 per cent in 2009. In the PA group, the share of wage earners fell from approximately 50 per cent in 2007 to under 40 per cent in 2009. Although the share of individuals in education did rise marginally for both groups, the individuals who were no longer employed in 2009 mainly received cash benefits or early-retirement benefits.

From 2007 to 2009, the general population also experienced a decline in the share of individuals who were wage earners as a consequence of the business-cycle setback. However, this decline was much smaller than that for the two ADHD groups. The numbers thus suggest that individuals with ADHD—perhaps as a consequence of their low average educational level—were hit much harder by the business-cycle setback than the rest of the population.

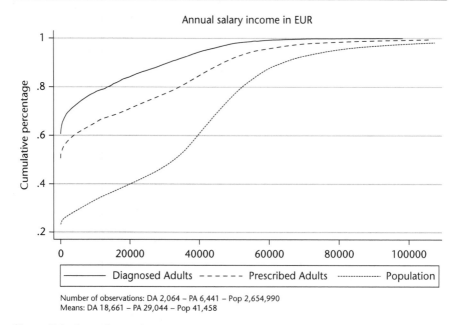

Figure 5.6. Annual wage income

Source: Statistics Denmark and own calculations.

Figure 5.6 shows the cumulative distributions of wage income for the three groups. The picture derived from this figure is consistent with that from Figure 5.5 because more than 60 per cent of the individuals in the DA group have no wage income. This is true for only slightly over 20 per cent of the general population. Moreover, the share of individuals with a wage income of more than 60,000 euros in 2009 was less than 10 per cent for the PA group and less than 5 per cent for the DA group, whereas approximately 15 per cent of the general population earned more than 60,000 euros.

Because of income redistribution in the Danish welfare state, individuals with no wage income are able to receive income transfer payments. The cumulative distributions in Figure 5.7 show the results if these income transfers are included in the actual income measure used.

A comparison of Figures 5.6 and 5.7 clearly shows the redistributive nature of the welfare state. Whereas the dotted curve for the general population moves only slightly, the dashed and solid curves for the two ADHD groups have moved to the right, which indicates that almost all individuals have a before-tax income of at least 20,000 euros when income transfers are included.[1] However, the main message remains the same: individuals with

---

[1] Those with an income below this level are most likely students or of a similar status.

Personal income in EUR

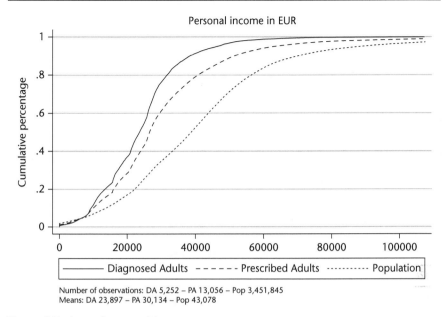

Number of observations: DA 5,252 – PA 13,056 – Pop 3,451,845
Means: DA 23,897 – PA 30,134 – Pop 43,078

Figure 5.7. Annual personal income
Source: Statistics Denmark and own calculations.

ADHD have a much lower income than the rest of the population, on average, even when income transfers are included in income.[2]

In sum, although some individuals with ADHD are able to work and earn a living, the figures in this section show that this is only true for a relatively small share of them. Moreover, those who do work earn much less, on average, than the rest of the population. However, some of the difference in income may be explained by the fact that individuals with ADHD have a much lower educational level than the rest of the population.

5.3 Criminal History

As discussed in Chapter 2, earlier studies have shown that individuals with ADHD are significantly more likely to be incarcerated because of criminal activity. This tendency may be consistent with the impulsivity aspect of the disorder, which may give rise to impulsive crimes. Moreover, Chapter 4 showed that a relatively large share of individuals with ADHD have problems

---

[2] The cumulative distribution of the hourly wage rate for the three groups is shown in the appendix to this chapter. This figure clearly shows that the hourly wage rate is also much lower for the ADHD groups than for the general population. This can be seen as a productivity indicator.

Table 5.3. Criminal offences

	Diagnosed adults		Prescribed adults		Population	
Individuals with no reported incident	2,119	39.75%	7,226	52.89%	3,205,630	80.22%
Individuals with reported incidents	3,212	60.25%	6,436	47.11%	790,216	19.78%
Average number of reported incidents	5.33		4.60		2.03	
Individuals with reported incidents in 2010	1,138	21.35%	2,005	14.68%	139,132	3.54%

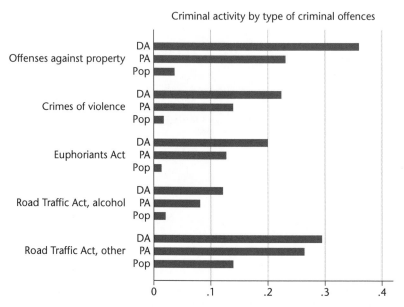

Figure 5.8. Average numbers of criminal offences, selected areas
Source: Statistics Denmark and own calculations.

with substance abuse. It could be hypothesized that the need to finance drug use leads to more crime.

Table 5.3 shows that individuals suffering from ADHD in Denmark are much more likely to have committed a crime than individuals in the general population. In fact, more than 60 per cent of the DA group have had some type of criminal conviction (including traffic violations). In the PA group, roughly half of the individuals have such a conviction; in the general population, less than 20 per cent of individuals had a criminal conviction in the period from 2001 to 2010.

In Figure 5.8, we examine the types of convictions. The figure shows the average number of convictions within specific areas. For example, individuals in the DA group have, on average, almost 0.4 convictions for offences against property and more than 0.2 convictions, on average, for violent crimes.

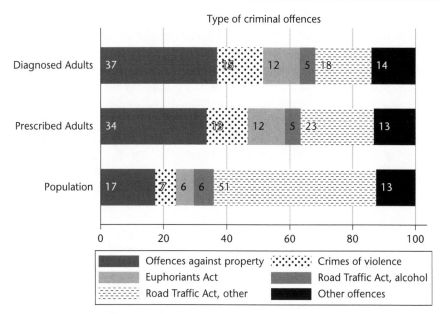

Figure 5.9. Distribution of criminal offences
Source: Statistics Denmark and own calculations.

Among all three groups, the average number of convictions is much higher for the two ADHD groups than for the rest of the population. It is notable, however, that the two ADHD groups do not differ substantially in criminal activity, as shown in Figure 5.8, and are much more similar than either group is with respect to the rest of the population in terms of number of crimes committed.

Having established that individuals with ADHD commit more recorded crimes than individuals in the rest of the population, we use Figure 5.9 to examine the distribution of the crimes committed. Figure 5.9 thus answers the question as to whether individuals with ADHD simply commit more crimes or whether they also commit crimes that are different to those committed by the rest of the population.

The figure clearly shows that individuals with ADHD do, in fact, commit different crimes than the rest of the population but that the crimes committed by the two ADHD groups are somewhat similar. Although more than half of the crimes committed by the rest of the population are traffic violations, these crimes constitute only 23 and 28 per cent of the crimes committed by the DA and PA groups, respectively. Moreover, the crimes of individuals with ADHD are much more likely to be either crimes against property or violent crimes, and these types of crimes are generally considered to be more serious than simple traffic violations.

We now turn to the issue of whether individuals with ADHD are also more likely to be the victim of a crime. Table 5.4 shows the share of individuals in the three groups who have been the victim of a crime.

The table shows that individuals in the DA group are more likely to be victims of a crime. Almost a third of the DA group has been the victim of a crime. For the PA group, the share of individuals who have been a victim of a crime is smaller but is still relatively high at 22 per cent.

Figure 5.10 shows the average number of times that individuals in the three groups have been the victim of different types of crimes. The figure shows that individuals in the DA group on average, have been victims of violent crimes almost 0.2 times, victims of property crimes 0.13 times, and victims of sexual crimes 0.02 times. These numbers are three to five times higher than those for

Table 5.4. Victim of a crime

	Diagnosed adults		Prescribed adults		Population	
Individuals with no reported incident	3,784	70.98%	10,687	78.22%	3,686,386	92.26%
Individuals with reported incidents	1,547	29.02%	2,975	21.78%	309,406	7.74%
Average number of reported incidents	1.71		1.54		1.26	
Individuals with reported incidents in 2010	203	3.81%	385	2.82%	41,157	1.05%

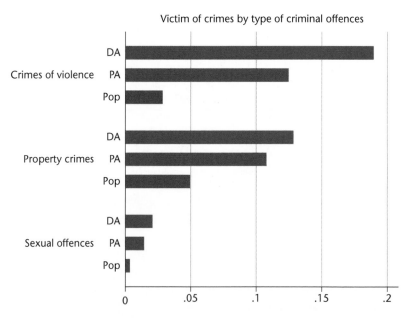

Figure 5.10. Average number of times the groups have been a victim of a crime
Source: Statistics Denmark and own calculations.

Type of criminal offences

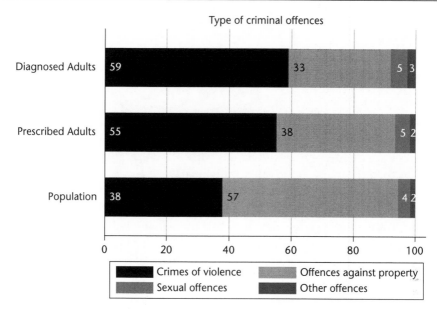

Figure 5.11. Distribution of crimes of which individuals have been victims
Source: Statistics Denmark and own calculations.

the general population. For individuals in the PA group, the risk of being the victim of a crime falls between the other two groups.

Finally, in Figure 5.11 we look at the distribution of the crimes committed against the individuals in the three groups.

This figure shows that individuals with ADHD are much more likely to be the victim of a violent crime than the rest of the population, as approximately 60 per cent of the crimes committed against individuals with ADHD are violent, compared with only 38 per cent of those committed against individuals in the rest of the population.

The distribution of crimes committed against individuals with ADHD is roughly the same between the two treatment groups, with only a slightly smaller share of violent crimes committed against individuals in the PA group compared with those against individuals in the DA group.

Regarding sexual crimes, the share is similar among the three groups, at approximately 5 per cent of all crimes committed.

Summing up, this section has shown that individuals with ADHD both commit more crimes and are more likely to become victims of a crime compared to the rest of the population. In fact, the risk is three to five times higher for individuals with ADHD than for individuals in the general population. Specifically, the crimes involving individuals with ADHD are more likely to be violent crimes or crimes against property, i.e. crimes directed against the individual.

5.4 Traffic Accidents

This section studies whether individuals with ADHD are more likely to be involved in traffic accidents than members of the general population and whether the accidents that individuals with ADHD are involved in are more serious than those involving other individuals.

Table 5.5 presents the share of individuals who have been involved in a traffic accident across the two ADHD groups and across the rest of the population. The numbers in the table show that individuals with ADHD are three to four times more likely to be involved in a traffic accident than an average person from the remaining population. More than 8 per cent of the DA group have been involved in a traffic accident, whereas only 7 per cent of the PA group and only 2 per cent of the individuals in the general population have been involved in a traffic accident.

It is also possible to observe the cause and outcome of traffic accidents. Figure 5.12 thus depicts the distribution of traffic accidents according to the degree of injury (top panel) and involvement of alcohol (bottom panel).

The top panel shows that accidents involving individuals with ADHD are more likely to cause injuries than those involving the rest of the population. Specifically, four out of five accidents involving individuals in the DA group led to injuries, whereas only three out of five accidents involving persons from the rest of the population led to injuries. The higher share of injuries among individuals in the DA group is caused by its larger share of both minor and more serious injuries.

From the bottom panel of Figure 5.12, we can infer that traffic accidents that involve individuals with ADHD are much more likely to involve alcohol. Whereas only 19 per cent of traffic accidents involving the general population involve drunk driving, the shares for individuals in the PA and DA groups are 34 and 41 per cent, respectively.

Table 5.5. Traffic accidents

	Diagnosed adults		Prescribed adults		Population	
Individuals with no reported incident	4,885	91.63%	12,772	93.49%	3,908,660	97.82%
Individuals with reported incidents	446	8.37%	890	6.51%	87,186	2.18%
Average number of reported incidents	1.12		1.11		1.04	
Individuals with reported incidents in 2010	35	0.66%	68	0.50%	5,269	0.13%

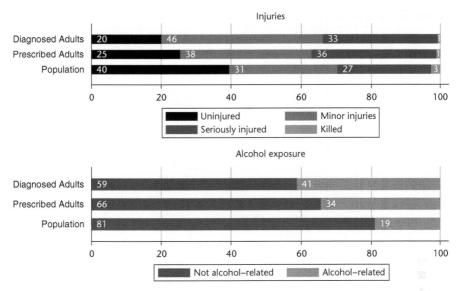

Figure 5.12. Distribution of traffic accidents

Source: Statistics Denmark and own calculations.

5.5 Childhood Outcomes

As ADHD is a development disorder with childhood onset, the individuals in both treatment groups have been affected by ADHD their entire lives. Hence, it is likely that the disorder will also have affected their performance during their childhood. In this section we will explore that further.

Table 5.6 shows that a relatively large percentage of the individuals with ADHD have been placed outside their home at some point in their childhood: almost 30 per cent of the DA group and almost 20 per cent of the PA group, compared to only 3 per cent of the general population.

Even though the individuals we are looking at are adults in 2010, we still have a small percentage of placements in 2010. This is due to 'aftercare' which is offered to some of the individuals who have been in placement when they were children.

We see the same picture in Table 5.7 for preventive measures.

The ADHD symptoms are also likely to affect performance during high school and we see that reflected in their grades (Figure 5.13).

A few points should be made to address the curves in Figure 5.13. Firstly, the curves in the figure obviously only concern the individuals who have actually been admitted to upper secondary education. This selection probably means that the individuals observed in the figures are among those with the mildest symptoms, although this cannot be confirmed from the data.

Table 5.6. Placements

	Diagnosed adults		Prescribed adults		Population	
Individuals with no reported incident	3,803	71.34%	10,995	80.48%	3,806,579	96.82%
Individuals with reported incidents	1,528	28.66%	2,667	19.52%	125,111	3.18%
Average number of reported incidents	2.46		2.24		1.94	
Individuals with reported incidents in 2010	145	2.72%	212	1.55%	7,358	0.19%

Table 5.7. Preventive measures

	Diagnosed adults		Prescribed adults		Population	
Individuals with no reported incident	4,256	79.83%	11,953	87.49%	3,858,043	98.13%
Individuals with reported incidents	1,075	20.17%	1,709	12.51%	73,647	1.87%
Average number of reported incidents	3.04		2.98		2.53	
Individuals with reported incidents in 2010	55	1.03%	79	0.58%	3,051	0.08%

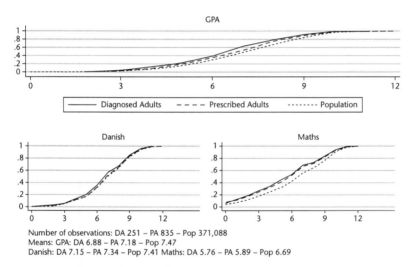

Number of observations: DA 251 – PA 835 – Pop 371,088
Means: GPA: DA 6.88 – PA 7.18 – Pop 7.47
Danish: DA 7.15 – PA 7.34 – Pop 7.41 Maths: DA 5.76 – PA 5.89 – Pop 6.69

Figure 5.13. Grades in high school[3]
Source: Statistics Denmark and own calculations.

Secondly, the overall picture from almost all the figures in this and the previous chapter is repeated when we look at grade point average (GPA). Those who are in the DA group on average have a lower GPA than those who are in the PA group, who in turn on average have a lower GPA than individuals from the rest of the population.

---

[3] The academic grading system in Denmark uses a seven-step scale. ECTS equivalents are the following: 12 (A), 10 (B), 7 (C), 4 (D), 02 (E), 00 (FX), -3 (F).

Thirdly, the lower panel of Figure 5.13 shows that individuals with ADHD seem to fall behind the general population more in mathematics than in Danish, as the curves for the DA and PA groups are much further to the left of the curve for the general population in mathematics.

5.6 Family Situation

Individuals in the DA and PA groups have fewer children on average than the general population, as shown in the left-hand panel of Figure 5.14. This is perhaps surprising, given that ADHD is associated with impulsiveness and perhaps also forgetfulness or risk-taking concerning birth control. However, here it is important to keep in mind the young age distribution among our ADHD groups.

The right-hand panel of Figure 5.14 shows the distribution of the number of different partners with whom you have children—given that you in fact do have children. This panel shows that while more than 90 per cent of individuals in the general population only have children with one partner, roughly 20 per cent of those in the DA group who have had children, have in fact had children with two partners and almost 5 per cent have had children with three

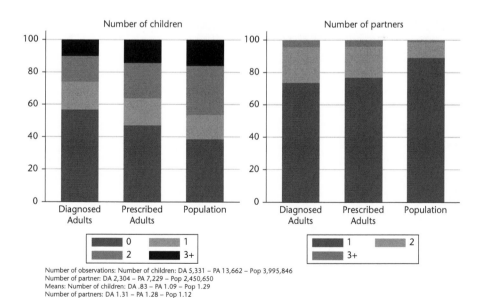

Number of observations: Number of children: DA 5,331 – PA 13,662 – Pop 3,995,846
Number of partner: DA 2,304 – PA 7,229 – Pop 2,450,650
Means: Number of children: DA .83 – PA 1.09 – Pop 1.29
Number of partners: DA 1.31 – PA 1.28 – Pop 1.12

Figure 5.14. Parenthood

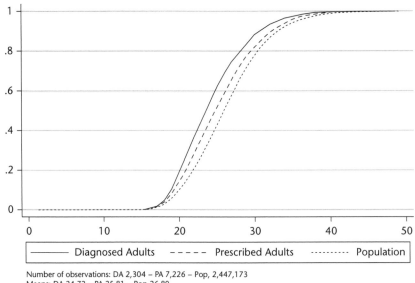

Number of observations: DA 2,304 – PA 7,226 – Pop, 2,447,173
Means: DA 24.72 – PA 25.81 – Pop 26.80

Figure 5.15. Age at first childbirth

different partners. A very similar picture can be found for individuals in the PA group who have children.

Moreover, if we again look at the subpopulation having children then there is a tendency for the ADHD groups to have those children early in life (see Figure 5.15). At age 25, over 60 per cent of the individuals in the DA group have become a parent, while the same is true for roughly half of the individuals in the PA groups and only about 40 per cent of the individuals in the rest of the population.

Tables 5.8 and 5.9 show the share of children of individuals with ADHD being either placed away from home or taking part in preventive measures compared to the same shares for children of the rest of the population. The tables clearly demonstrate that children of individuals with ADHD are more likely to be placed away from home or to take part in preventive measures.

For individuals in the DA group the likelihood that their children have at some point been placed away from home is approximately three times larger than for the rest of the population. For individuals in the PA group 13 per cent of the children have been placed away from home, compared to only 5 per cent among the general population.

For preventive measures the differences are even larger, with 23 per cent of children of individuals in the DA group having at some point been in a preventive measure, whereas less than 5 per cent of children of the general population have been so.

Table 5.8. Placements of children

	Diagnosed adults		Prescribed adults		Population	
Individuals with no reported incident	1,940	84.20%	6284	86.93%	2,319,200	94.64%
Individuals with reported incidents	364	15.80%	945	13.07%	131,450	5.36%
Average number of reported incidents	1.92		2.01		1.84	
Individuals with reported incidents in 2010	216	9.38%	470	6.50%	22,193	0.91%

Table 5.9. Children in preventive measures

	Diagnosed adults		Prescribed adults		Population	
Individuals with no reported incident	1,778	77.17%	5,783	80.00%	2,332,194	95.17%
Individuals with reported incidents	526	22.83%	1446	20.00%	118,456	4.83%
Average number of reported incidents	3.09		3.17		3.38	
Individuals with reported incidents in 2010	269	11.68%	566	7.83%	25,925	1.06%

5.7 Health Measures

Our treatment groups will by definition provide cost to the Danish health-care system, since they have been diagnosed with a permanent disorder and in most cases are also receiving medicine to treat it. Furthermore, our treatment groups have numerous comorbid diseases together with ADHD that need services from the Danish health-care system.

Figure 5.16 shows the average number of in-hospital days for the DA group, the PA group, and the general population in the left-hand panel and the average number of services received from GPs, specialist practitioners, psychologists, and others in the right-hand panel.

The left-hand figure shows that individuals from the two ADHD groups on average have had 4–5 in-hospital days in 2010 (with a slightly higher number of days for the PA group than the DA group), whereas the average for the general population is only two and a half days. From the right-hand panel of Figure 5.16 we can see that the number of services received in the primary health-care sector is also larger for individuals with ADHD than for members of the general population. The average number of GP services received for members of the PA group is thus roughly double that of the general population. For the DA group the number is almost three times as large as for the general population.

A further interesting fact arises from Figure 5.16. In the right-hand panel we can see that members of the PA groups received almost 5 services from psychologist practitioners in 2010. This is much higher than for both the DA group and also much higher than for members of the general population,

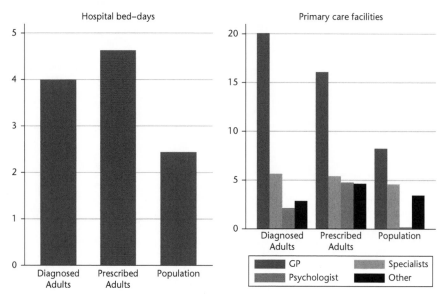

Number of observations: DA 5,331 – PA 13,662 – Pop 3,995,846

Figure 5.16. Use of health facilities
Source: Statistics Denmark, LPR, 2010.

who on average received less than 0.25 services from psychologist practitioners in 2010. While the difference between the PA group and the general population is probably well explained by the ADHD disorder, the explanation of difference between the PA group and the DA groups is probably due to the fact that members of the DA group receive psychological or psychiatric counselling in the secondary health-care sector instead.

Figure 5.17 shows the cumulative distribution of prescription medicine costs in 2010 for the three groups. The cumulative distribution is shown for both the out-of-pocket costs, the public subsidy, and the total cost. The figure clearly shows that individuals with ADHD have higher medicine costs than the general population, as the curves for the two ADHD groups lie clearly to the right of the curves for the general population. For example around 20 per cent of the individuals in the DA group had a total medicine cost of at least 2,700 euros in 2010, whereas only around 15 per cent of the PA group and a very small percentage of the general population had such a high cost.

5.8 Summary

In conclusion, the many tables and figures in this chapter paint a picture of hardship for individuals with ADHD. This chapter has shown that individuals

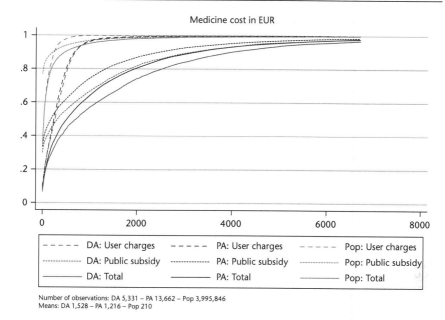

Number of observations: DA 5,331 – PA 13,662 – Pop 3,995,846
Means: DA 1,528 – PA 1,216 – Pop 210

Figure 5.17. Expenditures on medicine

with ADHD, on average, have lower education, are more likely to be out of the labour force, and earn significantly less than members of the general population. Moreover, individuals with ADHD are more likely to engage in criminal activity, and, when they do, these crimes are more serious than the crimes committed by other individuals, on average. This behaviour may perhaps be related to the fact that individuals with ADHD are also more likely to be victims of crimes, particularly violent crimes, than other individuals. Individuals with ADHD are more likely to be involved in traffic accidents than members of the general population, and the accidents that they are involved in are more likely to result in injuries and to be caused by drunk driving.

When it comes to family formation and family background, individuals with ADHD are more likely to be children of young parents and are more likely to become young parents themselves compared to the general population. Also, individuals with ADHD have a three- to four-fold increased likelihood of having been placed away from home at some point during their childhood compared to a member of the general population, and the children of persons with ADHD are also more likely to receive preventive measures or be placed away from home.

Finally, individuals with ADHD on average use both the primary and the secondary health-care sectors more than individuals from the general population, and the medicine costs for individuals with ADHD exceed those for members of the general public.

Appendix to Chapter 5: Cumulative Distribution of Hourly Wage Rate

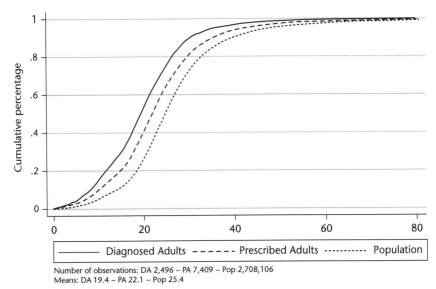

Number of observations: DA 2,496 – PA 7,409 – Pop 2,708,106
Means: DA 19.4 – PA 22.1 – Pop 25.4

Figure 5.A.1. Cumulative distribution of hourly wage rate

Source: Statistics Denmark and own calculations.

Part III
Methodology and Analytical Approach

MAIN IDEA: The main purpose of the third part of the book is to compare 'individuals diagnosed with ADHD later in life' with non-ADHD but otherwise similar individuals. Throughout the text, we refer to the former group as individuals with ADHD and the latter as non-ADHD individuals. The comparison is made along numerous dimensions that lead to private and social costs. The measures are related to labour-market status (occupational status), income and public transfers, education (highest completed level of education), crime and traffic accidents, childhood outcomes, family composition, and health measures.

COST ANALYSIS: The main purpose of this study is to measure the private and social costs of ADHD. In this respect, we are interested in the aggregate costs of individuals with ADHD. For example, one dimension of social costs is identified when we find that a higher share of individuals with ADHD participates in early-retirement schemes and that this higher share is associated with higher public expenditures. In this sense, we account for the total additional costs associated with the higher share of individuals participating in such schemes. An example of private costs is the tendency for reduced educational attainment, which leads to lower labour-market incomes.

MATCHING ANALYSIS: Inputs for the cost analysis are developed in two main parts. The first part is an empirical analysis that estimates differences in performance measures between the group of individuals with ADHD and the non-ADHD group. We refer to these differences as 'mean differences' throughout this study. The differences between the two groups are estimated with the primary aim of evaluating the extent to which individuals with ADHD differ from non-ADHD individuals who are otherwise similar. For example, we seek to answer the questions 'How much more likely are individuals with ADHD to receive benefits under an early retirement scheme?' and 'How much lower are the wages of employed individuals with ADHD compared with individuals without ADHD?'. The second part consists of the cost measures associated with these differences. This is presented in Part IV, which concerns measuring and aggregating the cost differences.

In the present analysis, we apply the so-called 'matching method' to identify pairs of individuals who are statistically identical with respect to observa-
bles but who differ in regard to whether they have been diagnosed with
ADHD. The matching thus involves pairing individuals with ADHD with
non-ADHD individuals based on a set of individual criterion variables that
ensure that the individuals are identical in a statistical sense. After the group of
non-ADHD individuals is identified, outcome variables for the pairs of individuals are compared.

In other words, the empirical methodology employed here compares a
treatment group (i.e., a patient group) to a control group (i.e., a group of
non-patients who are otherwise similar). In the empirical study, we apply
two treatment groups and a number of control groups. Next, we provide a
description of these groups; we first discuss the two treatment groups and then
proceed to discuss the control groups.

TREATMENT GROUPS: We employ two different patient groups based on
two different definitions of individuals with ADHD. The first group consists of
adults who received their diagnosis in the secondary mental-health sector.
This group is referred to as 'diagnosed adults' throughout the analysis and is
abbreviated as 'DA'. The diagnoses for this group of individuals are registered
in the Psychiatric Patient Register. The second group consists of adults who
have received methylphenidate, atomoxetine, or dexamphetamine. We refer
to this group as 'prescribed adults', with the abbreviation 'PA'. The use of these
types of medicines is registered in the Medicine Database. The approach for
this group of individuals is that they have received pharmacological treatment
for ADHD in the primary mental-health sector.[1] Before turning to the control
groups, we summarize the two treatment groups considered throughout the
analysis:

- **Diagnosed adults (DA):** adults who have been diagnosed with ADHD
  later in life (i.e., 18 years of age or older).
- **Prescribed adults (PA):** adults who have received methylphenidate,
  atomoxetine, or dexamphetamine later in life (i.e., 18 years of age or
  older).

CONTROL GROUPS: We compare the two treatment groups to a number of
control groups. In the baseline analysis in Chapter 7, we present the mean
differences in outcome measures between the treatment groups and our baseline control groups. There are two baseline control groups: the first control
group is selected such that the treatment group and the control group are

---

[1] In this group, we exclude individuals who were diagnosed with dementia and narcolepsy in
the secondary hospital system; these conditions are also treated with methylphenidate,
atomoxetine, and dexamphetamine.

similar with respect to *personal information and parental background information*. We refer to this control group as 'demographic controls' with the abbreviation 'C-Demo'. The selection of the second control group is based on *psychiatric diagnoses other than ADHD* in addition to personal information and parental background information. We refer to this control group as 'comorbidity control' with the abbreviation 'C-Comor'. In this respect, we account for comorbidity when considering the second control group. Comorbidity is found to be an important control variable.

Before turning to the other control groups, we summarize the two baseline control groups:

- **Demographic controls (C-Demo)**: matched controls selected from the adult population on the basis of demographic characteristics.

- **Comorbidity controls (C-Comor)**: matched controls selected from the adult population on the basis of demographic characteristics and comorbid psychiatric diagnoses.

Chapter 7 presents the baseline results of the analysis. The results indicate that individuals who have been diagnosed with ADHD later in life have weaker performance on a broad set of outcome measures compared with similar non-ADHD individuals. The differences between ADHD individuals and non-ADHD but otherwise identical groups of individuals are significant from both statistical and economic perspectives. Moreover, statistically and economically significant results showing weak performance are obtained even when we consider comorbidity. However, accounting for comorbidity reduces the negative effect considerably.

We also apply a number of control groups in addition to the baseline control groups. These additional control groups are motivated by the empirical challenge of *unobservable heterogeneity*. Next, we consider this issue and the associated control groups.

A sibling-based analysis: In Chapter 8, we consider a number of alternative control groups and perform additional estimations to evaluate the robustness of the baseline results presented in Chapter 7. We select matched non-ADHD individuals from the entire adult population in Chapter 7, whereas the matched control groups in Chapter 8 are selected from the *siblings* of the patients who have been diagnosed or have received methylphenidate, atomoxetine, or dex-amphetamine as adults. These additional control groups are introduced to assess and mitigate any differences between the two patient groups that are not related to ADHD. We now turn to the motivation for these control groups.

First, we describe the choice of control groups selected from the siblings of the treatment groups. Although we match individuals with ADHD with non-ADHD individuals who are otherwise similar, we cannot exclude the possibility that the two groups do not differ systematically. The use of matching methods enables us to remove observable differences across groups. However, we are unable to remove *unobservable* differences across groups. This inability becomes problematic if the group of individuals with ADHD is systematically different from non-ADHD individuals with respect to *unobserved* background variables. For example, it could be that individuals with ADHD are *systematically* raised under relatively difficult circumstances, implying that they have confronted more difficult initial conditions that could be reflected in worse outcomes with respect to educational attainment and labour-market performance compared with non-ADHD individuals. If unobserved systematic differences play an important role, then we cannot exclude the possibility that these unobserved background variables drive the mean differences between the treatment and control groups. Motivated by this possibility, we select additional control groups consisting of the siblings of the individuals with ADHD who have not been diagnosed with ADHD.

The advantage of using sibling-based control groups is that siblings are similar with respect to many of the aspects that are difficult to observe and that may influence the choice of education, income, and other outcomes. Such similarities may be observed, for example, in genetic and social-background factors during childhood and upbringing. In this sense, we reduce the possibility that unobserved differences play an important role in the differences observed between the treatment and control groups.

In this study, we select one control group from siblings of individuals with ADHD such that the treatment and control groups are similar with respect to personal information.[2] We refer to this group as the 'demographic sibling control' with the abbreviation 'Sib-Demo'.[3] The following sibling-based control group is used to mitigate the effects of unobservable heterogeneity:

- **Demographic sibling controls (Sib-Demo)**: matched controls selected from the siblings of individuals in the treatment group. Selection is based on demographic characteristics.

The overall impression of the sibling analysis is that the baseline results of Chapter 7 are robust to the inclusion of a sibling-based control group.

Motivations for the design of the analysis: The motivation for distinguishing between the two treatment groups throughout the analysis is that

---

[2] Many of the criteria are trivially controlled for, as much of the information is shared across siblings.

[3] In another sibling-based control group, we aim to control for psychiatric diagnoses other than ADHD as in Chapter 7. However, because we lack a sufficient number of siblings with other psychiatric diagnoses to perform the matching analysis, the method employed simply *excludes* individuals with ADHD and comorbid psychiatric diagnoses. This control group is referred to as 'comorbidity sibling control'. Since the results parallel those of Sib-Demo, the results are not included in Chapter 8.

the individuals in the two groups may differ with respect to performance. More precisely, we expect that the average individual belonging to DA has weaker performance than the average individual belonging to PA. Therefore, the division of individuals with ADHD into these two groups is important for the cost calculations presented in Part IV.

Another important aspect of this study is that we attempt to determine the true effects of ADHD symptoms on private and social costs. The study proposes a retrospective evaluation of these costs for individuals who have received an ADHD diagnosis in adulthood. Based on this empirical design, the analysis will allow us to examine the costs of ADHD while avoiding the contamination and bias of diagnosis and treatment for ADHD. This contribution is important in itself, and it is the correct benchmark for an evaluation of the costs of individuals with ADHD who have received treatment. This study's use of individuals with ADHD who were diagnosed or prescribed later in life is based on the hypothesis that DA individuals exhibit weaker performance outcomes than a similar group of adults diagnosed in childhood and that PA individuals exhibit weaker performance outcomes than a similar group of adults who were prescribed medication in childhood.

Investigation of the design of the analysis: This analytical approach is feasible because we can identify the two treatment groups (i.e., DA and PA) and the similar groups of adults diagnosed with or prescribed medication in childhood, respectively. We refer to the two additional groups as 'diagnosed children', abbreviated to 'DC', and 'prescribed children', abbreviated to 'PC'. The aim of Chapter 9 is to explore the two hypotheses outlined above. If these two hypotheses cannot be rejected, then this result supports the idea of distinguishing between those who accessed care earlier from those who were diagnosed later, and that the former group should be excluded from the analysis to obtain the true effect of ADHD on output. In addition, this result would also support the notion that DA individuals have weaker performance than their PA counterparts, thus reflecting the decision to distinguish between the two groups.

In summary, in addition to comparing DA and PA, we consider the following groups in our analytical approach:

- **Diagnosed children (DC)**: adults who were diagnosed with ADHD earlier in life (i.e., before the age of 18).
- **Prescribed children (PC)**: adults who received methylphenidate, atomoxetine, or dexamphetamine earlier in life (i.e., before the age of 18).

In Chapter 9, we are unable to reject either of the two hypotheses, thereby lending empirical support to the analytical design employed throughout the study.

A final comment concerning the analysis is that we do not know whether the population contains groups of undiagnosed but high-performing ADHD cases and, in that sense, whether the identified groups of individuals with ADHD consist of particularly low-performing individuals. In this case, the output effects for the average individual with ADHD will be overestimated relative to the 'true' average effect for individuals with ADHD. However, the aggregate private and social costs of ADHD will be underestimated when only a certain fraction of individuals with ADHD can be identified. In this sense, we estimate the aggregate costs for the group of individuals with ADHD whom we can identify and omit the costs for individuals with ADHD who were neither diagnosed nor prescribed medication.

STRUCTURE: Part III is outlined as follows:

- In Chapter 6 we present a non-technical introduction to the applied methodology and discuss econometric challenges. The target group for this chapter includes readers with an interest in these methodological issues. Readers may skip this chapter without any loss of comprehension.
- In Chapter 7 we present our baseline analysis by estimating differences in the means of the output measures for the treatment and control groups.
- In Chapter 8 we present the sibling-based analysis described above.
- In Chapter 9 we examine the design of our analytical approach.

6

Methodology and Econometric Challenges

In this chapter, we present our empirical methodology and discuss relevant methodological issues. The aim is to describe the applied methodology and to discuss methodological issues at a non-technical level. The target group of this chapter includes readers with an interest in these methodological issues. Other readers may skip this chapter without any loss of comprehension.

This chapter is structured as follows. First, we discuss our empirical approach to assess the differences between individuals with ADHD and non-ADHD individuals with the ultimate purpose of performing a cost analysis of ADHD. Second, we describe the chosen econometric methodology that we apply to estimate the differences. Third, we discuss an econometric challenge that we attempt to overcome by performing a sibling-based analysis. Fourth, we describe how we evaluate the methodology applied throughout this book.

6.1 Empirical Approach

The main purpose of this study is to assess the private and social costs of ADHD. To this end, we develop an approach to assess the direct and indirect effects of ADHD on a number of outcomes. If crime rates, for example, are higher for individuals diagnosed with ADHD, then we wish to capture the full costs of crime *associated with ADHD*, i.e., the direct effect of ADHD on crime and the indirect effects of ADHD on crime through, for example, lower levels of educational attainment and other relevant outcome measures. From a cost perspective, it is irrelevant whether the effect of ADHD is direct or indirect through, for example, educational attainment, but it is important to estimate the true cost associated with ADHD as accurately as possible.

Our approach can be illustrated using a simple linear example. Imagine that two output measures—education and crime—are affected by ADHD. In addition, imagine that education and crime are related as described by the following 'structural form':

$$crime = a_1 education + \beta_1 ADHD + \gamma_1 X$$

$$education = a_2 crime + \beta_2 ADHD + \gamma_2 X$$

The first equation indicates that ADHD has a direct effect on crime. This effect is captured by the parameter β_1; for example, this parameter captures the impulsivity effect of ADHD—individuals with ADHD are more likely to be unable to stop themselves from committing a crime than those without ADHD. Moreover, ADHD has a direct effect on education, which is depicted in the second equation and captured by β_2; for example, this parameter captures the inattention effect of ADHD—individuals with ADHD are more likely to daydream in school compared with individuals who do not have ADHD.

In addition to the direct effects, ADHD also affects crime through education in an effect that is captured by parameters a_1 and β_2, whereas education is affected by ADHD through crime in an effect that is captured by parameters a_2 and β_1. Thus, ADHD affects crime not only directly but also indirectly through educational attainment because lower education levels are statistically associated with criminal behaviour that is not directly related to ADHD but is affected indirectly by ADHD because of inattention during primary education, for example. In addition, crime and education are also affected by exogenous background variables included in X, which is a vector that includes personal information, parental/family information, and other relevant background information.

Because we are interested in the total effect of ADHD on both crime and education in the cost calculations, we apply the 'reduced form' of the two-equation system. That is, we estimate the following 'reduced-form' equations:

$$crime = \pi_1 ADHD + \mu_1 X$$

$$education = \pi_2 ADHD + \mu_2 X$$

where $\pi_1 = (\beta_1 + a_1\beta_2)/(1 - a_1 a_2)$, $\pi_2 = (\beta_2 + a_2\beta_1)/(1 - a_1 a_2)$, $\mu_1 = (\gamma_1 + a_1\gamma_2)/(1 - a_1 a_2)$ and $\mu_2 = (\gamma_2 + a_2\gamma_1)/(1 - a_1 a_2)$.

The parameter π_1 captures the *total* effect of ADHD on crime, which consists of the *direct* effect of ADHD and the *indirect* effect of ADHD through education. In the same manner, π_2 captures the *total* effect of ADHD on education, which consists of the *direct* effect of ADHD and the *indirect* effect of ADHD through crime.

We apply estimated versions of π parameters to perform the cost analyses. To illustrate the calculations in Chapter 10, we calculate the social costs of ADHD as follows:

$$social\ costs = \pi_1 P_{ADHD} C_{crime} + \pi_2 P_{ADHD} C_{education}$$

where P_{ADHD} is the adult ADHD population and $C_{i,}$ (i=crime, education) is the cost of cost category i per individual. Thus, $\pi_1 P_{ADHD}$ is the *expected additional number of individuals* in the treatment group—relative to the control group—who will engage in crime, implying that $\pi_1 P_{ADHD} C_{crime}$ represents the *expected additional costs* of crime generated by ADHD. The second term $\pi_2 P_{ADHD} C_{education}$ denotes the *expected additional costs* of education generated by ADHD. This latter cost may actually be a negative cost—or a benefit—if individuals with ADHD tend to be less educated than non-ADHD individuals. This effect will lead to cost savings in a country such as Denmark in which education at all levels is provided and financed by the government.

The π parameters are estimated using 'propensity score matching' in the empirical analysis below. The reason for this choice is that propensity score matching has important expositional advantages for the presentation of complex comparisons (see, for example, Angrist and Pischke, 2009). Moreover, the results obtained from a linear regression model and propensity score matching are also of similar quantitative magnitude.

6.2 A Non-technical Explanation of Propensity Score Matching

OVERVIEW: In this section, we present a non-technical explanation of propensity score matching. The methodology is described in Angrist and Pischke (2009), Rubin (1974), Rosenbaum and Rubin (1983), Heckman, Ichimura, and Todd (1998), and Heckman et al. (1998). The following propensity score matching procedure is used. First, we select a control group similar to the treatment group with respect to various observable aspects; this group is referred to as the *matched* control group. Second, the mean outcome measures for the treatment and matched control groups are compared. Third, we determine whether the mean difference (i.e., the difference between the two means) is significantly different from zero.

MATCHED CONTROL GROUP: The matched control group is selected by pairing each ADHD individual from the treatment groups with a non-ADHD individual who is similar with respect to the observable variables. The non-ADHD individuals are chosen from the unmatched control group, which is assumed to represent the non-ADHD adult Danish population in the baseline analysis of Chapter 7. Specifically, a non-ADHD individual is selected for the matched control group if he possesses the background characteristics that are the most similar to those of a specific individual with ADHD in the treatment group. This method is called 'nearest neighbour' propensity score matching. These selected individuals from the unmatched control group constitute the matched control group.

AVERAGE TREATMENT EFFECT ON THE TREATED (ATT): Having identified the matched control group, we can then estimate the extent to which the group of individuals with ADHD performs worse than an 'identical' control group of individuals without ADHD. The difference between the output measures for the treatment group and the matched control group is referred to as the 'average treatment effect on the treated' (ATT). More precisely, the ATT measures the difference in the mean outcomes between individuals assigned to the treatment group and those assigned to the control group. This measure is referred to as the mean difference.

DIFFICULT TASK: It should be emphasized that finding an *appropriate and convincing matched control group* is the most difficult task in matching. The main focus in this book is to identify precisely the most convincing matched control groups that are possible. One advantage of this study is that the control groups are selected from Danish register data that are based on highly detailed background information and that cover the full Danish population from 1980 onwards. We consider a large number of background variables to control for initial differences between ADHD individuals and non-ADHD individuals. Therefore, we consider the control groups to be of high quality in comparison with those used in other studies.

CAUSAL INTERPRETATION: The main objective of the analysis is to come as close as possible to a *causal interpretation* of the estimated mean differences, referring to the isolated effect of ADHD on the outcome measures.[1] Of course, this task is difficult to accomplish and requires the ability to observe 'sufficient characteristics' of all treatment and control groups. By 'sufficient characteristics', we mean that there are no remaining *omitted variables* of importance to the estimated mean differences between the treatment and control groups. If important omitted variables remain, then the mean differences would be overestimated or underestimated. In this case, part of the estimated mean difference would be related to circumstances other than ADHD and hence unrelated to the effect of ADHD. In technical terms, omitted variables result in biased estimates. Omitted variable bias is our main concern in this analysis, and so this issue will be discussed more fully in Section 6.3 and Chapter 8.

Specifically, in our search for an *appropriate control group*, we address unobservable heterogeneity, an important econometric challenge related to omitted variable bias. We consider unobservable heterogeneity in Section 6.3 and explain how we address it. We are of the opinion that we are able to address the challenge of unobservable heterogeneity relatively well through a sibling-based analysis in which we compare treatment groups to sibling-based matched control groups. We conclude that we are able to mitigate

---

[1] In *principle,* the ATT is understood as the *causal* effect of having ADHD if the *Strongly Ignorable Treatment Assignment assumption* is fulfilled; see the technical note at <http://www.cbs.dk/files/cbs.dk/adhd_technicalappendix.pdf>.

many problems related to omitted variables that often complicate causal interpretations.

OTHER ISSUES: Before we turn our attention to unobservable heterogeneity, we discuss additional issues that could complicate the causal interpretation. However, because we conclude that these issues are of less importance than omitted variable bias, we discuss these issues only in this section. One such issue that could be problematic for causal interpretations of the estimated mean differences between the treatment and control groups is measurement errors with respect to the background variables that are used to select a matched control group. We contend that measurement errors in the analysis are less of an issue in the present study because the analysis is performed using high-quality Statistics Denmark register data.

REVERSE CAUSALITY: Another issue is that we occasionally consider variables that are measured *after* an ADHD-diagnosed individual is born (rather than *before*) as a result of data availability. In the study, we only have data beginning in 1980, although many adults with ADHD were born before this year. In technical terms, we apply post-treatment variables rather than pre-treatment variables, which could introduce an estimation bias because post-treatment variables can be affected by ADHD. This reversed causality bias would result in an overestimated or underestimated effect of ADHD. Throughout the analysis, we include post-treatment variables that could lead to an underestimation of the effect of ADHD, as illustrated in the example that we now consider. We thereby obtain a conservative estimate of the costs of ADHD presented in Chapter 10 and thus do not further address this issue.

AN EXAMPLE: An example of a post-treatment variable applied in this study is a proxy for 'family situation', a variable that equals one if all siblings have the same parents and that is thought of as a measure of stability in the childhood household. The treatment and unmatched control groups differ substantially for this variable. As this variable may reflect inherent unobserved pre-treatment differences between the groups and effects of ADHD on the family situation, it may result in biased estimates of mean differences. We believe that the variable (primarily) proxies for the stability of the childhood household that is unrelated to ADHD, which motivates its inclusion in the analysis when selecting a matched control group whose difficulty with respect to 'family situation' is similar to that of the treatment group. If we are incorrect and ADHD primarily affects 'family situation', then we may be selecting a matched control group with an overly difficult 'family situation'. Because a difficult 'family situation' is associated with weak performance, we may underestimate the true effect of ADHD.

A FINAL CONCERN: A final concern relates to sample selection bias, in which individuals diagnosed with ADHD generally represent severe ADHD cases and there is a significant number of undiagnosed individuals with (less severe) ADHD in the population at large (see Dalsgaard et al., 2013). If this bias exists, then the analysis would overestimate the effect of ADHD on the outcome measures. However, we are less concerned about this problem because the main purpose of this study is to determine the *overall costs of ADHD*. Therefore, we may overestimate the average output effects for ADHD individuals in relation to the 'true' average effect for ADHD individuals. However, the aggregate private and social costs of ADHD will be underestimated when only a certain percentage of individuals with ADHD can be identified. In this sense, we estimate the aggregate costs for the group of ADHD individuals who have been identified and omit the costs for those ADHD individuals who have been neither diagnosed nor prescribed.

6.3 Unobservable Heterogeneity

INTRODUCTION: In this section, we discuss the challenges associated with unobservable heterogeneity and a possible solution. As the main purpose of the study is to perform a cost analysis, it is important to understand the extent to which the mean difference estimates can be given a causal interpretation, i.e., to what degree our analysis identifies the effects of ADHD per se, or whether these effects can be explained in other ways. In the following chapters, we attempt to explore possible biases that may influence the cost estimates in our attempt to discover the true costs of ADHD.

UNOBSERVED HETEROGENEITY: To illustrate the problem of *unobservable heterogeneity*, imagine that we estimate negative and statistically significant mean differences in the outcome variables between individuals with ADHD and similar individuals who do not have ADHD. Is this difference a consequence of ADHD, or is it a result of unobservable factors? Imagine further that we apply a rich set of background information for individuals with ADHD to select their matched control group. This background information could consist of parent-background variables, area of residence, number of siblings, and other information. Imagine also that we are unable to measure 'parental care and involvement'—which is especially important for outcomes later in life—in the childhood household. Consider that 'parental care and involvement' is systematically lower in households with ADHD children—for a reason that is not related to ADHD—compared with households whose children do not have ADHD but are otherwise similar. In this case, we do not know whether it is 'relatively low parental care and involvement in households' or ADHD per se that generates negative effects on the outcome measures.

This simple example illustrates the fundamental problem with *unobservable heterogeneity*. However, the challenge is even more substantial because we do not know what constitutes the *unobservable heterogeneity*. In Chapter 8, we address this aspect by comparing the treatment group of individuals with ADHD with their *siblings without ADHD* to compare individuals who have been raised in shared environments. The advantage of using sibling-based control groups is that siblings are similar with respect to many of the characteristics that we find difficult to observe, such as aspects that may influence the choice of education or income. For example, such differences may apply to genetic differences and social-background factors during childhood and upbringing. In this sense, we reduce the likelihood that unobserved differences play an important role in determining the observed differences between the treatment and control groups.

The sibling analysis does not necessarily remove all unobserved heterogeneity, as it addresses only unobserved differences within the family/household unit. Nevertheless, we must consider that other unobserved factors may play a role in the observed mean difference. For example, a non-shared environment that affects only one child in a family could be relevant (e.g., a unique relationship between a parent and a child). Another example is that a non-shared environment generated through differences outside of the family environment may also be important. Although measures of non-shared environment exist, they are rarely routinely collected or recorded and are therefore not available in the database for us to explore. In essence, non-shared environmental influences have been shown to interact with genetic effects to enhance the expression of both ADHD and conduct problems (Sonuga-Barke et al., 2008). However, it should be emphasized that *unobservable heterogeneity* is a problem only if it is *not* systematically distributed across the treatment and control groups. If, for example, 'parental care and involvement' were evenly distributed across individuals in the treatment and control groups, then this unobservable heterogeneity would be of no concern in the analysis.

The sibling-based analysis that is presented in Chapter 8 is considered to be particularly valuable and important because Danish households with children with ADHD are found to be more unstable than households without children with ADHD, and this difference is to some extent generated by poor child health in terms of ADHD. Kvist et al. (2013) conclude that poor child health in terms of ADHD results in reduced parental socioeconomic status specifically by lowering labour supply (and earnings) and reducing relationship stability.

7

Baseline Results

In this chapter, we report the results obtained when using formal estimation techniques. This chapter contains our baseline results. The overall findings suggest that individuals with ADHD exhibit weak performance on a large set of performance measures that are grouped based on occupational status, income, educational attainment, crime and traffic accidents, childhood outcomes, family composition, and health measures.

We perform the analysis using propensity score matching. First, we select a control group similar to the treatment group with respect to various observable aspects. This group is referred to as the *matched* control group. Second, the mean outcome measures for the treatment and matched control groups are compared. Finally, we determine whether the mean difference (i.e., the difference between the two means) is significantly different from zero.

The matched control group is selected by pairing each ADHD individual from the treatment groups with a non-ADHD individual who is similar with respect to observable variables. The non-ADHD individuals are chosen from the unmatched control group (in this chapter, the adult non-ADHD Danish population). Specifically, a non-ADHD individual is selected for the matched control group if he possesses the background characteristics that are most similar to those of a specific ADHD individual in the treatment group. This method is called 'nearest neighbour' propensity score matching. These selected individuals from the unmatched control group constitute the matched control group.

Having identified the matched control group, we can then estimate the extent to which the group of individuals with ADHD performs worse than an 'identical' control group of individuals without ADHD. The difference between the output measures for the treatment group and the matched control group is the mean difference.

Table 7.1. Comparisons in Chapter 7

Treatment group	Control group	Analysis
Diagnosed adults (DA) Prescribed adults (PA)	Demographic controls (C-Demo)	Baseline
Diagnosed adults (DA) Prescribed adults (PA)	Comorbidity controls (C-Comor)	Baseline + comorbidity control

Throughout this book, we employ two treatment groups that are defined as follows:

- **Diagnosed adults (DA)**: adults who have been diagnosed with ADHD later in life (i.e., 18 years of age or older).
- **Prescribed adults (PA)**: adults who have received methylphenidate, atomoxetine, or dexamphetamine later in life (i.e., 18 years of age or older).

In this chapter, we select two baseline control groups that are similar to the treatment group with respect to various observable variables. These *matched* control groups are selected according to the following:

- **Demographic controls (C-Demo)**: matched controls selected from the adult population on the basis of demographic characteristics.
- **Comorbidity controls (C-Comor)**: matched controls selected from the adult population on the basis of demographic characteristics and comorbid psychiatric diagnoses.

Having selected the treatment and control groups, we present the obtained baseline results regarding the estimated difference in mean outcome measures for the treatment and matched control groups. In this analysis, we also determine whether the mean difference is statistically significantly different from zero. The comparisons in this chapter are presented in Table 7.1.

The chapter is organized as follows. First, we present the selection of the matched control groups. Second, the results obtained for the mean differences between the treatment and matched control groups are presented. The samples of the two treatment groups are smaller than those presented in Part II because we can include individuals with ADHD only when information is available for all background variables considered. We are aware of the potential selection bias and a chapter appendix presents an analysis of the effect of the exclusion. Finally, we include an appendix table that provides a detailed description of the output measures considered.

7.1 Selecting Matched Control Groups

For the two matched control groups analysed in this chapter, individuals are selected from the Danish non-ADHD adult population. The implication of selecting individuals from this large group is that it is possible to find matched control groups whose observable characteristics are similar to those of the treatment group, even when considering rather specific background information.

The matched control groups will comprise individuals who are identical with respect to initial conditions such as age, gender, parental education, parental income level, and municipality of residence. In other words, we aim to find a group of individuals who are similar to the individuals in the treatment group in many dimensions—except that they do not have ADHD.

An important aspect of the full-population data is that we are able to control for comorbidity as measured by *psychiatric diagnoses other than ADHD*, in addition to a broad set of information for personal and family-background variables.[1] This capability is important because many individuals with ADHD have one or more psychiatric diagnoses in addition to ADHD. If we were unable to account for other psychiatric diagnoses, then we would not be able to determine whether weak performance results from ADHD itself or from other psychiatric diagnoses, or from a combination of the two. We find that accounting for other psychiatric diagnoses—or comorbidity—is highly important, as this type of background information often explains a large share of the mean differences between groups. It should be noted that if the ADHD diagnosis is what causes other psychiatric diagnoses, then this effect should be part of the cost calculation in Part IV. However, if there is no clear link, then one should be cautious in interpreting the results. In reality, research literature does not exist that would allow us to identify with considerable certainty causal relationships between ADHD and later comorbidity. In fact a recent study by Copeland et al. (2013) has shown that while individuals with ADHD show very high continuity of psychiatric problems over time, the causal relationship between early ADHD and other later psychiatric problems is very difficult to establish. It has been found, however, that comorbidity rates in adults with ADHD are high, with individuals experiencing one or more psychiatric disorders during their lifespan, including mood and anxiety disorders and substance-abuse disorders (Garcia et al., 2012; Kessler et al., 2006; Sobanski, 2006).

---

[1] The information on comorbid psychiatric diagnoses stem from the Psychiatric Patient Register. It should be emphasized that there may be a lack of registration of comorbidity by clinicians. See the discussion of this in Chapter 3.

Below, we list the background variables used to select the matched control groups. We group the variables into demographic controls and psychiatric diagnoses.

7.1.1 *Demographic Controls*

The background variables for the first control group are as follows:[2]

- Personal information for individuals measured by the following:
  - o Gender
  - o Age in 2010
  - o Nationality (native, immigrant, or descendant)
  - o Region of residence in 2010
  - o Adopted (whether individuals are adopted or not)
- Parental/family information:
  - o Mother's and father's educational attainment
  - o Mother's and father's age at parenthood
  - o Stable family situation (this variable equals one if all siblings have the same parents)
  - o Number of siblings
  - o Birth order (first born, second born, etc.)
  - o Mother's and father's real income during the individual's childhood
  - o Mother's and father's psychiatric diagnoses

According to this list of background variables, the treatment and matched control groups will be similar with respect to personal-background information. Moreover, we include parental/family information. The variables indicating a stable family situation and psychiatric diagnoses are included as proxies for stability in the childhood household.

Table 7.2 presents the characteristics of the treatment groups and the matched and unmatched control groups. The left part of the table presents the results for DA, whereas the results for PA are presented in the right part. The matched control group is based on demographic controls (C-Demo), i.e., the control group is selected based on personal information and parental/family information. The table reads as follows: for the variable gender, the first row presents the difference between the treatment group and the *unmatched* control group. The table indicates that the DA group is 64 per cent male compared to 51 per cent in the unmatched control group, whereas the PA group is 58 per cent male. This difference in gender results in large percentage differences between the treatment groups and the control group—a difference

---

[2] Some of the background variables are post-treatment variables, which may result in underestimated mean differences. See Chapter 2 for a discussion.

Table 7.2. Reduction in bias—Demographic controls (C-Demo)

Variable	Sample	Diagnosed adults			Prescribed adults		
		Treated	Control	% bias	Treated	Control	% bias
Gender	Unmatched	0.64	0.51	26.80***	0.58	0.51	15.60***
	Matched	0.64	0.63	1.70	0.58	0.59	-0.20
Age (2010)	Unmatched	29.28	33.64	-52.00***	31.94	33.64	-19.50***
	Matched	29.28	29.37	-1.10	31.94	32.03	-1.00
Native	Unmatched	0.98	0.97	8.30***	0.98	0.97	7.40***
	Matched	0.98	0.98	-0.40	0.98	0.98	-1.70
Immigrant	Unmatched	0.01	0.02	-5.20**	0.01	0.02	-5.20***
	Matched	0.01	0.01	1.80	0.01	0.01	1.60
Descendant	Unmatched	0.01	0.01	-6.60***	0.01	0.01	-5.30***
	Matched	0.01	0.01	-1.40	0.01	0.01	0.80
Capital Region of Denmark	Unmatched	0.20	0.30	-24.20***	0.26	0.30	-9.30***
	Matched	0.20	0.20	0.20	0.26	0.26	-0.70
Central Denmark Region	Unmatched	0.47	0.29	37.30***	0.36	0.29	13.90***
	Matched	0.47	0.49	-3.30	0.36	0.35	1.00
North Denmark Region	Unmatched	0.05	0.09	-16.20***	0.11	0.09	4.40***
	Matched	0.05	0.04	3.00	0.11	0.11	-0.50
Region Zealand	Unmatched	0.12	0.15	-8.60***	0.17	0.15	5.50***
	Matched	0.12	0.12	1.30	0.17	0.17	-0.60
Region of Southern Denmark	Unmatched	0.16	0.16	-0.70	0.10	0.16	-16.90***
	Matched	0.16	0.15	0.70	0.10	0.10	0.60
Siblings	Unmatched	2.23	1.85	26.60***	2.09	1.86	17.30***
	Matched	2.23	2.24	-1.00	2.09	2.08	0.50
Stable family situation	Unmatched	0.59	0.80	-48.10***	0.65	0.80	-33.70***
	Matched	0.59	0.58	1.90	0.65	0.66	-1.40
Mother's education length	Unmatched	132.34	135.64	-9.10***	133.36	135.66	-6.20***
	Matched	132.34	132.58	-0.70	133.36	132.84	1.40
Father's education length	Unmatched	135.05	142.66	-20.20***	139.11	142.67	-9.20***
	Matched	135.05	135.68	-1.70	139.11	138.32	2.00

Mother's age at parenthood	Unmatched	22.58	23.76	-30.20***	22.90	23.76	-21.30***
	Matched	22.58	22.61	-0.70	22.90	22.88	0.40
Father's age at parenthood	Unmatched	25.50	26.50	-21.10***	25.75	26.50	-15.60***
	Matched	25.50	25.56	-1.20	25.75	25.69	1.20
Mother's income	Unmatched	2.4E+04	2.4E+04	2.80	2.4E+04	2.4E+04	0.90
	Matched	2.4E+04	2.4E+04	-0.10	2.4E+04	2.4E+04	-0.90
Father's income	Unmatched	3.5E+04	4.2E+04	-25.80***	3.8E+04	4.2E+04	-11.00***
	Matched	3.5E+04	3.5E+04	-1.30	3.8E+04	3.8E+04	1.60
Mother's psychiatric diagnoses: One	Unmatched	0.09	0.04	16.70***	0.07	0.04	11.50***
	Matched	0.09	0.08	3.80	0.07	0.06	3.20*
Mother's psychiatric diagnoses: More than one	Unmatched	0.14	0.07	23.00***	0.13	0.07	19.40***
	Matched	0.14	0.13	1.30	0.13	0.13	0.00
Father's psychiatric diagnoses: One	Unmatched	0.07	0.04	13.90***	0.06	0.04	9.30***
	Matched	0.07	0.07	2.70	0.06	0.06	-0.10
Father's psychiatric diagnoses: More than one	Unmatched	0.12	0.06	21.20***	0.10	0.06	15.00***
	Matched	0.12	0.10	4.00	0.10	0.09	1.20
Adoption	Unmatched	0.98	0.99	-8.50***	0.98	0.99	-6.80***
	Matched	0.98	0.99	-2.60	0.98	0.99	-1.40
First-born	Unmatched	0.45	0.45	0.50	0.46	0.45	2.60**
	Matched	0.45	0.46	-2.50	0.46	0.46	-0.60

Note: 4,452 observations in DA; 10,258 observations in PA. Method: T-test for differences in means. Significance level: 0.05(*), 0.01(**), 0.001(***).

Source: Statistics Denmark

that is referred to as a bias of 26.8 per cent between DA and the unmatched control group and a bias of 15.6 per cent between PA and the unmatched control group. Regarding bias, the number of asterisks indicates whether the bias is statistically significantly different from zero. A higher number of asterisks (up to three) indicates greater statistical significance. However, a lack of asterisks indicates that the bias is not statistically significantly different from zero. It is evident from the table that the biases are highly statistically significantly different from zero.

In the second row, the difference in gender shares between the DA and C-Demo—the *matched* control group—and PA and C-Demo are presented. It is evident that C-Demo has nearly the same gender shares as DA and PA. In this case, the biases are only 1.7 per cent and –0.2 per cent, respectively, and both are statistically insignificant. In other words, the matching procedure of choosing the 'nearest neighbour' of every individual in the treatment groups removes all significant biases, except for mother's psychiatric diagnosis, which is significant at a relatively low level, and only so for the PA group. Therefore, the treatment groups and the control groups have similar characteristics with respect to observable characteristics.

The overall impression of Table 7.2 is that significant biases in the difference between the treatment and unmatched control groups are removed in the matched control groups. This is a helpful consequence of the large number of non-ADHD individuals to draw from when constructing the matched control group. In other words, by applying matching procedures and having access to an enormous amount of information on the entire adult population of Denmark, we are able to select control groups that are highly similar to the treatment groups based on observable information.

7.1.2 *Addressing Comorbidity*

To address comorbidity, we employ information on 'other psychiatric diagnoses' as selection criteria in addition to the demographic controls applied above when matching the control groups to the treatment groups.

We include information on the following aggregate ICD-10 codes:[3]

- F10–F19: Mental and behavioural disorders resulting from psychoactive substance use
- F20–F29: Schizophrenia, schizotypal, and delusional disorders
- F30–F39: Mood [affective] disorders

---

[3] More precisely, we perform the matching based on dummy variables for the diagnoses. The aggregate ICD-10 codes are selected based on the descriptive statistics set out in Part II.

Table 7.3. Reduction in comorbidity bias—Demographic and comorbidity controls

Variable	Sample	Diagnosed adults			Prescribed adults		
		Treated	Control	% bias	Treated	Control	% bias
Substance	Unmatched	0.35	0.04	84.30***	0.23	0.04	55.10***
	Matched: C-Demo	0.35	0.07	77.50***	0.23	0.06	50.40***
	Matched: C-Comor	0.35	0.35	0.30	0.23	0.22	0.30
Schizophrenia	Unmatched	0.13	0.01	45.70***	0.07	0.01	27.80***
	Matched: C-Demo	0.13	0.02	43.20***	0.07	0.02	25.50***
	Matched: C-Comor	0.13	0.12	4.50	0.07	0.06	2.00
Mood	Unmatched	0.27	0.03	68.90***	0.19	0.03	50.50***
	Matched: C-Demo	0.27	0.05	65.80***	0.19	0.04	48.90***
	Matched: C-Comor	0.27	0.28	−4.40	0.19	0.19	−0.40
Stress	Unmatched	0.36	0.06	79.90***	0.26	0.06	57.00***
	Matched: C-Demo	0.36	0.07	75.60***	0.26	0.07	54.70***
	Matched: C-Comor	0.36	0.37	−4.20	0.26	0.26	−1.40
Personality	Unmatched	0.24	0.02	69.70***	0.16	0.02	50.30***
	Matched: C-Demo	0.24	0.03	67.60***	0.16	0.02	48.50***
	Matched: C-Comor	0.24	0.23	3.90	0.16	0.14	4.60*

Note: 4,452 observations in DA; 10,258 observations in PA. Method: T-test for differences in means. Significance level: 0.05(*), 0.01(**), 0.001(***).
Source: Statistics Denmark

- F40–F48: Neurotic, stress-related, and somatoform disorders
- F60–F69: Disorders of adult personality and behaviour

The characteristics of the treatment and control groups are presented in Table 7.3. More precisely, we present the matches between DA and C-Comor and those between PA and C-Comor. We present only the characteristics for psychiatric diagnoses that were not considered in the matching presented in Table 7.2.

The comorbidity biases between the treatment groups and the unmatched control groups are large, especially for DA. For example, 35 per cent of the DA individuals have diagnoses of 'mental and behavioural disorders resulting from psychoactive substance use'. For the unmatched control group, this share is only 4.4 per cent. The biases are smaller for PA but nevertheless still large. These biases are reduced when considering C-Demo, but the bias remains large and significant. Controlling for comorbidity when selecting the matched control group results in insignificant biases for all diagnoses except 'disorders of adult personality and behaviour' for PA, which exhibits relatively low significance.

It is crucial to be able to account for comorbidity, because we are able to disentangle the effect of other psychiatric diagnoses on performance from the direct effect of ADHD. In situations in which it was not possible to account for comorbidity, we compared output measures (e.g., education, labour-market performance) for a group of individuals of which a high share have diagnoses related to substance abuse to a matched control group of which a much lower share has such diagnoses. Such a scenario is problematic because we do not know whether the potentially poor performance of the treatment group is related to substance abuse or to ADHD.

When we apply other psychiatric diagnoses as background variables, all biases related to these variables are removed for DA. This procedure implies that characteristics with respect to other psychiatric diagnoses are similar in DA and C-Comor. That is, the share of individuals with psychiatric diagnoses related to substance use equals 35 per cent in both groups, the share of individuals with schizophrenia equals 13 per cent, and so on for other conditions.

For PA, it is possible to remove the biases for four out of five diagnoses when selecting C-Comor. For 'disorders of adult personality and behaviour' a bias remains. However, this bias is substantially reduced, implying that the treatment and control groups are also more similar with respect to this diagnosis.

After presenting tests for the applied matching criteria leading to the matched control groups, we turn our attention to the results for the outcome variables.

7.2 Mean Differences Between the Treatment and Control Groups

In this section, we present the estimated mean differences for the matching analysis. The results are presented using the following three measures: the mean outcomes for the treatment and the control group as well as the difference between the two. The latter measure is referred to as the *mean difference*, and we evaluate whether it is significantly different from zero. If the mean difference is significantly different from zero, then we can conclude that the means for the two groups are significantly different.[4]

The presentation of the outcome measures will be organized along a number of dimensions. These outcomes are grouped according to the following:

- **Occupational status**: self-employed, wage employed, students, unemployed, welfare, activation programmes, sickness subsidy, retirement scheme, and outside labour market.

- **Income and public transfers**: personal income, annual wage income, hourly wage, taxes, student grants, social-security benefits, sickness benefits, and retirement benefits.

---

[4] In this book, we estimate mean differences for the 2009 and 2010 outcomes. A cleaner strategy than the one applied would be to focus on the years prior to diagnosis only. We have performed a robustness analysis where we apply outcome measures for the year prior to the year of diagnosis. The analysis has been performed on the same outcome measures as in this chapter. The overall impression is that it to a large extent confirms the baseline results presented in this chapter.

- **Educational attainment**: highest level of education completed.

- **Crime and traffic accidents**: criminal offences, victim of a crime, and traffic accidents.

- **Childhood outcomes**: placement away from home, involvement in preventive measures as a child, age at grade 9, age when graduating from secondary education, secondary graduation marks (GPA, maths, and Danish), and disruption in education.

- **Family composition**: fraction with children, age at parenthood, number of children (fewer than or more than four children), placement of children, preventive measures, and number of partners (one partner or more than one partner).

- **Health measures**: bed-days in hospital, DRG/DAGS,[5] treatment in primary-care facilities (GPs, specialists, psychologists, and others), and prescription drugs.

The detailed explanations of the outcome measures are presented in Table 7.A.2 in the appendix to this chapter.

7.2.1 Occupational Status

The occupational status for 2009 is presented in Table 7.4. The table is organized as follows: Column 1 contains the *names of the dependent variables*, and Column 2 contains information on the *control groups*. Columns 3–6 contain the mean values for DA, the three control groups, the *mean difference* between the treatment and the specific control group, and information on statistical significance. Columns 7–10 contain similar information for PA.[6]

The three rows corresponding to 'wage employed' present information regarding the share of wage-employed individuals in 2009 for the different groups. It is evident that only 25 per cent of DA and 36 per cent of PA are wage employed. This result is in contrast to 75 per cent among the adult population, which leads to large differences between the treatment groups and the adult population (approximately 50 and 40 percentage points).

In the second and third rows on wage employment data, the treatment groups are compared to C-Demo and C-Comor. The difference between the

---

[5] DAGS (Danish outpatient grouping system) and DRG (diagnosis-related grouping system) are systems to classify hospital cases into groups. The purpose is to identify the 'products' that a hospital provides. One example of a 'product' is an appendectomy. It is used for reimbursement, to replace 'cost-based' reimbursement. DRGs are assigned by program based on ICD (International Classification of Diseases) diagnoses, procedures, age, sex, discharge status, and the presence of complications or comorbidities.
[6] The number of asterisks indicates whether the mean difference is significantly different from zero. A higher number of asterisks (up to three) indicates greater statistical significance. Conversely, in the absence of asterisks, the mean difference is not significantly different from zero.

125

Table 7.4. Baseline results—Occupational status

Variable	Sample	Diagnosed adults				Prescribed adults			
		Treated	Control	Difference	S.E.	Treated	Control	Difference	S.E.
Self-employed	Unmatched	0.02	0.04	-0.03***	0.00	0.03	0.04	-0.02***	0.00
	C-Demo	0.02	0.03	-0.02***	0.00	0.03	0.04	-0.01***	0.00
	C-Comor	0.02	0.02	-0.01**	0.00	0.03	0.03	0.00	0.00
Wage employed	Unmatched	0.25	0.75	-0.50***	0.01	0.36	0.75	-0.39***	0.00
	C-Demo	0.25	0.68	-0.43***	0.01	0.36	0.72	-0.36***	0.01
	C-Comor	0.25	0.52	-0.27***	0.01	0.36	0.62	-0.26***	0.01
Student	Unmatched	0.05	0.06	-0.01	0.00	0.05	0.06	-0.01***	0.00
	C-Demo	0.05	0.07	-0.02***	0.01	0.05	0.06	-0.01*	0.00
	C-Comor	0.05	0.06	-0.01*	0.00	0.05	0.06	-0.01*	0.00
Unemployed	Unmatched	0.05	0.03	0.02***	0.00	0.05	0.03	0.02***	0.00
	C-Demo	0.05	0.04	0.01	0.00	0.05	0.03	0.01***	0.00
	C-Comor	0.05	0.04	0.01*	0.00	0.05	0.04	0.01*	0.00
Welfare	Unmatched	0.23	0.02	0.21***	0.00	0.16	0.02	0.15***	0.00
	C-Demo	0.23	0.03	0.20***	0.01	0.16	0.02	0.14***	0.00
	C-Comor	0.23	0.08	0.15***	0.01	0.16	0.06	0.10***	0.00
Activation programmes	Unmatched	0.16	0.03	0.13***	0.00	0.12	0.03	0.10***	0.00
	C-Demo	0.16	0.04	0.12***	0.01	0.12	0.04	0.09***	0.00
	C-Comor	0.16	0.08	0.08***	0.01	0.12	0.05	0.07***	0.00
Sickness subsidy	Unmatched	0.06	0.01	0.05***	0.00	0.05	0.01	0.04***	0.00
	C-Demo	0.06	0.01	0.05***	0.00	0.05	0.01	0.04***	0.00
	C-Comor	0.06	0.03	0.03***	0.00	0.05	0.02	0.03***	0.00
Retirement scheme	Unmatched	0.13	0.03	0.10***	0.00	0.12	0.03	0.09***	0.00
	C-Demo	0.13	0.03	0.10***	0.01	0.12	0.03	0.09***	0.00
	C-Comor	0.13	0.10	0.02***	0.01	0.12	0.07	0.05***	0.00
Outside labour market	Unmatched	0.06	0.04	0.03***	0.00	0.06	0.04	0.02***	0.00
	C-Demo	0.06	0.05	0.01**	0.00	0.06	0.04	0.01***	0.00
	C-Comor	0.06	0.05	0.01	0.01	0.06	0.05	0.01***	0.00

Note: Occupational status in November 2009. 4,452 observations in DA; 10,258 observations in PA. Method: Propensity score matching. Significance level: 0.05(*), 0.01(**), 0.001(***).

Source: Statistics Denmark

adult population—the unmatched control group—and C-Demo controls is moderate. Using demographic controls reduces the difference between the treatment and control groups by only 3 to 7 percentage points. In this sense, there remain large differences between the group of adult individuals with ADHD and their matched control group.

With comorbidity controls, the comparison also accounts for psychiatric diagnoses other than ADHD. It is evident from the third row on wage-employed individuals that it is crucial to consider other such diagnoses. For the control group relevant for DA, the share of wage employed decreases by more than 15 percentage points to approximately 52 per cent, whereas the share declines by approximately 10 percentage points for the control group relevant for PA. Although the shares of individuals who are wage employed decrease considerably when comorbidity is considered, substantial differences persist between the treatment and control groups. This result implies that the individuals in the treatment groups were less likely to be employed in 2009 than the similar but non-ADHD groups.

Another important occupational status category is the early-retirement scheme. 12–13 per cent of the DA and PA individuals benefit from this scheme. These figures represent substantial differences from the Danish adult population, of whom approximately 3 per cent benefit from the scheme. The corresponding shares for C-Comor controls are approximately 10 per cent and 7 per cent.

Similar results are obtained for the other occupational-status categories. This finding implies that individuals who are diagnosed with ADHD later in life receive welfare benefits, sickness payments, or government training pro-grammes to a much greater extent than non-ADHD but similar individuals. However, the mean shares of unemployed people in the treatment groups are not (particularly) different from those in the control groups, probably because many of the individuals in the treatment groups are considered unemployable and are therefore moved to other support schemes.

We must be cautious, however, when interpreting the results in Table 7.4, as we may exaggerate the effect of ADHD as a consequence of choosing the year 2009 for the comparison. A concern with the baseline results for occupational status presented is whether individuals with ADHD have become marginalized during the financial crisis to a greater extent than non-ADHD but otherwise similar individuals. The presented results apply for 2009, i.e., a year after the onset of the financial crisis. As it is well known that many workers have lost their jobs during this crisis—especially unskilled jobs in industry—it is interesting to investigate the impact on individuals diagnosed with ADHD later in life to evaluate whether they have had different development in their labour-market attachment compared to individuals in the control groups. Consequently, we have investigated whether the *development* of labour-market attachment has changed more for individuals with ADHD or for non-ADHD individuals during the financial crisis. The results show that the share of wage employed among ADHD individuals has dropped faster than among non-ADHD individuals during the period between 2007 and 2009.

Due to space limitations, we do not present the results of this analysis in this book. However, we apply more conservative estimates for occupational status obtained on 2007 data in the robustness checks in the cost analysis in Part IV.

7.2.2 Income

Income measures, taxes, and public transfers for 2010 are presented in Table 7.5. The measures employed are personal income, annual wage income, hourly wage, income taxes paid, student grants, social-security benefits, sickness benefits, and retirement benefits.

The overall impression of the table is that individuals with ADHD have lower incomes, pay fewer taxes, and receive more benefits. This result is evident when DA is compared with either C-Demo or C-Comor. This difference is also evident when PA is compared with either C-Demo or C-Comor, and the mean differences are lower when compared with C-Comor.

Income, taxes, and public transfers are conditional on occupational status, i.e. the difference in annual wage income is presented for the subpopulation of wage workers, the difference in sickness benefits is presented for the subpopulation receiving sickness benefits, etc.

Compared with the demographic controls, personal income is up to one-third lower for the treatment groups compared with the control group. For PA individuals, income is approximately 20 per cent lower than that for individuals in the C-Comor group. Annual wage income is between 30 per cent and 45 per cent lower for PA and DA compared with C-Demo and approximately 20 per cent and 40 per cent lower compared with C-Comor, respectively. The hourly wage rate is 5 per cent to 10 per cent lower for DA and PA compared with the control groups.

7.2.3 Educational Attainment

Educational attainment is presented in Table 7.6. The measures employed are the shares of the groups that have a certain level of educational attainment. The overall impression is that individuals with ADHD are less educated than non-ADHD individuals.

It is evident that large shares of both treatment groups have low levels of formal education when we compare with either control group (i.e., C-Demo or C-Comor). Specifically, substantial shares of individuals with ADHD have completed only elementary school: 68 per cent and 52 per cent in the two treatment groups compared with approximately 21 per cent in the adult

Table 7.5. Baseline results—Income, taxes, and public transfers

Variable	Sample	Diagnosed adults				Prescribed adults			
		Treated	Control	Difference	S.E.	Treated	Control	Difference	S.E.
Personal income	Unmatched	23,773	43,051	-19,278***	832	28,936	43,224	-14,288***	47
	C-Demo	23,773	36,253	-12,480***	497	28,936	39,638	-10,703***	351
	C-Comor	23,773	36,802	-13,029*	6,112	28,936	36,601	-7666***	621
Annual wage income	Unmatched	18,709	40,249	-21,541***	762	27,478	40,249	-12,770***	455
	C-Demo	18,709	34,921	-16,212***	788	27,478	39,031	-11,553***	520
	C-Comor	18,709	29,874	-11,165***	681	27,478	35,393	-7914***	509
Hourly wage	Unmatched	19.21	24.55	-5.34***	0.38	21.46	24.55	-3.10***	0.23
	C-Demo	19.21	21.66	-2.45***	0.37	21.46	23.43	-1.97***	0.26
	C-Comor	19.21	20.42	-1.21**	0.37	21.46	23.13	-1.68***	0.33
Income taxes paid	Unmatched	5,835	13,682	-7,847***	349	7,770	13,754	-5984***	837
	C-Demo	5,835	11,227	-5,392***	197	7,770	12,362	-4592***	144
	C-Comor	5,835	11,299	-5,464*	2,597	7,770	11,067	-3296***	259
Student grants	Unmatched	5,774	5,396	378*	155	6,600	5,396	1,204***	103
	C-Demo	5,774	5,574	200	275	6,600	5,543	1,057***	198
	C-Comor	5,774	5,590	184	287	6,600	5,781	819***	204
Social-security benefits	Unmatched	8,073	6,319	1,754***	143	8,012	6,319	1,693***	112
	C-Demo	8,073	5,647	2,426***	201	8,012	6,349	1,662***	159
	C-Comor	8,073	6,453	1,620***	206	8,012	6,691	1,321***	160
Sickness benefits	Unmatched	36.55	24.07	12.48***	0.82	34.11	24.07	10.03***	0.53
	C-Demo	36.55	23.47	13.09***	1.27	34.11	23.95	10.16***	0.81
	C-Comor	36.55	28.85	7.70***	1.33	34.11	26.80	7.31***	0.84
Retirement benefits	Unmatched	21,895	21,462	432	238	21,464	21,471	-7***	165
	C-Demo	21,895	22,101	-207	330	21,464	21,851	-387***	232
	C-Comor	21,895	22,799	-904**	312	21,464	21,874	-410***	232

Note: Personal income, annual salary, income taxes paid, student grant, social-security benefits, sickness benefits, and retirement benefits in 2010; hourly wage in November 2007. 4,451 observations in DA (1,782 employees; 2,143 hourly wage observations; 521 receiving student grants; 1,898 receiving social-security benefits; 1,567 receiving sickness benefits; 805 receiving retirement benefits). 10,258 observations in PA (5,011 employees; 5,745 hourly wage observations; 1,192 receiving student grants; 3,154 receiving social-security benefits; 3,758 receiving sickness benefits; 1,706 receiving retirement benefits). Method: Propensity score matching. Significance level: 0.05(*), 0.01(**), 0.001(***).

Source: Statistics Denmark

Table 7.6. Baseline results—Educational attainment

Variable	Sample	Diagnosed adults				Prescribed adults			
		Treated	Control	Difference	S.E.	Treated	Control	Difference	S.E.
Elementary school (Folkeskole)	Unmatched	0.68	0.21	0.47***	0.01	0.52	0.21	0.31***	0.00
	C-Demo	0.68	0.32	0.36***	0.01	0.52	0.27	0.26***	0.01
	C-Comor	0.68	0.43	0.24***	0.01	0.52	0.35	0.17***	0.01
Secondary education	Unmatched	0.06	0.14	-0.08***	0.01	0.08	0.14	-0.06***	0.00
	C-Demo	0.06	0.14	-0.08***	0.01	0.08	0.13	-0.05***	0.00
	C-Comor	0.06	0.13	-0.07***	0.01	0.08	0.12	-0.04***	0.00
Vocational education	Unmatched	0.20	0.34	-0.14***	0.01	0.27	0.34	-0.08***	0.00
	C-Demo	0.20	0.35	-0.15***	0.01	0.27	0.35	-0.09***	0.01
	C-Comor	0.20	0.29	-0.09***	0.01	0.27	0.32	-0.06***	0.01
Short further	Unmatched	0.01	0.05	-0.04***	0.00	0.02	0.05	-0.03***	0.00
	C-Demo	0.01	0.04	-0.02***	0.00	0.02	0.05	-0.02***	0.00
	C-Comor	0.01	0.03	-0.02***	0.00	0.02	0.04	-0.02***	0.00
Medium further	Unmatched	0.03	0.13	-0.10***	0.01	0.06	0.13	-0.07***	0.00
	C-Demo	0.03	0.08	-0.05***	0.01	0.06	0.11	-0.05***	0.00
	C-Comor	0.03	0.06	-0.03***	0.00	0.06	0.09	-0.03***	0.00
Bachelor	Unmatched	0.00	0.03	-0.03***	0.00	0.02	0.03	-0.02***	0.00
	C-Demo	0.00	0.03	-0.02***	0.00	0.02	0.03	-0.01***	0.00
	C-Comor	0.00	0.02	-0.02***	0.00	0.02	0.02	-0.01***	0.00
Long further	Unmatched	0.01	0.08	-0.08***	0.00	0.03	0.08	-0.06***	0.00
	C-Demo	0.01	0.05	-0.04***	0.00	0.03	0.06	-0.03***	0.00
	C-Comor	0.01	0.03	-0.02***	0.00	0.03	0.05	-0.02***	0.00

Note: Highest completed level of education as of 2010. 4,325 observations in DA, 10,048 observations in PA. Method: Propensity score matching. Significance level: 0.05(*), 0.01(**), 0.001(***).

Source: Statistics Denmark

Danish population. This result implies mean differences of 47 and 31 percentage points respectively. Moreover, approximately a quarter of the individuals with ADHD have a vocational education.

When treatment groups are compared to C-Demo, the mean differences are reduced somewhat but not substantially. For elementary school, the mean differences decline by 11 and 5 percentage points for DA and PA respectively. When compared with C-Comor, the mean differences are reduced further, declining by an additional 12 and 9 percentage points to 24 and 17 percentage points. In total, the mean differences for elementary school are nearly halved when moving from the comparison of the unmatched control group to C-Comor.

However, the lower mean differences for elementary school indicate that the mean differences between ADHD individuals and non-ADHD individuals for the other educational attainment categories are also numerically lower.

7.2.4 Crime and Traffic Accidents

Measures of criminal offences, being the victim of a crime, and traffic accidents are presented in Table 7.7. Compared with the control groups, large shares of individuals with ADHD have been convicted of a crime, have been the victim of a crime, or have been involved in a traffic accident. This result is observed regardless of whether comorbidity is considered.

It is evident that 60 per cent of the diagnosed adults have been convicted of criminal offences, whereas the corresponding share is 50 per cent for prescribed adults. By contrast, the share of the non-ADHD adult Danish population is 25 per cent. Although the shares for the matched control groups are higher, the mean differences are still large and amount to 15 to 20 percentage points when comorbidity is considered.

Similar results are obtained for both 'victims of a crime' and 'traffic accidents'. When comorbidity is considered, the mean differences decline but remain large and significantly different from zero.

7.2.5 Childhood Outcomes

Table 7.8 presents the results for a number of outcome measures related to childhood outcomes. These variables include placement away from home, participation in preventive measures as a child, age at grade 9, age when graduating from secondary education, grades from secondary education (GPA, maths, and Danish), and educational disruptions.

Individuals with ADHD have poor childhood outcomes compared with their non-ADHD counterparts. A larger share of ADHD individuals were placed away from home, were involved in preventive measures, and had educational

Table 7.7. Baseline results—Crime and traffic

Variable	Sample	Diagnosed adults				Prescribed adults			
		Treated	Control	Difference	S.E.	Treated	Control	Difference	S.E.
Criminal offences	Unmatched	0.60	0.25	0.35***	0.01	0.50	0.25	0.25***	0.00
	C-Demo	0.60	0.33	0.28***	0.01	0.50	0.30	0.20***	0.01
	C-Comor	0.60	0.41	0.19***	0.01	0.50	0.36	0.14***	0.01
Victim of a crime	Unmatched	0.29	0.10	0.18***	0.00	0.24	0.10	0.13***	0.00
	C-Demo	0.29	0.14	0.15***	0.01	0.24	0.13	0.11***	0.01
	C-Comor	0.29	0.21	0.08***	0.01	0.24	0.16	0.07***	0.01
Traffic accidents	Unmatched	0.09	0.03	0.06***	0.00	0.07	0.03	0.04***	0.00
	C-Demo	0.09	0.05	0.04***	0.01	0.07	0.04	0.04***	0.00
	C-Comor	0.09	0.06	0.02***	0.01	0.07	0.05	0.03***	0.00

Note: At least one registered incident in the period 2001–2010. 4,452 observations in DA, 10,258 observations in PA. Method: Propensity score matching. Significance level: 0.05(*),0.01(**), 0.001(***).

Source: Statistics Denmark

Table 7.8. Baseline results—Childhood performance

Variable	Sample	Diagnosed adults				Prescribed adults			
		Treated	Control	Difference	S.E.	Treated	Control	Difference	S.E.
In placement as a child	Unmatched	0.28	0.05	0.24***	0.00	0.21	0.05	0.17***	0.00
	C-Demo	0.28	0.11	0.18***	0.01	0.21	0.09	0.13***	0.00
	C-Comor	0.28	0.17	0.11***	0.01	0.21	0.13	0.08***	0.01
Involved in preventive measures as a child	Unmatched	0.20	0.03	0.17***	0.00	0.14	0.03	0.11***	0.00
	C-Demo	0.20	0.09	0.11***	0.01	0.14	0.06	0.08***	0.00
	C-Comor	0.20	0.12	0.08***	0.01	0.14	0.08	0.06***	0.00
Age in grade 9 (*)	Unmatched	15.29	15.07	0.22***	0.01	15.23	15.07	0.16***	0.01
	C-Demo	15.29	15.14	0.16***	0.02	15.23	15.13	0.10***	0.01
	C-Comor	15.29	15.19	0.11***	0.02	15.23	15.14	0.08***	0.01
Age when graduating from secondary education	Unmatched	19.69	18.74	0.95***	0.07	19.40	18.75	0.65***	0.04
	C-Demo	19.69	18.98	0.71***	0.16	19.40	19.13	0.27*	0.11
	C-Comor	19.69	19.20	0.49*	0.20	19.40	19.08	0.31***	0.10
Secondary graduation marks	Unmatched	6.88	7.48	-0.60***	0.12	7.17	7.48	-0.32***	0.07
	C-Demo	6.88	7.52	-0.64***	0.18	7.17	7.74	-0.58***	0.10
	C-Comor	6.88	7.33	-0.45**	0.17	7.17	7.58	-0.41***	0.10
Secondary graduation marks (Maths)	Unmatched	5.81	6.72	-0.91***	0.23	5.91	6.72	-0.81***	0.13
	C-Demo	5.81	6.73	-0.92**	0.34	5.91	6.99	-1.08***	0.19
	C-Comor	5.81	6.39	-0.58	0.36	5.91	6.87	-0.96***	0.20
Secondary graduation marks (Danish)	Unmatched	7.11	7.43	-0.33*	0.15	7.31	7.43	-0.13***	0.08
	C-Demo	7.11	7.33	-0.22***	0.22	7.31	7.66	-0.35**	0.11
	C-Comor	7.11	7.81	-0.71***	0.20	7.31	7.72	-0.42***	0.12
Educational disruption	Unmatched	0.51	0.14	0.37***	0.01	0.39	0.14	0.25***	0.01
	C-Demo	0.51	0.19	0.32***	0.02	0.39	0.16	0.24***	0.01
	C-Comor	0.51	0.32	0.19***	0.02	0.39	0.22	0.17***	0.01

Note: Measures related to childhood performance. 4,452 observations in DA (2,345 observations from primary education; 234 observations from secondary education; 216 Danish graduation marks; 195 Maths graduating marks). 10,258 observations in PA (5,148 observations from primary education; 760 observations from secondary education; 687 Danish graduation marks; 598 Maths graduating marks). Method: Propensity score matching. Significance level:0.05(*),0.01(**),0.001(***).(*) Results from another sample indicate that children having ADHD will typically have a late start in primary education.

Source: Statistics Denmark

disruptions; the individuals were also on average older when they graduated from elementary school. Other data sources indicate that ADHD individuals on average have a later school start, which may be due to immaturity. Poor performance is documented irrespective of whether comorbidity is considered.

Moreover, individuals with ADHD have relatively lower secondary school grades in general and specifically in maths and Danish. However, the mean differences are not statistically significant for DA individuals because of the low number of observations.

7.2.6 Family Composition

Table 7.9 presents the results for a number of outcome measures related to family composition. These variables are the fraction of individuals with children, age at parenthood, the number of children (fewer than or more than four children), placement of children, preventive measures, the number of partners, and the fraction with more than one partner.

There is no strong evidence that the decision to become a parent is affected by ADHD. However, ADHD individuals tend to be younger when they become parents and have more children. Moreover, there is a tendency for individuals with ADHD to have more partners compared with those without ADHD. Individuals with ADHD have their children placed outside of the home more often, and more preventive measures are also implemented.

7.2.7 Health Measures

Table 7.10 presents the results for a number of outcome measures related to health. These variables are hospital bed days, DRG/DAGS, treatment in primary-care facilities (GPs, specialists, psychologists, and others), and prescription drugs (user charges and public subsidy).

The main result is that individuals with ADHD make much broader use of the primary health-care system. Moreover, these individuals also use the secondary health-care sector more frequently, as measured by the number of hospital bed days. The significance of the latter result disappears when C-Comor is used as a comparison, but costs remain significant, which may be explained by longer (or more demanding) admissions.

7.3 Summary

In this chapter, we have presented the baseline results of the propensity score matching. In summary, the results indicate weak performance on the part of the two treatment groups considered: adults who have been diagnosed with

Table 7.9. Baseline results—Family composition (adulthood)

Variable	Sample	Diagnosed adults				Prescribed adults			
		Treated	Control	Difference	S.E.	Treated	Control	Difference	S.E.
Fraction of parents	Unmatched	0.42	0.55	-0.13***	0.01	0.48	0.55	-0.06***	0.00
	C-Demo	0.42	0.41	0.01	0.01	0.48	0.50	-0.02*	0.01
	C-Comor	0.42	0.38	0.03**	0.01	0.48	0.48	0.01	0.01
Age at parenthood	Unmatched	24.50	27.76	-3.26***	0.11	25.54	27.76	-2.22***	0.07
	C-Demo	24.50	26.37	-1.87***	0.15	25.54	27.07	-1.53***	0.10
	C-Comor	24.50	25.61	-1.12***	0.15	25.54	26.62	-1.08***	0.10
Number of children	Unmatched	1.90	2.00	-0.10***	0.02	2.00	2.00	0.01	0.01
	C-Demo	1.90	1.84	0.06	0.03	2.00	1.92	0.08***	0.02
	C-Comor	1.90	1.78	0.12***	0.03	2.00	1.90	0.11***	0.02
Fewer than four children	Unmatched	0.94	0.96	-0.02***	0.00	0.93	0.96	-0.02***	0.00
	C-Demo	0.94	0.97	-0.03***	0.01	0.93	0.96	-0.02***	0.00
	C-Comor	0.94	0.95	-0.02*	0.01	0.93	0.95	-0.02***	0.00
Placement of children	Unmatched	0.13	0.02	0.11***	0.00	0.09	0.02	0.08***	0.00
	C-Demo	0.13	0.03	0.10***	0.01	0.09	0.02	0.07***	0.00
	C-Comor	0.13	0.07	0.06***	0.01	0.09	0.05	0.04***	0.01
Preventive measures	Unmatched	0.17	0.03	0.14***	0.00	0.14	0.03	0.11***	0.00
	C-Demo	0.17	0.03	0.14***	0.01	0.14	0.03	0.11***	0.01
	C-Comor	0.17	0.06	0.11***	0.01	0.14	0.06	0.08***	0.01
Number of partners	Unmatched	1.31	1.11	0.20***	0.01	1.28	1.11	0.17***	0.00
	C-Demo	1.31	1.12	0.19***	0.02	1.28	1.12	0.16***	0.01
	C-Comor	1.31	1.17	0.13***	0.02	1.28	1.17	0.12***	0.01
More than one partner	Unmatched	0.26	0.10	0.16***	0.01	0.24	0.10	0.14***	0.00
	C-Demo	0.26	0.11	0.15***	0.01	0.24	0.11	0.13***	0.01
	C-Comor	0.26	0.15	0.11***	0.01	0.24	0.15	0.09***	0.01

Note: Measures related to the situation in the family. 4,452 observations in DA (1,863 having children); 10,258 observations in PA (4,963 having children). Method: Propensity score matching. Significance level: 0.05(*), 0.01(**), 0.001(***).

Source: Statistics Denmark

Table 7.10. Baseline results—Health measures

Variable	Sample	Diagnosed adults				Prescribed adults			
		Treated	Control	Difference	S.E.	Treated	Control	Difference	S.E.
Hospital bed days	Unmatched	4.17	2.32	1.85***	0.29	3.65	2.32	1.34***	0.19
	C-Demo	4.17	2.19	1.98**	0.73	3.65	2.08	1.57***	0.27
	C-Comor	4.17	3.87	0.30	0.78	3.65	3.16	0.49	0.34
DRG/DAGS	Unmatched	147	88	59***	6	136	88	48***	4
	C-Demo	147	83	64***	8	136	86	50***	6
	C-Comor	147	118	29***	8	136	116	20**	7
Treatment in primary-care facilities: GP	Unmatched	20.12	8.40	11.72***	0.18	16.87	8.40	8.47***	0.12
	C-Demo	20.12	8.49	11.63***	0.51	16.87	8.18	8.69***	0.23
	C-Comor	20.12	12.33	7.79***	0.55	16.87	10.99	5.88***	0.25
Treatment in primary-care facilities: Specialists	Unmatched	5.55	4.69	0.86***	0.13	5.48	4.69	0.79***	0.09
	C-Demo	5.55	3.94	1.61***	0.28	5.48	4.48	1.00***	0.14
	C-Comor	5.55	5.12	0.43	0.34	5.48	4.93	0.54***	0.16
Treatment in primary-care facilities: Psychologist	Unmatched	2.27	0.24	2.02***	0.03	5.35	0.24	5.11***	0.03
	C-Demo	2.27	0.23	2.04***	0.12	5.35	0.25	5.10***	0.24
	C-Comor	2.27	0.50	1.77***	0.13	5.35	0.24	5.11***	0.03
Treatment in primary-care facilities: Other	Unmatched	2.84	3.18	-0.34	0.18	4.35	3.18	1.17***	0.12
	C-Demo	2.84	2.60	0.24	0.27	4.35	2.67	1.68***	0.18
	C-Comor	2.84	2.65	0.18	0.26	4.35	3.27	1.08***	0.20
Prescription drugs: User charges	Unmatched	342	76	265***	2	335	76	259***	1
	C-Demo	342	65	276***	6	335	73	261***	4
	C-Comor	342	123	219***	7	335	105	230***	4
Prescription drugs: Public subsidy	Unmatched	1,129	91	1,039***	10	901	91	811***	7
	C-Demo	1,129	72	1,057***	30	901	84	817***	18
	C-Comor	1,129	356	773***	36	901	205	696***	20
Prescription drugs: Total	Unmatched	1,539	169	1,370***	11	1,278	169	1,109***	7
	C-Demo	1,539	140	1,399***	34	1,278	160	1,118***	20
	C-Comor	1,539	491	1,048***	41	1,278	318	960***	22

Note: Health-related measures in 2010. 4,452 observations in DA; 10,258 observations in PA. Method: Propensity score matching. Significance level: 0.05(*), 0.01(**), 0.001(***).
Source: Statistics Denmark

ADHD later in life and adults who have been prescribed methylphenidate, atomoxetine, or dexamphetamine later in life. The results suggest that individuals with ADHD have weak performance on a number of performance measures that are grouped on the basis of occupational status, income and public transfers, educational attainment, crime and traffic accidents, childhood outcomes, family composition, and health measures. This performance is observed when accounting for a wide range of demographic control variables and after matched control groups are selected using comorbid psychiatric diagnoses as selection criteria in addition to demographic control variables. Independent of the matched control group considered, the mean differences between the treatment and matched control groups are large and statistically significant.

However, there is an important limitation of the results. We have selected matched control groups based on observed variables alone. Although the list of variables is long, we are unable to exclude the possibility that there are important background variables that we were unable to consider. For example, genetic differences and social-background factors during childhood and upbringing may be important conditions that we have not controlled for. In this sense, we cannot exclude the possibility that that the treatment and control groups do systematically differ because of *unobservable heterogeneity*. We address this issue in Chapter 8.

Appendix to Chapter 7: Effects of Excluding Individuals from Treatment Groups

Below, we describe the differences between the treatment groups analysed in this chapter and the groups identified in Part II. Because we require highly detailed background information for the treatment groups to be able to select matched treatment groups, we must exclude a number of ADHD individuals from the analysis in this chapter. Below, we describe the change in the treatment groups and evaluate the consequences of the characteristics of the treatment groups. The overall result is that the characteristics of DA do not change significantly, despite our exclusion of more than 15 per cent of the original treatment group of ADHD individuals. For the PA individuals, we are forced to omit 25 per cent of the sample. The characteristics of these samples thus change to some extent.

In addition, the appendix provides a detailed description of the outcome variables considered.

A.7.1 Comparing Treatment

The matching analysis is based on the two groups of individuals diagnosed with ADHD later in life identified in Part II. These two groups are referred to as follows:

- **DA**: consists of 5,331 individuals. A total of 879 individuals are omitted from the sample because we do not have all the relevant background information that is needed to select the matched control groups.

- **PA**: consists of 13,662 individuals. A total of 3,404 individuals are omitted from the sample because we do not have all the relevant background information that is needed to select the matched control groups.

The following table indicates which of the background variables lead to the restrictions. The restrictions are primarily the result of missing parental information.

In the table below, we present the means for the full sample and the excluded sample. The excluded sample is older than the full sample; this result holds for DA and to an even greater extent for PA. PA also exhibits a change in gender composition. We believe that these differences are the primary explanation for the remaining differences (differences in outcome variables). By excluding some of the older individuals in our sample the outcome variables are affected due to cohort effects.

Consistent with the change in age profile, what we observe for the outcome variables is a (relatively small) drop in employment, a larger drop in retirement, an increase in the share of students, an increase in the share receiving welfare benefits, and an increase in the share in government activation programmes. We observe a drop in income levels but a relatively stable situation for welfare transfers (more so with regard to student grants, less so with regard to retirement benefits). More people have not had their first child, and the average number of children is lower. PA shifts towards a lower level of education, more criminal activity, more placements, and less use of the primary health system and GPs, but more use of specialists and psychologists, and more money spent on prescription drugs.

We would like to stress that this does not make our matching invalid, as the matched control group is restricted likewise. We select individuals from the population who are similar to our treatment groups based on demographic variables. However, our final objective is to measure the private and social cost of the identified group of adult-diagnosed ADHD individuals in Denmark in 2010. By applying the mean differences—estimated for a younger group—on the entire group there is a potential bias. To explain this, let us say for the sake of argument that the severity of ADHD decreases with age. When comparing a 50-year-old individual diagnosed with ADHD with a 50-year-old individual not diagnosed with ADHD, the differences in performance might be less than the differences between 25-year-old individuals with and without an ADHD diagnosis. Then, by excluding elderly people in the estimation, we (upwardly) bias the effect for the entire group identified in Part II, as the excluded sample is not as severely affected in 2010. However, the opposite could also be argued: despite the fact that our cost estimates refer to 2010, the outcome is accumulated over a lifetime. For example, the personal income in 2010 is accumulated over a lifetime with and without ADHD, and the wage income in 2010 is an effect of accumulated knowledge gained over the lifetime with and without ADHD. In other words, the effect of ADHD is potentially even larger for the 50-year-old compared to the 25-year-old. The point is that we have no knowledge on whether the analysis is upwardly or downwardly biased and such an analysis is outside the scope of this study.

A.7.2 Detailed Description of the Variables

Table 7.A.1. Background variables

Personal information	Description	Number of observations	
		Diagnosed Adults	Prescribed Adults
Gender	Personal information is observed from the statistics of the population. The entire panel from 1980 to 2010 are considered. Age in 2010 is a constructed variable. Region of residence is picked from the statistics in 2010.	5,331	13,662
Age in 2010		5,331	13,662
Nationality		5,331	13,661
Region of residence in 2010		5,236	13,003
Adopted	The variable adopted indicates if the individual is adopted. Information is from the fertility database.	5,159	12,669

Parental/family information	Description	Number of observations	
		Diagnosed Adults	Prescribed Adults
Mother's and father's educational attainment	Parents are indentified from the statistics of the population. Where possible this data is updated by data from the fertility database. Level of education is from the register of education. Age at parenthood and real yearly income are constructed variables. The real yearly income is the average personal income during the childhood of the individual (where information is observed). Income is measured in 2000 prices, deflated by the Consumer Price Index. Information about psychiatric diagnoses is from the psychiatric register.	5,060 (mother) 4,825 (father)	12,378 (mother) 11,687 (father)
Mother's and father's age at parenthood		5,191 (mother) 5,018 (father)	12,678 (mother) 12,235 (father)
Mother's and father's real yearly income		5,047 (mother) 4,895 (father)	11,709 (mother) 11,338 (father)
Mother's and father's psychiatric diagnoses		5,331 (mother) 5,331 (father)	13,662 (mother) 13,662 (father)
Stable family situation	Stable family situation is a constructed variable that equals 1 if both of the parents are registered and none of the siblings are half-siblings.	5,231	12,829
Number of siblings	Number of siblings is calculated based on information from the statistics of the population. This variable includes children of the mother, as well as of the father.	5,231	12,829
Birth order	Birth order indicates the individual's position in the group of siblings (i.e. first-born, second-born, etc.). Information is from the fertility database.	5,147	12,569

Table 7.A.2. Selection due to missing information

Variables	Diagnosed adults			Prescribed adults		
	Full sample	Excluded sample	T-test	Full sample	Excluded sample	T-test
Age	29.28	34.05***		31.94	42.06***	
Gender	0.64	0.65		0.59	0.54***	
Self-employed	0.02	0.02		0.03	0.05***	
Wage employed	0.25	0.24		0.36	0.38	
Student	0.05	0.04		0.05	0.03***	
Unemployed	0.05	0.05		0.05	0.04	
Welfare	0.23	0.20*		0.16	0.12***	
Activation programmes	0.16	0.14		0.12	0.08***	
Sickness subsidy	0.06	0.04**		0.05	0.05	
Retirement scheme	0.13	0.22***		0.12	0.20***	
Outside labour market	0.06	0.07		0.06	0.06	
Personal income	23,773	24,616		28,936	33,811***	
Annual wage income	18,709	19,815		27,478	34,363***	
Income taxes paid	5,835	5,928		7,770	9,875***	
Student grants	5,774	5,833		6,600	5,818	
Social-security benefits	8,073	8,887*		8,012	8,672*	
Sickness benefits	36.61	37.98		34.62	32.25	
Retirement benefits	21,895	22,762		21,464	20,072***	
Elementary school	0.68	0.63*		0.52	0.41***	
Secondary school	0.06	0.06		0.08	0.07*	
Vocational education	0.20	0.23		0.27	0.28	
Short further	0.01	0.01		0.02	0.03*	
Medium further	0.03	0.05		0.06	0.12***	
Bachelor	0.01	0.01		0.02	0.12	
Long further	0.01	0.01		0.03	0.08***	
Criminal offences	0.60	0.60		0.50	0.37***	
Victim of a crime	0.29	0.30		0.24	0.16***	
Traffic accidents	0.09	0.07		0.07	0.10***	
In placement as a child	0.28	0.30		0.21	0.14***	
Involved in preventive measures	0.20	0.20		0.14	0.08***	
Age in grade 9	15.30	15.30		15.23	15.26***	
Age when graduating from secondary education	19.69	19.53		19.40	20.41***	
Secondary graduation marks	6.88	6.82		7.17	7.33***	
Educational disruption	0.44	0.44		0.34	0.25***	
Fractions of parents	0.42	0.50***		0.48	0.67***	
Number of children	1.90	2.03*		2.01	2.17***	
Placement of children	0.15	0.21**		0.12	0.16***	
Preventive measures	0.16	0.21*		0.13	0.15	
Number of partners	1.31	1.34		1.28	1.26***	
Hospital bed days	4.17	3.12		3.65	7.57***	
DRG/DAGS	147	146		136	178***	
Treatment in primary care: GP	20.12	19.76		0.20	0.32***	
Treatment in primary care: Specialists	5.55	6.21		5.48	5.18***	
Treatment in primary care: Psychologist	2.27	1.42**		5.35	3.04***	
Treatment in primary care: Other	2.84	2.99		4.35	5.52***	
Prescription drugs	1,539	1,473		1,278	1,031***	

Table 7.A.3. Outcome variables

Occupational status	Database	Description	Unit
Self-employed	Integrated Database for Labour Market Research (IDA). Main occupation in November	Identified using pstill 11, 12, 14, 19, 20. Includes self-employed as well as assisting spouse	Exclusive categories. Dummy indicator for occupational status in November 2009
Wage employed		Identified using pstill 31–37. Includes all wage employed workers: skilled or unskilled workers from regular staff to CEOs	
Student		Identified using pstill 91. Includes all students	
Unemployed		Identified using pstill 40, 52. Includes all unemployed	
Welfare		Identified using pstill 95. Includes all individuals receiving social security benefits	
Activation programmes		Identified using pstill 45, 46, 49, 57. Includes individuals in an activation programme, i.e. short-term employment without salary, mandatory educational programme, etc.	
Sickness subsidy		Identified using pstill 43. Includes all individuals receiving sickness benefits	
Retirement scheme		Identified using pstill 50, 92, 93, 94. Includes all individuals in a pension scheme	
Outside labour market		Identified using pstill 90. Includes individuals defined as outside the labour market	

Income, taxes, and public transfers	Database	Description	Unit
Personal income	Income Database (INDH) and the register of sickness benefits	The total of earned income, public transfers, property income, etc. directly attributable to the specific person	EUR
Annual wage income		Taxable wages incl. benefits, tax-free salary, and value of stock options	EUR
Hourly wage		An estimate of the average hourly wage for main and secondary occupation	EUR
Income taxes paid		Taxes, labour-market contributions, and pension	EUR
Student grants		Income transfer available to almost all individuals currently in education	EUR
Social-security benefits		In the absence of other income sources individuals are entitled to an income transfer	EUR
Sickness benefits		A transfer available to employed or unemployed individuals in a period of sickness	Number of days
Retirement benefits		Pension income given to individuals who have been assessed and been found to have lost the ability to work	EUR

(continued)

Table 7.A.3. Continued

Educational attainment	Database	Description	Unit
	Educational Database. Highest attained educational level in October. We apply the classification: Forspalte1		Exclusive categories. Dummy indicator for highest attained education level in October 2010
Elementary school		Identified using h1 10. Contains all individuals who in October 2010 have elementary school as highest obtained level of education	
Secondary school		Identified using h1 20 and 25. Contains all individuals who in October 2010 have secondary school as highest obtained level of education	
Vocational education		Identified using h1 35. Contains all individuals who in October 2010 have vocational education as highest obtained level of education	
Short further		Identified using h1 40. Contains all individuals who in October 2010 have short further education as highest obtained level of education	
Medium further		Identified using h1 50. Contains all individuals who in October 2010 have a bachelor degree (non-academic) as highest obtained level of education	
Bachelor		Identified using h1 60. Contains all individuals who in October 2010 have a bachelor degree as highest obtained level of education	
Long further		Identified using h1 65. Contains all individuals who in October 2010 have long further education as highest obtained level of education	

Crime and Traffic	Database	Description	Unit
	Criminal register and traffic-accident register		Non-exclusive categories. Dummy indicator for at least one incident in the period from 2001 to 2010
Criminal offences		Identified if there is a record in the criminal register in the period from 2001 to 2010. Includes violations of the Danish Penal Code, the Road Traffic Act, etc.	
Victim of a crime		Identified if there is a record in the criminal register for a conviction in the period from 2001 to 2010. Includes violent crimes under the Danish Penal Code	
Traffic accidents		Identified if there is a record in the traffic-accident register in the period from 2001 to 2010. Includes accidents involving personal injury	

Childhood performance	Database	Description	Unit
In placement as a child	Placement register	Identified using pgf 100–199 and 346. Includes permanent or time-limited foster care, imprisonment, youth sanction, etc.	Dummy indicator for at least one placement
Involved in preventive measures		Identified using pgf 200–299. Includes counselling, day-to-day help, financial support for boarding school, etc.	Dummy indicator for at least one preventive measure
Age in grade 9	Student register	Calculated based on information from the student register when udel = 9	Age in grade 9
Age when graduating from secondary education		Calculated based on information from the student register when individual obtained the diploma	Age when graduating
Secondary graduation marks		Secondary graduation marks are registered from 1978	Grade: 0–12
Educational disruption		Identified from the student register when udd has a h1 20 or 25 and audd has a h10	Grade: 0–12

Family composition	Database	Description	Unit
Fractions of parents	Population statistics	Identified from population statistics	Dummy indicator if a parent
Age at parenthood		Calculated based on information from population statistics	Age at parenthood
Number of children		Calculated based on information from population statistics	Number of children
Placement of children	Placement register	Identified using pgf 100–199 and 346. Includes permanent or time-limited foster care, imprisonment, youth sanction, etc.	Dummy indicator for at least one placement
Preventive measures		Identified using pgf 200–299. Includes counselling, day-to-day help, financial support for boarding school, etc.	Dummy indicator for at least one preventive measure
Number of partners	Population statistics	Calculated based on information from population statistics	Number of partners

Health measures	Database	Description	Unit
Hospital bed days DRG/DAGS	National Patients Register	Registered in the National Patient Register DRG/DAGS is a tool used to analyse the costs and activity at the hospitals. The system consists of DRG used for inpatients and DAGS used for outpatients.	Number of days EUR
Treatment in primary-care facilities	Public Health Insurance Register	Tool used for payment to health providers, such as doctors, dentists, etc.	Number of services
Prescription drugs	Medicines database	User charges, public subsidy, and total prices are registered in the medicines database	EUR

8

A Sibling-Based Analysis—Addressing Unobserved Heterogeneity

In this chapter, we present a sibling-based analysis in which we compare the two treatment groups to sibling-based matched control groups. The advantage of this analysis is that siblings are similar with respect to many of the aspects that are difficult to observe. These aspects may influence characteristics concerning education and income, among others. For example, genetic differences and social-background factors during childhood and upbringing are similar across siblings. In this sense, we reduce the likelihood of unobserved differences between the treatment and control groups playing an important role in determining the mean differences obtained. Thus, we attempt to explore possible biases that may influence the cost estimates to approximate the true costs of ADHD as accurately as possible.

The overall finding is that even when we consider siblings, ADHD individuals exhibit weak performance compared with their non-ADHD siblings with respect to a large number of performance measures that are grouped around occupational status, income and public transfers, educational attainment, crime and traffic accidents, childhood outcomes, family composition, and health measures. Ultimately, the results presented in Chapter 7 are robust to the use of sibling-based matched control groups. In this sense, employing the cost estimates presented in Chapter 7 in the cost calculations is considered a valid approach.

In more technical terms, the challenge that we address is *unobservable heterogeneity*. Because the main purpose of the study is to prepare a cost-benefit analysis, it is important to understand the extent to which the estimation of the mean difference can be given a *causal* interpretation, i.e., to what extent our analysis identifies the effects of ADHD per se, or whether these mean differences can be explained in other ways.

To illustrate the problem of unobservable heterogeneity, recall the weak performance that was observed in Chapter 7 for ADHD individuals relative to non-ADHD individuals who are otherwise similar. Is this difference a consequence of ADHD, or is it a result of unobservable factors? Imagine that we are unable to measure 'parental care and involvement' in the childhood household and that this factor is especially important for outcomes later in life. Consider the possibility that 'parental care and involvement' is systematically lower in households with children with ADHD—for reasons that are not related to ADHD—compared with households whose children do not have ADHD but are otherwise similar. In this case, we do not know whether it is 'relatively low parental care and involvement in households', ADHD per se, or a combination of the two that generates the negative effects on outcome measures observed in Chapter 7.

This simple example illustrates the fundamental problem with unobservable heterogeneity. However, the challenge is even greater because we do not know what constitutes the unobserved heterogeneity. Therefore, we compare the ADHD individuals to control groups composed of individuals who are as similar as we can imagine, namely, the *siblings of ADHD individuals*. The following applied control group based on siblings is used:

- **Demographic sibling controls (Sib-Demo)**: matched controls selected from same-gender siblings of individuals in the treatment group.

More precisely, we compare DA and PA with sibling-based matched control groups and apply three different definitions of siblings. The first definition refers to siblings of the same gender and the same biological mother and father but without an ADHD diagnosis. The second definition is the more narrow definition of (same-gender) twins (i.e., siblings born in the same calendar year). The third definition, which we apply for reasons explained below, is half-siblings (i.e., same-gender siblings with the same biological mother but different fathers). We refer to the three sibling groups as follows: (i) siblings, (ii) twins, and (iii) half-siblings.

The motivation for including half-siblings is that the mean differences between individuals with ADHD and similar non-ADHD individuals may be underestimated when full sisters and full brothers are included in the control groups, as ADHD is partly a genetic disorder with relatively high heritability estimates. In Chapter 2, we cited the work of Biederman (2005) that calculates a mean heritability estimate of 0.77, meaning that the twin of an ADHD child has a 77 per cent likelihood of also having the disorder. In this sense, results using the control group consisting of twins could be especially underestimated as a result of undiagnosed ADHD in the control group. Moreover, the parents and siblings of children with ADHD have been found to have a two- to eight-fold increased risk of ADHD. Because heritability is more likely to run through the father (Kustanovich et al., 2003), we consider half-siblings with the same mother but different fathers, as we expect that the described underestimation problem will be less severe.

145

The property of heritability just described is used for formulating the following two hypotheses: (i) same-gender siblings with the same mother and father are relatively genetically uniform, implying that we expect differences between ADHD individuals and their siblings to be relatively low; and (ii) half-siblings are less genetically uniform than siblings, and we expect pairs of half-siblings to have larger differences than siblings. It is exactly this pattern that is documented in many of the tables presented in this chapter.

We have also performed the sibling-based analysis taking comorbidity into account. Comorbidity is difficult to account for in this analysis because there are few siblings with other relevant psychiatric diagnoses to choose from, implying that we cannot remove significant biases in the matched control groups. As a consequence, we simply *exclude* ADHD and non-ADHD individuals with other psychiatric diagnoses from the analysis. Because the results based on the matched control groups selected from the siblings of individuals in the treatment group and excluding individuals with other psychiatric diagnoses than ADHD are similar to the results obtained when these individuals are included, we do not present the results in this study.

The sibling analysis is a sophisticated way to handle unobserved heterogeneity, but it should be emphasized that there are also limitations associated with it.

We eliminate a large number of observations from our analysis. More than 90 per cent of our ADHD group do have a sibling. However, we also require that the sibling has to be of the same gender and either (i) have the same biological mother and father, or (ii) have the same biological mother and a different biological father. Furthermore, we require that the sibling does not have a diagnosis of ADHD. This is quite restrictive for our sample and effectively means that we have less than 40 per cent of our original sample for the sibling analysis, and less than 10 per cent of our sample for the half-sibling analysis.

When we apply twins as a control group the size of the sample reduces dramatically. However, the advantage of this twin comparison between ADHD and non-ADHD individuals is that they are as similar as possible— i.e., they have a shared environment as they are raised in the same household during the exact same period of time.

As the main objective of this chapter is to address unobserved heterogeneity, we believe that the three sibling analyses together constitute a superior econometric method, albeit that the mean differences are estimated with less precision than the baseline estimates due to the limited number of observations. Moreover, selecting ADHD individuals may also result in sample selection bias.[1] To explain this bias, imagine that parents of an only child have

---

[1] In the following tables we exclude estimates based on less than 30 observations.

more time to handle conflicts associated with an ADHD disease of the child compared to parents with more than one child to take care of. This potentially means that the selected group (children with siblings) are worse off than the excluded sample without siblings. The bias could also have the opposite direction if siblings have a symptom-reducing effect on ADHD.

Another limitation of the sibling analysis has to do with what is feasible due to data limitation. As noted above, we attempt to control for unobserved heterogeneity within the family/household by comparing siblings. Clearly, this procedure eliminates only the unobserved effects of a shared environment. Unobservable heterogeneity that is not associated with a shared environment is not considered. If such effects are important, then they could influence the estimates. For example, a non-shared environment that affects only one child in a family could be relevant (e.g., a unique relationship between a parent and a child). Furthermore, a non-shared environment generated through differences outside of the family environment may also be important. Although measures of a non-shared environment exist, they are rarely routinely collected or recorded and are therefore unavailable in the database. In essence, non-shared environmental influences have been shown to interact with genetic effects to enhance the expression of both ADHD and conduct problems (Sonuga-Barke et al., 2008). However, it should be emphasized that unobservable heterogeneity is a problem only if it is not systematically distributed across the treatment and the control groups. If, for example, 'parental care and involvement' were evenly distributed across individuals in the treatment group and the control group, then this unobservable heterogeneity would be of no concern in the analysis.

The sibling analysis is considered to be particularly valuable because Danish households with children who have ADHD are found to be more unstable than households without children with ADHD, and this difference partly results from poor child health in terms of ADHD. Kvist et al. (2013) conclude that poor child health in terms of ADHD results in reduced parental socioeconomic status by reducing labour supply (and earnings) and relationship stability. Moreover, Danish parents of children with ADHD are more likely to divorce and to encounter greater difficulties in the labour market, among other problems. This means that a comparison across families could be counterfactual.

While we recognize the limitations of the sibling analysis, this analysis is thought to be of very high quality—especially as a complement to the baseline analysis. In other words, we address unobserved heterogeneity issues raised in the more robust baseline analysis.

In the following sections, we present the results of the analysis using various groups of siblings as control groups. In Section 8.1, we present the results that do not account for comorbidity. The results are summarized in Section 8.2.

The following comparisons will be applied in this chapter: DA and PA are compared to Sib-Demo to take unobserved heterogeneity into account.

8.1 Empirical Results from the Sibling-Based Analysis

In this section, we present the results from the matching analysis based on the siblings of ADHD individuals. As in Section 7.2, the results are presented using the mean outcomes for the treatment and control groups as well as the difference between the two (i.e., the mean difference and whether it is significantly different from zero). If the mean difference is significantly different from zero, then we can conclude that the means for the two groups are significantly different.

The outcome measures will be presented using the same structure as in Chapter 7. Hence, these outcomes are grouped according to occupational status, income and public transfers, educational attainment, crime and traffic accidents, childhood outcomes, family composition, and health measures.

8.1.1 *Occupational Status*

The results concerning occupational status in 2009 are presented in Table 8.1. The table is organized as follows: Column 1 contains the names of the dependent variables, and Column 2 contains information on the control groups considered. Columns 3–6 contain mean values for DA, the control group, the mean difference between the two groups, and information on the standard error of the estimate. Four results are presented for each output measure: (i) the baseline mean difference from Chapter 7, (ii) the mean difference for the *twin-based* matched control group, (iii) the *sibling-based* control group, and (iv) the *half-sibling-based* control group. Columns 7–10 contain similar information for the PA group.

The baseline results are relatively robust to the use of sibling-based matched control groups. To review the main baseline results, the overall impression of Chapter 7 was that individuals with ADHD are markedly less likely to be wage employed and that they rely on the early-retirement scheme to a greater extent than those without ADHD. The aim of this chapter is to determine whether these results change in quantitative and/or qualitative terms when we alter the control group by exclusively considering siblings as a comparison.

For DA, the qualitative results are essentially unchanged when we select the control group from *half-siblings* rather than from the adult Danish population. This finding suggests that the baseline results are robust. Note that the treatment group is reduced in size and now includes only 365 individuals with ADHD, implying that most of these individuals have no half-siblings. For

Table 8.1. Sibling results—Occupational status

Variable	Sample	Diagnosed adults				Prescribed adults			
		Treated	Control	Difference	S.E.	Treated	Control	Difference	S.E.
Self-employed	Baseline	0.02	0.03	-0.02***	0.00	0.03	0.04	-0.01***	0.00
	Twins	0.00	0.03	-0.03	0.03	0.04	0.02	0.01	0.03
	Siblings	0.02	0.04	-0.02***	0.01	0.03	0.04	-0.01*	0.00
	Half-siblings	0.01	0.03	-0.02*	0.01	0.02	0.04	-0.01	0.01
Wage employed	Baseline	0.25	0.68	-0.43***	0.01	0.36	0.72	-0.36***	0.01
	Twins	0.32	0.61	-0.29*	0.12	0.46	0.64	-0.18*	0.08
	Siblings	0.27	0.65	-0.37***	0.02	0.38	0.68	-0.30***	0.01
	Half-siblings	0.18	0.64	-0.46***	0.03	0.28	0.61	-0.33***	0.02
Student	Baseline	0.05	0.07	-0.02***	0.01	0.05	0.06	-0.01*	0.00
	Twins	0.00	0.03	-0.03	0.03	0.04	0.04	0.00	0.03
	Siblings	0.04	0.05	-0.02*	0.01	0.05	0.05	0.00	0.00
	Half-siblings	0.05	0.05	0.00	0.02	0.04	0.05	-0.01	0.01
Unemployed	Baseline	0.05	0.04	0.01	0.00	0.05	0.03	0.01***	0.00
	Twins	0.03	0.06	-0.03	0.06	0.07	0.06	0.01	0.04
	Siblings	0.05	0.04	0.00	0.01	0.05	0.04	0.01	0.00
	Half-siblings	0.05	0.06	-0.01	0.02	0.04	0.04	0.01	0.01
Welfare	Baseline	0.23	0.03	0.20***	0.01	0.16	0.02	0.14***	0.00
	Twins	0.19	0.06	0.13	0.08	0.11	0.06	0.05	0.04
	Siblings	0.22	0.04	0.18***	0.01	0.14	0.03	0.11***	0.01
	Half-siblings	0.27	0.05	0.22***	0.03	0.22	0.06	0.16***	0.02
Activation programmes	Baseline	0.16	0.04	0.12***	0.01	0.12	0.04	0.09***	0.00
	Twins	0.19	0.00	0.19***	0.07	0.10	0.01	0.08*	0.03
	Siblings	0.16	0.06	0.10***	0.01	0.12	0.05	0.07***	0.01
	Half-siblings	0.16	0.06	0.11***	0.02	0.16	0.08	0.08***	0.02

(continued)

Table 8.1. Continued

Variable	Sample	Diagnosed adults				Prescribed adults			
		Treated	Control	Difference	S.E.	Treated	Control	Difference	S.E.
Sickness subsidy	Baseline	0.06	0.01	0.05***	0.00	0.05	0.01	0.04***	0.00
	Twins	0.13	0.06	0.06	0.08	0.02	0.04	−0.01	0.03
	Siblings	0.06	0.01	0.05***	0.01	0.05	0.02	0.04***	0.00
	Half-siblings	0.06	0.01	0.05***	0.01	0.05	0.01	0.04***	0.01
Retirement scheme	Baseline	0.13	0.03	0.10***	0.01	0.12	0.03	0.09***	0.00
	Twins	0.13	0.06	0.06	0.08	0.12	0.07	0.05	0.05
	Siblings	0.13	0.05	0.09***	0.01	0.13	0.04	0.08***	0.01
	Half-siblings	0.14	0.04	0.10***	0.02	0.11	0.06	0.05***	0.01
Outside labour market	Baseline	0.06	0.05	0.01**	0.00	0.06	0.04	0.01***	0.00
	Twins	0.06	0.04	0.03***	0.00	0.04	0.05	−0.01	0.03
	Siblings	0.05	0.05	0.00	0.01	0.05	0.04	0.00	0.00
	Half-siblings	0.08	0.06	0.01	0.02	0.07	0.05	0.01	0.01

Note: Occupational status in November 2009. DA: 4,452 observations in baseline, 31 twins, 1,632 siblings, and 365 half-siblings. PA: 10,258 observations in baseline, 84 twins, 3,992 siblings, and 767 half-siblings. Method: Propensity score matching. Significance level: 0.05(*), 0.01(**), 0.001(***).

Source: Statistics Denmark

siblings and twins, the qualitative results remain unchanged. The results for PA are presented in the last four columns of Table 8.1. The qualitative results from the baseline analysis remain valid. Specifically, individuals with ADHD are much less likely to be wage employed and are more reliant on the early-retirement scheme than those without ADHD.

For some of the groups of siblings, the quantitative magnitude of the results changes in the form of reduced mean differences. For example, the difference in the share of wage-employed individuals in the DA group declines from 43 percentage points to 37 percentage points for 'siblings' and to 29 percentage points for 'twins'. The mean difference for twins is not as significant as those for the other control groups. However, although twins are reduced to 31 and 84 pairs, the difference remains significantly different from zero at the 10 per cent significance level. For the two groups of half-siblings, the difference remains substantial and very close in magnitude to the baseline result of Chapter 7.

However, a number of factors should be considered when interpreting the results for the siblings. First, ADHD is a hereditary disorder, implying that we may include undiagnosed ADHD individuals in the control groups comprising the siblings of individuals with ADHD. Thus, although we are able to account for unobservable heterogeneity in the form of a shared environment, we increase the risk of selecting siblings with undiagnosed ADHD, which would entail underestimated differences. This risk is reduced considerably when we base the matched control groups on half-siblings with the same mother, as the heritability is more likely to be passed down from fathers (Kustanovich et al., 2003). However, the *same environment property* of this group is not as clear as for the full-sibling analyses.

Second, and especially for the group of 'twins', recall that we reduce the number of individuals or observations considerably. For DA, the baseline analysis consists of 4,452 individuals with ADHD, the sibling-based analysis consists of 1,632 individuals with ADHD, the half-sibling-based analysis consists of 365 individuals with ADHD, and the 'twins' analysis consists of 31 individuals with ADHD. Reducing the number of observations means that the mean difference is estimated with less precision, as is evident in the last column, which presents the standard error (S.E.) of the mean difference. The standard error increases when the number of individuals in the analysis is reduced.

For the other occupational status variables, we find that higher shares of individuals with ADHD are on the early-retirement scheme and more frequently receive sickness subsidies, welfare, and activation programmes. Moreover, the differences from the baseline case are relatively small.

Nevertheless, our interpretation of the results presented in Table 8.1 is that the mean differences serve as important conservative estimates and that the qualitative insights of the baseline results presented in Table 7.4 hold for the matched control groups based on siblings by accounting for some unobserved heterogeneity.

8.1.2 *Income*

We now turn our attention to income measures, tax payments, and benefits received. The main impression from the baseline analysis was that individuals with ADHD reported lower income levels, paid less in taxes, and received higher benefits. In Table 8.2 we present the results for the analysis in which matched control groups are selected from the siblings of individuals with ADHD. All of the conclusions remain qualitatively unchanged; however, the quantitative magnitudes of the mean differences are reduced, especially for the income measures for which the differences are halved relative to the baseline estimates.

8.1.3 *Education*

Next, we turn our attention to the highest level of education completed. The main impression from the baseline analysis was that individuals with ADHD have lower educational attainment than comparable non-ADHD individuals. One-half to two-thirds of ADHD individuals had only completed elementary school. These shares exceed the baseline matched control, resulting in mean differences of 25 and 36 percentage points (see Table 8.3). These results point to the fact that ADHD individuals are educated to a much lower degree than their non-ADHD counterparts.

We also present results for the analyses using matched control groups selected from the siblings of individuals with ADHD. It is seen that the baseline results are relatively robust to the use of the sibling-based analysis. The results resemble those for educational attainment in the baseline analysis. As for occupational status, we find very robust results suggesting that the results for the baseline case and half-siblings are very similar, whereas mean differences for siblings and twins are lower.

8.1.4 *Crime*

The measures for criminal offences, being the victim of a crime, and traffic accidents are presented in Table 8.4. The results presented for siblings are relatively similar to the baseline results. More precisely, larger shares of individuals in the treatment groups have been convicted of a crime, have been the victim of a crime, or have been involved in a traffic accident. However, the mean differences are not statistically significant for twins. Again, there are

Table 8.2. Sibling results—Income, taxes, and public transfers

Variable	Sample	Diagnosed adults				Prescribed adults			
		Treated	Control	Difference	S.E.	Treated	Control	Difference	S.E.
Personal income	Baseline	23,773	36,253	-12,480***	497	28,936	39,638	-10,703***	351
	Twins	26,846	35,619	-8,774*	4,141	30,605	32,092	-1,487	2,777
	Siblings	25,243	33,564	-8,321***	660	29,833	37,472	-7,640***	540
	Half-siblings	22,704	30,505	-7,801***	1,528	25,457	29,904	-4,447***	897
Annual wage income	Baseline	18,709	34,921	-16,212***	788	27,478	39,031	-11,553***	520
	Twins					28,248	30,369	-2,120	4,088
	Siblings	20,791	31,558	-10,767***	897	27,198	35,876	-8,678***	681
	Half-siblings	17,894	27,012	-9117***	1,845	22,166	28,560	-6,394***	1,290
Hourly wage	Baseline	19.21	21.66	-2.45***	0.37	21.46	23.43	-1.97***	0.26
	Twins					21.33	21.67	-0.34	2.06
	Siblings	19.72	22.05	-2.33	0.69	22.33	24.59	-2.26***	0.46
	Half-siblings	19.36	21.88	-2.52	1.51	19.74	22.46	-2.72*	1.15
Income taxes paid	Baseline	5,835	11,227	-5,392***	197	7,770	12,362	-4,592***	144
	Twins	7,661	11,322	-3,662*	1,775	8,879	9,462	-583	1,139
	Siblings	6,863	10,365	-3,501***	283	8,667	12,119	-3,452***	230
	Half-siblings	6,124	9,644	-3,520***	668	7,001	8,876	-1,875***	363
Student grants	Baseline	5,774	5,574	200	275	6,600	5,543	1,057***	198
	Twins								
	Siblings	4,909	5,423	-514	723	4,437	4,731	-294	356
	Half-siblings								
Social-security benefits	Baseline	8,073	5,647	2,426***	201	8,012	6,349	1,662***	159
	Twins								
	Siblings	6,433	5,285	1,148	739	8,546	6,878	1,668*	655
	Half-siblings	5,282	5,226	55	1,280	7,688	5,931	1,757	1,087

(continued)

Table 8.2. Continued

Variable	Sample	Diagnosed adults				Prescribed adults			
		Treated	Control	Difference	S.E.	Treated	Control	Difference	S.E.
Sickness benefits	Baseline	36.55	23.47	13.09***	1.27	34.11	23.95	10.16***	0.81
	Twins								
	Siblings	23.78	22.69	1.10***	3.27	27.78	21.83	5.96**	2.23
	Half-siblings					31.85	25.16	6.68	7.29
Retirement benefits	Baseline	21,895	22,101	−207***	330	21,464	21,851	−387	232
	Twins								
	Siblings					18,987	19,648	−661	1014
	Half-siblings								

Note: Personal income, annual salary, income taxes paid, student grants, social-security benefits, sickness benefits, and retirement benefits in 2010; hourly wage in November 2007. DA: 4,451 observations in baseline, 31 twins, 1,632 siblings, and 366 half-siblings (1,782 employees in baseline, 18 twins, 902 siblings, and 183 half-siblings; 2,143 hourly wage observations in baseline, 13 twins, 689 siblings, and 115 half-siblings; 521 receiving student grants in baseline, 1 twins, 67 siblings, and 11 half-siblings; 1,898 receiving social-security benefits in baseline, 3 twins, 111 siblings, and 34 half-siblings; 1,567 receiving sickness benefits in baseline, 3 twins, 187 siblings, and 22 half-siblings; 805 receiving retirement benefits observations in baseline, 0 twins, 29 siblings, and 1 half-siblings). PA: 10,258 observations in baseline, 84 twins, 3,989 siblings, and 769 half-siblings (5,011 employees in baseline, 53 twins, 2,393 siblings, and 406 half-siblings; 5,745 hourly wage observations in baseline, 46 twins, 1,962 siblings, and 286 half-siblings; 1,192 receiving student grants in baseline, 8 twins, 161 siblings, and 22 half-siblings; 3,154 receiving social-security benefits in baseline, 3 twins, 177 siblings, and 52 half-siblings; 3,758 receiving sickness benefits in baseline, 10 twins, 458 siblings, and 59 half-siblings; 1,706 receiving retirement benefits in baseline, 2 twins, 79 siblings, and 11 half-siblings). Method: Propensity score matching. Significance level: 0.05(*), 0.01(**), 0.001(***).

Source: Statistics Denmark

Table 8.3. Sibling results—Educational attainment

Variable	Sample	Diagnosed adults				Prescribed adults			
		Treated	Control	Difference	S.E.	Treated	Control	Difference	S.E.
Elementary school (Folkeskole)	Baseline	0.68	0.32	0.36***	0.01	0.52	0.27	0.26***	0.01
	Twins	0.70	0.50	0.20	0.13	0.46	0.30	0.16*	0.08
	Siblings	0.65	0.38	0.27***	0.02	0.49	0.29	0.20***	0.01
	Half-siblings	0.80	0.49	0.31***	0.04	0.66	0.42	0.24***	0.03
Secondary education	Baseline	0.06	0.14	-0.08***	0.01	0.08	0.13	-0.05***	0.00
	Twins	0.00	0.10	-0.10	0.06	0.06	0.09	-0.02	0.04
	Siblings	0.06	0.11	-0.05***	0.01	0.08	0.11	-0.03***	0.01
	Half-siblings	0.03	0.08	-0.05**	0.02	0.06	0.11	-0.06***	0.01
Vocational education	Baseline	0.20	0.35	-0.15***	0.01	0.27	0.35	-0.09***	0.01
	Twins	0.13	0.27	-0.13	0.10	0.32	0.43	-0.11	0.08
	Siblings	0.22	0.32	-0.09***	0.02	0.28	0.36	-0.08***	0.01
	Half-siblings	0.17	0.31	-0.15***	0.03	0.24	0.32	-0.08***	0.02
Short further	Baseline	0.01	0.04	-0.02***	0.00	0.02	0.05	-0.02***	0.00
	Twins	0.07	0.03	0.03	0.06	0.04	0.01	0.02	0.02
	Siblings	0.01	0.04	-0.03***	0.01	0.03	0.04	-0.01	0.00
	Half-siblings	0.00	0.02	-0.02*	0.01	0.01	0.02	-0.02*	0.01
Medium further	Baseline	0.03	0.08	-0.05***	0.01	0.06	0.11	-0.05***	0.00
	Twins	0.10	0.10	0.00	0.08	0.07	0.07	0.00	0.04
	Siblings	0.04	0.09	-0.05***	0.01	0.07	0.11	-0.04***	0.01
	Half-siblings	0.01	0.06	-0.05***	0.01	0.02	0.08	-0.06***	0.01
Bachelor	Baseline	0.00	0.03	-0.02***	0.00	0.02	0.03	-0.01***	0.00
	Twins	0.00	0.00	0.00	0.00	0.01	0.05	-0.04	0.03
	Siblings	0.01	0.02	-0.02***	0.00	0.02	0.03	-0.01***	0.00
	Half-siblings	0.00	0.01	-0.01	0.00	0.01	0.01	0.00	0.00
Long further	Baseline	0.01	0.05	-0.04***	0.00	0.03	0.06	-0.03***	0.00
	Twins	0.00	0.00	0.00	0.00	0.02	0.04	-0.01	0.03
	Siblings	0.01	0.04	-0.03***	0.01	0.03	0.06	-0.03***	0.00
	Half-siblings	0.00	0.03	-0.03**	0.01	0.01	0.03	-0.03***	0.01

Note: Highest completed level of education as of 2010. DA: 4,325 observations in baseline, 30 twins, and 337 half-siblings. PA: 10,048 observations in baseline, 81 twins, 3,890 siblings, and 722 half-siblings. Method: Propensity score matching. Significance level: 0.05(*), 0.01(**), 0.001(***).

Source: Statistics Denmark

Table 8.4. Sibling results—Crime and traffic

Variable	Sample	Diagnosed adults				Prescribed adults			
		Treated	Control	Difference	S.E.	Treated	Control	Difference	S.E.
Criminal Offences	Baseline	0.60	0.33	0.28***	0.01	0.50	0.30	0.20***	0.01
	Twins	0.71	0.48	0.23	0.12	0.51	0.44	0.07	0.08
	Siblings	0.60	0.40	0.20***	0.02	0.49	0.34	0.14***	0.01
	Half-siblings	0.62	0.40	0.22***	0.04	0.61	0.41	0.20***	0.03
Victim of a crime	Baseline	0.29	0.14	0.15***	0.01	0.24	0.13	0.11***	0.01
	Twins	0.42	0.23	0.19	0.12	0.29	0.27	0.01	0.07
	Siblings	0.16	0.12	0.03	0.03	0.22	0.14	0.08***	0.01
	Half-siblings	0.30	0.18	0.13***	0.03	0.31	0.18	0.12***	0.02
Traffic Accidents	Baseline	0.09	0.05	0.04***	0.01	0.07	0.04	0.04***	0.00
	Twins	0.03	0.03	0.00	0.05	0.08	0.06	0.02	0.04
	Siblings	0.08	0.05	0.04***	0.01	0.07	0.04	0.03***	0.01
	Half-siblings	0.11	0.05	0.06**	0.02	0.10	0.05	0.05***	0.01

Note: At least one registered incident in the period 2001–2010. DA: 4,452 observations in baseline, 31 twins, 1,632 siblings, and (355, 369, 365) half-siblings. PA: 10,258 observations in baseline, 84 twins, 3,992 siblings, and (759, 764, 766) half-siblings. Method: Propensity score matching. Significance level: 0.05(*), 0.01(**), 0.001(***).

Source: Statistics Denmark

indications suggesting that half-siblings have larger mean differences than siblings and that siblings have larger mean differences than twins.

8.1.5 *Childhood Outcomes*

Table 8.5 presents the results for a number of outcome measures related to childhood outcomes. These variables are placement away from home, participation in preventive measures as a child, age at grade 9, age when graduating from secondary education, grades from secondary education (GPA, Maths, and Danish), and educational disruptions. Again, the sibling-based analyses report results that are relatively robust compared to the baseline analysis for most output measures. However, the same results were not found for specific grades because of the limited number of observations.

8.1.6 *Family Composition*

Table 8.6 presents the results for a number of outcome measures related to family composition. These variables are the fraction of individuals with children, age at parenthood, number of children (fewer than or more than four children), placement of children, preventive measures, and the number of partners and the fraction with more than one partner. The baseline results are relatively robust to the use of sibling-based matched control groups.

8.1.7 *Health Measures*

Table 8.7 presents the results for a number of outcome measures related to health. These variables are hospital bed days, DRG/DAGS, treatment in primary-care facilities (GPs, specialists, psychologists, and others), and prescription drugs (user charges and public subsidy). The baseline results are relatively robust to the use of sibling-based matched control groups.

8.2 Summary

In this chapter, we perform a sibling-based analysis in which we compare the treatment groups to sibling-based matched control groups. The overall finding of the analysis is that ADHD individuals exhibit weak performance compared with non-ADHD siblings on a large number of performance measures. The performance measures are grouped on the basis of occupational status, income and public transfers, educational attainment, crime and traffic accidents, childhood outcomes, family composition, and health measures. Ultimately, the results presented in Chapter 7 are robust to the use of sibling-based

Table 8.5. Sibling results—Childhood performance

Variable	Sample	Diagnosed adults				Prescribed adults			
		Treated	Control	Difference	S.E.	Treated	Control	Difference	S.E.
In placement as a child	Baseline	0.28	0.11	0.18***	0.01	0.21	0.09	0.13***	0.00
	Twins	0.42	0.39	0.03	0.13	0.26	0.19	0.07	0.06
	Siblings	0.27	0.15	0.13***	0.01	0.19	0.11	0.08***	0.01
	Half-siblings	0.48	0.29	0.19***	0.04	0.41	0.27	0.14***	0.02
Involved in preventive measures as a child	Baseline	0.20	0.09	0.11***	0.01	0.14	0.06	0.08***	0.00
	Twins	0.13	0.10	0.03	0.08	0.13	0.05	0.08	0.04
	Siblings	0.18	0.09	0.09***	0.01	0.11	0.06	0.05***	0.01
	Half-siblings	0.31	0.20	0.10**	0.03	0.25	0.15	0.10***	0.02
Age in grade 9 (*)	Baseline	15.29	15.14	0.16***	0.02	15.23	15.13	0.10***	0.01
	Twins								
	Siblings	15.22	15.15	0.07*	0.03	15.18	15.12	0.07**	0.02
	Half-siblings								
Age when graduating from secondary education	Baseline	19.69	18.98	0.71***	0.16	19.40	19.13	0.27*	0.11
	Twins								
	Siblings	19.68	18.76	0.93*	0.47	19.36	18.76	0.60*	0.26
	Half-siblings								
Secondary graduation marks	Baseline	6.88	7.52	-0.64***	0.18	7.17	7.74	-0.58***	0.10
	Twins								
	Siblings	7.17	7.73	-0.56	0.42	7.66	7.92	-0.26	0.21
	Half-siblings								
Secondary graduation marks (Maths)	Baseline	5.81	6.73	-0.92**	0.34	5.91	6.99	-1.08***	0.19
	Twins								
	Siblings	6.76	6.76	0.00	0.79	6.71	7.01	-0.30	0.50
	Half-siblings								

Secondary graduation marks (Danish)	Baseline	7.11	7.33	-0.22	0.22	7.31	7.66	-0.35**	0.11
	Twins								
	Siblings	6.94	7.45	-0.52	0.59	7.77	7.90	-0.14	0.29
	Half-siblings								
Educational disruption	Baseline	0.51	0.19	0.32***	0.02	0.39	0.16	0.24***	0.01
	Twins								
	Siblings	0.37	0.16	0.21***	0.04	0.28	0.12	0.16***	0.02
	Half-siblings				0.45	0.22	0.23**	0.08

Note: Measures related to childhood performance. DA: 4,452 observations in baseline, 31 twins, 1,632 siblings and 363 half-siblings - 2,345 observations from primary education in baseline, 5 twins, 474 siblings, and 16 half-siblings - 234 observations from secondary education in baseline, 0 twins, 41 siblings, and 0 half-siblings - 216 Danish graduation marks in baseline, 0 twins, 33 siblings, and 0 half-siblings - 195 Math observations in baseline, 0 twins, 34 siblings, and 0 half-siblings. PA: 10,258 observations in baseline, 84 twins, 3,992 siblings, and 764 half-siblings - 5,148 observations from primary education in baseline, 27 twins, 1,201 siblings, and 28 half-siblings - 760 observations from secondary education in baseline, 2 twins, 143 siblings, and 1 half-siblings - 687 Danish graduation marks in baseline, 1 twins, 115 siblings, and 1 half-siblings - 598 Math observations in baseline, 1 twins, 98 siblings, and 1 half-siblings.

Source: Statistics Denmark

Table 8.6. Sibling results—Family composition (adulthood)

Variable	Sample	Diagnosed adults				Prescribed adults			
		Treated	Control	Difference	S.E.	Treated	Control	Difference	S.E.
Fraction of parents	Baseline	0.42	0.41	0.01	0.01	0.48	0.50	-0.02*	0.01
	Twins	0.55	0.58	-0.03	0.13	0.44	0.46	-0.02	0.08
	Siblings	0.49	0.51	-0.02	0.02	0.53	0.55	-0.03*	0.01
	Half-siblings	0.47	0.42	0.04	0.04	0.48	0.44	0.04	0.03
Age at parenthood	Baseline	24.50	26.37	-1.87***	0.15	25.54	27.07	-1.53***	0.10
	Twins					26.70	24.47	2.23	1.22
	Siblings	25.06	25.76	-0.70*	0.28	25.72	26.49	-0.76***	0.17
	Half-siblings	22.97	24.25	-1.28	0.72	23.71	25.14	-1.42**	0.49
Number of children	Baseline	1.90	1.84	0.06	0.03	2.00	1.92	0.08***	0.02
	Twins					1.83	2.23	-0.40	0.25
	Siblings	2.04	2.12	-0.07	0.06	2.15	2.13	0.02	0.03
	Half-siblings	1.91	2.12	-0.21	0.17	1.97	1.84	0.13	0.10
Fewer than four children	Baseline	0.94	0.97	-0.03***	0.01	0.93	0.96	-0.02***	0.00
	Twins					0.97	0.97	0.00	0.05
	Siblings	0.93	0.92	0.00	0.02	0.92	0.92	0.00	0.01
	Half-siblings	0.96	0.91	0.04	0.04	0.92	0.95	-0.03	0.03
Placement of children	Baseline	0.13	0.03	0.10***	0.01	0.09	0.02	0.07***	0.00
	Twins					0.13	0.03	0.10	0.07
	Siblings	0.12	0.04	0.08***	0.00	0.09	0.04	0.05***	0.01
	Half-siblings	0.16	0.03	0.13**	0.05	0.16	0.07	0.09***	0.03
Preventive measures	Baseline	0.17	0.03	0.14***	0.01	0.14	0.03	0.11***	0.01
	Twins					0.27	0.00	0.27**	0.08
	Siblings	0.19	0.06	0.13***	0.02	0.15	0.05	0.09***	0.01
	Half-siblings	0.17	0.09	0.08	0.05	0.23	0.05	0.18***	0.03

Number of partners	Baseline	1.31	1.12	0.19***	0.02	1.28	1.12	0.16***	0.01
	Twins					1.20	1.23	-0.03	0.12
	Siblings	1.35	1.25	0.10**	0.03	1.31	1.20	0.10***	0.02
	Half-siblings	1.37	1.22	0.15	0.09	1.35	1.19	0.16**	0.06
More than one partner	Baseline	0.26	0.11	0.15***	0.01	0.24	0.11	0.13***	0.01
	Twins					0.20	0.20	0.00	0.11
	Siblings	0.30	0.22	0.08**	0.03	0.26	0.18	0.08***	0.01
	Half-siblings	0.34	0.21	0.13	0.08	0.28	0.17	0.11**	0.04

Note: Measures related to the situation in the family. DA: 4,452 observations in baseline, 31 twins, 1,632 siblings, and 359 half-siblings (1,863 having children in baseline, 16 twins, 571 siblings, and 77 half-siblings). PA: 10,258 observations in baseline, 84 twins, 3,992 siblings, and 764 half-siblings (4,963 having children in baseline, 30 twins, 1,565 siblings, and 193 half-siblings). Method: Propensity score matching. Significance level: 0.05(*), 0.01(**), 0.001(***).

Source: Statistics Denmark

Table 8.7. Sibling results—Health measures

Variable	Sample	Diagnosed adults				Prescribed adults			
		Treated	Control	Difference	S.E.	Treated	Control	Difference	S.E.
Hospital bed days	Baseline	4.17	2.19	1.98**	0.73	3.65	2.08	1.57***	0.27
	Twins	4.44	0.69	3.74	2.55	7.21	2.93	4.28	3.80
	Siblings	5.80	2.11	3.69	1.90	3.98	2.39	1.59***	0.48
	Half-siblings	3.71	5.71	-2.01	2.88	3.52	2.29	1.23	0.64
DRG/DAGS	Baseline	147	83	64***	8	136	86	50***	6
	Twins	88	33	55	45	277	153	124	169
	Siblings	149	90	58***	13	142	111	30**	11
	Half-siblings	141	113	28	27	132	102	30	18
Treatment in primary-care facilities: GP	Baseline	20.12	8.49	11.63***	0.51	16.87	8.18	8.69***	0.23
	Twins	18.03	5.68	12.35***	3.67	13.01	11.77	1.24	2.05
	Siblings	20.20	9.29	10.91***	0.70	17.18	9.50	7.68***	0.38
	Half-siblings	20.18	9.76	10.42***	1.42	17.90	9.42	8.49***	0.86
Treatment in primary-care facilities: Specialists	Baseline	5.55	3.94	1.61***	0.28	5.48	4.48	1.00***	0.14
	Twins	4.03	2.77	1.26	1.25	5.46	5.75	-0.29	1.05
	Siblings	5.58	4.07	1.51***	0.41	5.66	4.72	0.94***	0.22
	Half-siblings	5.25	3.71	1.54*	0.77	5.34	4.24	1.10**	0.42
Treatment in primary-care facilities: Psychologist	Baseline	2.27	0.23	2.04***	0.12	5.35	0.25	5.10***	0.24
	Twins	2.16	0.00	2.16**	0.83	6.54	2.67	3.87	2.69
	Siblings	2.25	0.27	1.98***	0.19	5.56	0.39	5.17***	0.52
	Half-siblings	3.20	0.27	2.92***	0.92	4.89	0.48	4.41***	0.29
Treatment in primary-care facilities: Other	Baseline	2.84	2.60	0.24	0.27	4.35	2.67	1.68***	0.18
	Twins	10.19	5.45	4.74	4.94	4.89	2.69	2.20	1.92
	Siblings	2.93	2.56	0.37	0.40	4.29	3.07	1.23***	0.29
	Half-siblings	1.86	2.06	-0.20	0.66	4.39	2.93	1.46*	0.64
Prescription drugs: User charges	Baseline	342	65	276***	6	335	73	261***	4
	Twins	293	50	242***	56	298	105	192***	31
	Siblings	354	76	279***	11	338	88	250***	6
	Half-siblings	331	68	263***	21	313	88	225***	15

Prescription drugs: Public subsidy								
Baseline	1129	72	1057***	30	901	84	817***	18
Twins	1091	256	835*	376	895	193	702***	182
Siblings	1234	151	1083***	53	923	142	781***	29
Half-siblings	990	144	846***	105	779	107	672***	60
Prescription drugs: Total								
Baseline	1539	140	1399***	34	1278	160	1118***	20
Twins	1540	306	1234**	448	1246	304	942***	211
Siblings	1661	230	1431***	60	1309	233	1075***	33
Half-siblings	1411	217	1194***	123	1139	198	941***	69

Note: Health-related measures in 2010. DA: 4,452 observations in baseline, 31 twins, 1,632 siblings, and (356, 366, 357, 368) half-siblings. PA: 10,258 observations in baseline, 84 twins, 3,992 siblings, and (763, 766, 771, 764) half-siblings. Method: Propensity score matching. Significance level: 0.05(*), 0.01(**), 0.001(***).

Source: Statistics Denmark

matched control groups. In this sense, using the estimates presented in Chapter 7 in the cost calculations is considered a valid approach. Therefore, the main result suggests that *unobservable heterogeneity* is not a major problem.

The results presented in this chapter are surprisingly robust. ADHD is a hereditary disorder and the hereditary property is more likely to be passed down from fathers (Kustanovich et al., 2003). This property is used for the following two hypotheses: (i) same-gender siblings are relatively genetically uniform, implying that we expect differences between ADHD individuals and their same-gender siblings to be relatively low; and (ii) half-siblings are less genetically uniform than full siblings, and we expect pairs of half-siblings to have larger differences than siblings. It is exactly this pattern that is documented in many of the tables presented in this chapter.

9

Evaluating the Analytical Approach

The analytical approach that we employ is based on two hypotheses with respect to individuals with ADHD. The first hypothesis states that DA individuals exhibit weaker performance than PA individuals. The second hypothesis states that DA individuals exhibit weaker performance than a similar group of adults diagnosed in childhood and that PA individuals exhibit weaker performance than a similar group of adults who were prescribed medication as children. In this chapter, we present empirical evidence for these hypotheses in support of our analytical approach.

We thus introduce two additional control groups referred to as 'diagnosed children' (abbreviated to 'DC') and 'prescribed children' (abbreviated to 'PC'):

- **Diagnosed children (DC)**: adults who were diagnosed with ADHD earlier in life (i.e., before the age of 18).

- **Prescribed children (PC)**: adults who received methylphenidate, atomoxetine, or dexamphetamine earlier in life (i.e., before the age of 18).

These new control groups are identified in exactly the same way as the treatment groups but were identified or prescribed in childhood instead of adulthood.

The motivation for distinguishing between the two treatment groups throughout the analysis is that the individuals in the two groups may differ with respect to performance. More precisely, we expect that the average individual in the DA sample shows weaker performance than the average PA individual. This expectation is supported by the empirical analysis below. Therefore, dividing the individuals with ADHD into the two groups is important for the cost calculations.

Another important consideration is that we attempt to determine the true effects of ADHD symptoms on private and social costs. The study design proposes a retrospective evaluation of these costs for individuals who receive a diagnosis of ADHD in adulthood. Based on this empirical design, our retrospective analysis allows us to examine the costs of ADHD while avoiding the contamination and bias of ADHD diagnosis and treatment. This contribution is important in itself, and it is the correct benchmark for an evaluation of the costs of individuals with ADHD who have received treatment.

The main impression of the analysis in this chapter is that DA individuals exhibit weaker performance than PA and DC individuals. Moreover, PA individuals to some extent show weaker performance than PC individuals.

9.1 Investigating the Two Hypotheses

As in previous chapters, we present the results for the different groups of outcome measures: occupational status, income and public transfers, education, crime and traffic accidents, childhood outcomes, family composition, and health measures.[1]

9.1.1 Occupational Status

The results regarding occupational status in 2009 are presented in Table 9.1. The table is organized as follows: Column 1 contains the names of the dependent variables, and Column 2 contains information on the groups being compared (DA and PA refer to the two treatment groups, and DC and PC refer to the counterparts of the two treatment groups that have been diagnosed in childhood). Columns 3–4 present the difference between the two groups and information on the statistical significance when comorbidity is not considered. Columns 5–6 present similar information when accounting for comorbidity.

A number of interesting results are evident from Table 9.1. First, DA individuals are less likely to be wage employed and more frequently rely on welfare than PA individuals. As in the baseline analysis of Chapter 7, the mean differences are reduced when comorbidity is considered. Second, individuals with ADHD who are diagnosed later in life (i.e., DA and PA) are less likely to be wage employed than those diagnosed early in life (i.e., DC and PC). The difference is reduced to some extent when comorbidity is considered. Individuals with ADHD who are diagnosed early in life (i.e., DC and PC) more frequently rely on early-retirement schemes than those diagnosed later in life (i.e., DA and PA). By contrast, DA and PA are more likely to participate in welfare schemes

---

[1] In this chapter, we estimate using OLS instead of matching. The reason for not using matching is that we are not selecting a matched control group as we are using two groups of ADHD individuals, the full population of DC and PC, in the estimation.

Table 9.1. Selection results—Occupational status

Variable	Sample	Diagnosed adults		Prescribed adults	
		Difference	S.E.	Difference	S.E.
Self-employed	DA–PA	0.00	0.00	0.00	0.00
	DA–DC	0.00	0.00	0.00	0.00
	PA–PC	0.00	0.01	0.01	0.01
Wage employed	DA–PA	−0.08***	0.01	−0.04***	0.01
	DA–DC	−0.10***	0.01	−0.07***	0.01
	PA–PC	−0.08***	0.02	−0.05**	0.02
Student	DA–PA	0.00	0.00	0.00	0.00
	DA–DC	0.01	0.01	0.01	0.01
	PA–PC	−0.01	0.01	0.00	0.01
Unemployed	DA–PA	0.00	0.00	0.01	0.00
	DA–DC	0.00	0.01	0.00	0.01
	PA–PC	0.00	0.01	0.00	0.01
Welfare	DA–PA	0.05***	0.01	0.03***	0.01
	DA–DC	0.10***	0.01	0.08***	0.01
	PA–PC	0.07***	0.01	0.05***	0.01
Activation programmes	DA–PA	0.02***	0.01	0.02***	0.01
	DA–DC	0.02*	0.01	0.02*	0.01
	PA–PC	0.03*	0.01	0.02*	0.01
Sickness subsidy	DA–PA	0.01	0.00	0.01	0.00
	DA–DC	0.03***	0.01	0.03***	0.01
	PA–PC	0.02*	0.01	0.02*	0.01
Retirement scheme	DA–PA	0.02**	0.01	−0.01	0.01
	DA–DC	−0.06***	0.01	−0.08***	0.01
	PA–PC	−0.05***	0.01	−0.07***	0.01
Outside labour market	DA–PA	0.00	0.00	0.00	0.00
	DA–DC	0.01	0.01	0.01	0.01
	PA–PC	0.03**	0.01	0.02**	0.01

Note: Occupational status in November 2009. 4,452 observations in DA, 3,558 observations in DC, 10,258 observations in PA, 1,442 observations in PC. Method: OLS. Significance level: 0.05(*), 0.01(**), 0.001(***).

Source: Statistics Denmark

than DC and PC. These differences may be a consequence of different labour-market policies at different times.

In summary, there is some evidence that DA and PA individuals exhibit weaker performance than DC and PC individuals in the sense that DA and PA individuals are less often wage employed.

9.1.2 *Income*

Table 9.2 presents the results for income, taxes, and public transfers. It is evident that DA individuals have lower income, pay fewer taxes, and receive less in cash and sickness benefits compared with PA individuals. In this sense, DA individuals show weaker performance than PA individuals do. Moreover, there is evidence that DA individuals exhibit weaker performance than their

Table 9.2. Selection results—Income, taxes, and public transfers

Variable	Sample	Diagnosed adults		Prescribed adults	
		Difference	S.E.	Difference	S.E.
Personal income	DA–PA	−2,546***	319	−1,666***	321
	DA–DC	−2,638***	324	−2,139***	328
	PA–PC	−1,314*	620	−467	616
Annual wage income	DA–PA	−5,620***	587	−3,941***	588
	DA–DC	−3,419***	636	−2,350***	641
	PA–PC	−796	950	112	938
Hourly wage	DA–PA	−0.96**	0.34	−0.80*	0.34
	DA–DC	0.75	0.42	0.80	0.43
	PA–PC	1.66*	0.65	1.80**	0.65
Income taxes paid	DA–PA	−1,062***	128	−696***	129
	DA–DC	−1,058***	116	−848***	117
	PA–PC	−430	252	−89	251
Student grants	DA–PA	−402	281	−405	285
	DA–DC	236	239	165	245
	PA–PC	698*	304	741*	304
Social-security benefits	DA–PA	627***	169	441**	169
	DA–DC	978***	226	695**	225
	PA–PC	843**	327	650*	326
Sickness benefits	DA–PA	1.03	1.23	1.22	1.24
	DA–DC	15.58***	3.12	16.19***	3.15
	PA–PC	14.48***	4.24	14.38***	4.25
Retirement benefits	DA–PA	192	289	66	291
	DA–DC	−1,477**	557	−1,531**	571
	PA–PC	−3,090***	748	−3,681***	748

Note: Personal income, annual salary, income taxes paid, student grants, social-security benefits, sickness benefits, and retirement benefits in 2010; hourly wage in November 2007. 4,451 observations in DA (1,782 employees; 2,143 hourly wage observations; 521 receiving student grant; 1,898 receiving social security benefits; 1,567 receiving sickness benefits; 805 receiving retirement benefits); 3,558 observations in DC (1,888 employees; 1,460 hourly wage observations; 899 receiving student grant; 1,268 receiving social-security benefits; 420 receiving sickness benefits; 301 receiving retirement benefits); 10,258 observations in PA (5,011 employees; 5,745 hourly wage observations; 1,192 receiving student grant; 3,154 receiving social-security benefits; 3,757 receiving sickness benefits; 1,706 receiving retirement benefits); 1,442 observations in PC (801 employees; 617 hourly wage observations; 453 receiving student grant; 441 receiving social-security benefits; 0 receiving sickness benefits; 128 receiving retirement benefits). Method: OLS. Significance level: 0.05(*), 0.01(**), 0.001(***).

Source: Statistics Denmark

counterparts diagnosed in childhood, whereas this pattern is less pronounced for PA individuals.

9.1.3 *Education*

Table 9.3 presents the results for educational attainment. The results are mixed in the sense that the share of DA individuals who have completed elementary school only (with no further qualifications) is larger than that of PA individuals. Moreover, DA individuals are more likely to have graduated from elementary school only, compared to their counterparts diagnosed in

Table 9.3. Selection results—Educational attainment

Variable	Sample	Diagnosed adults		Prescribed adults	
		Difference	S.E.	Difference	S.E.
Elementary school (Folkeskole)	DA–PA	0.08***	0.01	0.06***	0.01
	DA–DC	0.03**	0.01	0.01	0.01
	PA–PC	−0.01	0.02	−0.03*	0.01
Secondary education	DA–PA	−0.02**	0.00	−0.01**	0.00
	DA–DC	0.01	0.01	0.01	0.01
	PA–PC	0.02	0.01	0.02*	0.01
Vocational education	DA–PA	−0.03***	0.01	−0.02**	0.01
	DA–DC	−0.04***	0.01	−0.03*	0.01
	PA–PC	−0.02	0.01	−0.01	0.01
Short further	DA–PA	−0.01*	0.00	0.00	0.00
	DA–DC	0.00	0.00	0.00	0.00
	PA–PC	0.00	0.00	0.00	0.00
Medium further	DA–PA	−0.01*	0.00	−0.01	0.00
	DA–DC	0.00	0.00	0.00	0.00
	PA–PC	0.00	0.01	0.00	0.01
Bachelor	DA–PA	−0.01***	0.00	−0.01**	0.00
	DA–DC	0.00	0.00	0.00	0.00
	PA–PC	0.01	0.00	0.01	0.00
Long further	DA–PA	−0.01***	0.00	−0.01*	0.00
	DA–DC	0.00	0.00	0.00	0.00
	PA–PC	0.00	0.01	0.01	0.01

Note: Highest completed level of education as of 2010. 4,325 observations in DA; 3,408 observations in DC; 10,048 observations in PA; 1,403 observations in PC. Method: OLS. Significance level: 0.05(*), 0.01(**), 0.001(***).

Source: Statistics Denmark

childhood (i.e., DC). By contrast, there is no important difference between PA and PC individuals in this respect. However, the proportions for elementary school are balanced when secondary education (high school) and vocational education are also considered.

The difference between the DA group and the PA group is smaller when comorbidity is considered. The difference between DA and DC disappears when we account for comorbidity. We obtain the *opposite result* when comparing PA and PC, which implies that a higher share of PC individuals' highest completed level of education is elementary school.

Many of these differences are the result of higher shares of secondary education and vocational education.

9.1.4 *Crime and Traffic*

The results for criminal offences, being the victim of a crime, and traffic accidents are presented in Table 9.4. The table suggests that DA individuals are more likely to engage in criminal behaviour than PA individuals. The effect is nearly halved when comorbidity is considered. DA individuals are more

Table 9.4. Selection results—Crime and traffic

Variable	Sample	Diagnosed adults		Prescribed adults	
		Difference	S.E.	Difference	S.E.
Criminal offences	DA–PA	0.06***	0.01	0.03***	0.01
	DA–DC	0.14***	0.01	0.10***	0.01
	PA–PC	0.11***	0.02	0.09***	0.02
Victim of a crime	DA–PA	0.03***	0.01	0.01	0.01
	DA–DC	0.04**	0.01	0.01	0.01
	PA–PC	0.04**	0.01	0.02	0.01
Traffic accidents	DA–PA	0.00	0.00	0.00	0.00
	DA–DC	0.01	0.01	0.00	0.01
	PA–PC	0.02**	0.01	0.02*	0.01

Note: At least one registered incident in the period 2001–2010. 4,452 observations in DA; 3,558 observations in DC; 10,258 observations in PA; 1,442 observations in PC. Method: OLS. Significance level: 0.05(*), 0.01(**), 0.001(***).
Source: Statistics Denmark

likely to engage in criminal behaviour than DC individuals, and PA individuals are more likely to engage in criminal behaviour than PC individuals. There are no differences in the 'victim of a crime' and 'traffic accidents' measures between the groups of individuals with ADHD when comorbidity is considered.

9.1.5 Childhood Outcomes

Table 9.5 presents the results for a number of outcome measures related to childhood outcomes. These variables include placement away from home, participation in preventive measures as a child, age at grade 9, age when graduating from secondary education, grades from secondary education (GPA, Maths, and Danish), and educational disruptions.

DA individuals exhibit poorer childhood outcomes compared to PA individuals. A larger share of DA individuals have been placed away from home, have been involved in preventive measures, and had educational disruptions, and DA individuals were on average older when graduating from elementary school. Poor performance is documented irrespective of whether comorbidity is considered.

When comparing DA and PA to DC and PC, we find that the two latter groups are more likely to be placed away from home, to be involved in preventive measures, to experience disruptions in their educational disruptions, and to be older when graduating from elementary school. These differences may be a consequence of different social and school policies at different times.

Table 9.5. Selection results—Childhood performance

Variable	Sample	Diagnosed adults		Prescribed adults	
		Difference	S.E.	Difference	S.E.
In placement as a child	DA–PA	0.05***	0.01	0.03***	0.01
	DA–DC	−0.13***	0.01	−0.16***	0.01
	PA–PC	−0.11***	0.01	−0.12***	0.01
Involved in preventive measures as a child	DA–PA	0.02**	0.01	0.01*	0.01
	DA–DC	−0.14***	0.01	−0.15***	0.01
	PA–PC	−0.11***	0.01	−0.11***	0.01
Age in grade 9 (*)	DA–PA	0.03*	0.01	0.03*	0.01
	DA–DC	−0.20***	0.03	−0.20***	0.03
	PA–PC	−0.09***	0.03	−0.09***	0.03
Age when graduating from secondary education	DA–PA	0.22	0.14	0.24	0.14
	DA–DC	−0.12	0.18	−0.13	0.18
	PA–PC	−0.09	0.17	−0.07	0.17
Secondary graduation marks	DA–PA	−0.17	0.13	−0.19	0.14
	DA–DC	0.03	0.22	−0.06	0.23
	PA–PC	0.14	0.19	0.13	0.19
Secondary graduation marks (Maths)	DA–PA	0.07	0.29	0.08	0.31
	DA–DC	0.56	0.46	0.59	0.48
	PA–PC	0.08	0.39	0.04	0.40
Secondary graduation marks (Danish)	DA–PA	−0.10	0.17	−0.18	0.18
	DA–DC	0.11	0.29	−0.04	0.31
	PA–PC	0.26	0.23	0.25	0.23
Educational disruption	DA–PA	0.08***	0.02	0.05**	0.02
	DA–DC	0.22***	0.03	0.19***	0.04
	PA–PC	0.17***	0.03	0.16***	0.03

Note: Measures related to childhood performance. 4,452 observations in DA (2,345 observations from primary education; 234 observations from secondary education; 216 Danish graduation marks and 195 Maths graduation marks); 3,558 observations in DC (1,741 observations from primary education; 218 observations from secondary education; 189 Danish graduation marks and 198 Maths graduation marks); 10,258 observations in PA (5,148 observations from primary education; 760 observations from secondary education; 687 Danish graduation marks and 598 Maths graduation marks); 1,442 observations in PC (820 observations from primary education; 143 observations from secondary education; 129 Danish graduation marks and 131 Maths graduation marks). Method: OLS. Significance level: 0.05(*), 0.01(**), 0.001(***).
Source: Statistics Denmark

9.1.6 *Family Composition*

Table 9.6 presents the results for a number of outcome measures related to family composition. These variables are the fraction of individuals with children, age at parenthood, number of children (fewer than or more than four children), placement of children, preventive measures, the number of partners, and the fraction with more than one partner.

Relatively few differences between the groups are significantly different from zero. We find that DA individuals are more likely to be parents compared with PA individuals. Moreover, the children of DA individuals are more frequently placed away from home and receive preventive measures, and these parents have a relatively high number of partners. In the remaining

Table 9.6. Selection results—Family composition (adulthood)

Variable	Sample	Diagnosed adults		Prescribed adults	
		Difference	S.E.	Difference	S.E.
Fraction of parents	DA–PA	0.01*	0.01	0.03***	0.01
	DA–DC	0.05***	0.01	0.06***	0.01
	PA–PC	0.02	0.01	0.03*	0.01
Age at parenthood	DA–PA	−0.40***	0.11	−0.33**	0.12
	DA–DC	0.29	0.33	0.34	0.33
	PA–PC	0.55	0.62	0.64	0.62
Number of children	DA–PA	0.01	0.03	0.04	0.03
	DA–DC	0.01	0.07	0.03	0.07
	PA–PC	0.04	0.13	0.06	0.13
Fewer than four children	DA–PA	−0.01	0.01	−0.01	0.01
	DA–DC	0.02	0.02	0.02	0.02
	PA–PC	0.00	0.04	0.00	0.04
Placement of children	DA–PA	0.04***	0.01	0.02*	0.01
	DA–DC	−0.02	0.03	−0.04	0.03
	PA–PC	−0.04	0.05	−0.07	0.05
Preventive measures	DA–PA	0.05***	0.01	0.04***	0.01
	DA–DC	0.01	0.03	0.00	0.03
	PA–PC	−0.04	0.06	−0.06	0.06
Number of partners	DA–PA	0.05***	0.02	0.04*	0.02
	DA–DC	−0.02	0.05	−0.03	0.05
	PA–PC	0.07	0.08	0.05	0.08
More than one partner	DA–PA	0.04***	0.01	0.03**	0.01
	DA–DC	0.00	0.04	−0.01	0.04
	PA–PC	0.07	0.06	0.05	0.06

Note: Measures related to the situation in the family. 4,452 observations in DA (1,863 having children); 3,558 observations in DC (197 having children); 10,258 observations in PA (4,963 having children); 1,442 observations in PC (50 having children). Method: OLS. Significance level: 0.05(*), 0.01(**), 0.001(***).

Source: Statistics Denmark

comparisons, there are no significant differences, except for a greater tendency of DA individuals to be parents compared with their counterparts diagnosed in childhood.

9.1.7 *Health Measures*

Table 9.7 presents the results for a number of outcome measures related to health. These variables are hospital bed days, DRG/DAGS, treatment in primary-care facilities (GPs, specialists, psychologists, and others), and prescription drugs (user charges and public subsidy).

The overall impression is that DA individuals have more GP visits and fewer psychologist visits than PA individuals. Moreover, these individuals tend to take more prescription drugs.

Comparing DA and PA to DC and PC, we find that the adult groups have more visits—with both GPs and psychologists—and take more prescription drugs than their counterparts diagnosed in childhood.

Table 9.7. Selection results—Health measures

Variable	Sample	Diagnosed adults		Prescribed adults	
		Difference	S.E.	Difference	S.E.
Hospital bed days	DA–PA	0.85	0.62	0.59	0.63
	DA–DC	0.37	1.06	−0.06	1.08
	PA–PC	0.14	0.82	−0.07	0.82
DRG/DAGS	DA–PA	12	9	7	9
	DA–DC	20	12	8	12
	PA–PC	12	17	7	17
Treatment in primary care facilities: GP	DA–PA	3.26***	0.44	1.79***	0.44
	DA–DC	5.17***	0.74	3.56***	0.74
	PA–PC	3.19***	0.65	2.14***	0.64
Treatment in primary care facilities: Specialists	DA–PA	0.25	0.24	−0.12	0.25
	DA–DC	0.99*	0.41	0.45	0.42
	PA–PC	0.66	0.36	0.44	0.36
Treatment in primary-care facilities: Psychologist	DA–PA	−3.08***	0.38	−3.12***	0.39
	DA–DC	1.23***	0.28	1.09***	0.28
	PA–PC	4.84***	0.76	4.89***	0.77
Treatment in primary care facilities: Other	DA–PA	−0.75**	0.26	−0.66*	0.27
	DA–DC	−0.11	0.37	−0.05	0.37
	PA–PC	−0.40	0.51	−0.32	0.51
Prescription drugs: User charges	DA–PA	19	52	1	7
	DA–DC	127	73	107***	10
	PA–PC	111	90	98***	12
Prescription drugs: Public subsidy	DA–PA	283	245	145***	32
	DA–DC	282	351	133**	46
	PA–PC	133	413	53	54
Prescription drugs: Total	DA–PA	331	275	166***	36
	DA–DC	450	397	270***	52
	PA–PC	271	465	170**	61

Note: Health- related measures in 2010. 4,452 observations in DA; 3,558 observations in DC; 10,258 observations in PA; 1,442 observations in PC. Method: OLS. Significance level: 0.05(*), 0.01(**), 0.001(***).

Source: Statistics Denmark

9.2 Summary

The analytical approach applied throughout this book is based on two hypotheses with respect to individuals with ADHD. The first hypothesis states that DA individuals exhibit weaker performance than PA individuals. The second hypothesis states that DA individuals exhibit weaker performance than a similar group of adults who were diagnosed as children and that PA individuals show weaker performance than a similar group of adults who were prescribed ADHD medication as children. In this chapter, we present empirical support for these hypotheses, thereby providing empirical support for our analytical approach.

Part IV
The Costs of ADHD

MAIN CONTENT: The main purpose of this part of the book is to present cost calculations based on differences between groups of individuals with ADHD and non-ADHD individuals. Also, this part contains a discussion of the cost-calculation method and a listing of the data sources for the cost data used. Finally, this part contains the conclusions and the recommendations based on the results set out in this book. Moreover, we discuss the results we have obtained in relation to the existing literature, their generalizability beyond Denmark, and also the limitations and strengths of research based on register data.

Inputs for the cost analysis are developed in two steps. The first step is an empirical analysis that estimates differences in performance measures between the groups of individuals with ADHD and the non-ADHD groups who are otherwise similar. The second step consists of evaluating the cost measures associated with these differences.

For the first step we apply the so-called 'matching method' to identify pairs of individuals who are statistically identical with respect to background characteristics but who differ in whether they have been diagnosed with ADHD. The matching thus involves pairing individuals with ADHD with non-ADHD individuals based on a set of individual criterion variables that ensure that the individuals are identical in a statistical sense. After the group of non-ADHD individuals is identified, outcome variables for the pairs of individuals are compared. The second step consists of the cost measures associated with these differences. As a consequence, the cost calculations are *not* based directly on the differences between groups presented in Chapter 5 but on the estimation results of Part III.

METHOD: When calculating the private and social costs of ADHD and finding the cost of illness for adults with ADHD, we are faced with a basic choice between two methods, the incidence-based or life-cycle method and the prevalence-based or cross-section method. The main idea behind the incidence-based or life-cycle method is to calculate the cost that can be attributed to a representative individual over the course of his or her life, while the prevalence-based or cross-section method takes as its starting point the available population of individuals in a single year.

We use the cross-section method, because this method makes the best use of data and because the group of adults with ADHD—with only a relatively small share of individuals older than 35—is simply not mature enough to make good life-cycle estimates.

RESULTS: The main findings from the cost calculations in Chapter 10 are:

- There are large private and social costs of ADHD in Denmark. The overall yearly costs to society are estimated at around 340 million euros per year when using non-ADHD siblings as the control group.

- The private costs of ADHD to individuals with ADHD are large in terms of loss of wage income. However, a part of this loss is covered by the receipt of income-replacement transfers and the fact that a lower income also results in lower tax payments, such that the total individual private costs are smaller. Nevertheless, compared to their non-ADHD siblings, individuals with ADHD still experience a loss of approximately 650 euros per month after taxes.

- The public costs of ADHD are also large. Not only does the public sector lose tax revenue and pay out income-replacement benefits, but it also incurs large indirect costs for crime committed by individuals with ADHD and for traffic accidents involving persons with ADHD. There are also increased costs due to medical treatments and placements, but these are of a smaller magnitude. When compared to non-ADHD siblings, the average individual public costs of ADHD are thus 9200 euros per year.

- Controlling for comorbidity leads to a significant reduction in the measured cost. This is particularly true for individuals in the DA group, but also to a smaller extent for individuals in the PA group. The main reason for this result is that the loss of work income is markedly smaller when controlling for comorbidity.

RECOMMENDATIONS AND FUTURE CONSIDERATIONS: Based on the estimated private and social costs for adults with ADHD, we present a number of recommendations and future considerations in Chapter 11. Among these are:

- Greater consideration needs to be given to the careers advice and early work-training opportunities provided for individuals with ADHD. This includes identification of ADHD and other mental-health problems in job centres so that individuals with ADHD can be guided towards occupations where they can apply their skills effectively and find a place in the workforce that complements their symptoms.

- Greater consideration needs to be given to the role of ADHD symptoms in crime. Identification and treatment of ADHD symptoms in the prison populations may help to reduce the cycle of reoffending and the high costs attributed to the judicial and prison systems. Identifying the role of comorbidity as a contributing factor will be important in this context.

- Greater access to psycho-education for parents and partners to help them understand the impact of ADHD on behaviour—i.e., why individuals with ADHD behave in the way that they do—would be a good first step, and would be welcomed.

- Increased access to care is required for children and adolescents with or at risk of ADHD.

- Future consideration should be given to the fact that professionals working in adult mental health, and health services generally, often remain unaware of the clinical presentation and the consequences of ADHD in adults. This includes the recognition of ADHD in the context of substance abuse and as a comorbid disorder associated with other mental-health disorders (e.g. depression and anxiety).

10

The Calculation of Private and Social Costs

10.1 Introduction

The purpose of this chapter is twofold. The first section of the chapter presents the basic design of the calculations of private and social costs in finding the cost of illness (COI) for adults with ADHD. In addition, this section contains the sources of cost measures for the various areas covered by the calculations. Finally, there is a brief discussion of the choice of comparison groups for the calculation of costs.

The second section pieces together the estimates of Part III and the monetary sources listed in the first section to arrive at the total private and social costs of ADHD.

10.2 Methodology and Sources for Cost Calculations

10.2.1 *Definition of Types of Costs*

By *the private costs of ADHD* we understand all costs for the individuals themselves. This means that the private costs include the following areas: loss of work income, income-replacement transfers, individual costs of being a victim of a crime,[1] and private costs of prescription medicine.

The public costs of ADHD are all costs paid by the local or central government. This includes income transfers, the cost of crime (police and correctional system), the cost of state education, the cost of traffic accidents, the cost of foster care and preventive measures, and the cost of publicly provided health care including subsidies for prescription medicine.

---

[1] Strictly speaking the victim costs are not paid entirely by the individuals themselves, but since these costs arise due to the fact that they have been the victim of a crime, we have chosen to present them along with the other private costs. A similar argument can be made for defining the costs of crimes committed and the costs of traffic accidents as public costs, since they are related to costs incurred by both the public sector and other individuals.

The social costs of ADHD are the total costs of ADHD to society as a whole. In other words, the term 'social costs' represents the sum of the private costs of ADHD that individuals with ADHD sustain *plus* the sum of public costs of ADHD paid by local or central government.

It should be mentioned that some income transfers to ADHD individuals are not counted as public costs because they are redistributions between groups within the private sector. This is, for example, the case when unemployment benefits are financed through privately organized unemployment insurance.

Also, it can be relevant to distinguish between the *direct costs*, which are costs that can be attributed to a single payer such as a health-insurance company or an individual, and *indirect costs*, which are costs that are paid by others such as a government or employer (Costa et al., 2012; Damm et al., 2009).

10.2.2 *Method of Calculation*

When calculating the private and social costs of ADHD, we are faced with a basic choice between two cost-of-illness methods, the *incidence-based* or *life-cycle method* and the *prevalence-based* or *cross-section method* (Hodgson and Meiners, 1982).[2] Below we describe both these methods, discuss their strengths and weaknesses, and argue for the choice of method used in this book.

INCIDENCE-BASED OR LIFE-CYCLE METHOD

The main idea behind the incidence-based or life-cycle method is to calculate the cost that can be attributed to a representative individual over the course of his or her life, hence the term 'life-cycle'. Thus, the life-cycle method answers the question 'What will be the total cost for an average individual over the entire lifespan?'

The main advantage of this method is its general appeal. It is easy to understand and interpret the results of this method. For example, if the resulting number is 1000 euros, then we can compare this number to other costs that occur during a lifetime. Also, the incidence-based method may provide a baseline against which new interventions may be measured (Drummond, 1992; Tarricone, 2006; World Health Organization, 2009).

However, when it comes to the practical implementation of the life-cycle method, lack of availability of suitable data often limits the possible calculations. As very few data sources contain actual information about individuals over their entire lifespans, it is in practice not possible to carry out a 'perfect'

---

[2] The terms 'cross-section' and 'life-cycle' are most frequently used in economics, whereas in epidemiology the normal terminology is 'incidence-based' and 'prevalence-based'.

life-cycle calculation. Therefore in most applications, life-cycle calculations are done using a less-than-perfect method.[3]

There are two main methods used to approximate the available data to a life-cycle calculation. Firstly, one can limit the lifespan considered. Thus, a life-cycle calculation may not in fact cover the entire life-cycle, but rather a limited number of years, say ages 18–30 or 50–80, depending on the area under consideration.

Secondly, one can approximate a life-cycle calculation by using different persons' observations in the same year as an approximation of the life-cycle. This method is only feasible if it is possible to control for background variables and pool together individuals of the 'same type' to complete the life-cycle perspective.

In fact, often a combination of the two methods is used. If, for example, data are available for a period of five years, then the life-cycle perspective may be constructed by following one individual during a period of his or her life between the ages of 20 and 24 years, then combining these data with data from another individual who was aged 25–29 years during the data period available, and further combining with data from a third person who was aged 30–34 years, and so on. In order for these combinations to constitute a valid approximation of a true life-cycle perspective, one generally needs to control for a number of background variables, such as gender, education level, and comorbidity. Otherwise, the combined individuals do not give a reasonable approximation of a single life-cycle.

However, even in the case where the less-than-perfect methods are used, the life-cycle method still needs to use data for a broad range of ages to construct a stylized life-cycle. If the population at hand simply does not contain information about the relevant individuals for a long enough age span, then the life-cycle method is hard to use.

As can be seen from the above explanation, the main weakness of the incidence-based or life-cycle method is data availability. In some cases, the lack of data may be due to the fact that sufficiently detailed data are simply not available, and in other cases the lack of data may be caused by the fact that the available population is simply not sufficiently mature to make a complete life-cycle calculation. This is the case if the population at hand has a skewed age distribution or perhaps a skewed distribution with respect to the time of diagnosis.

---

[3] When using the cost calculations for cost-benefit analysis, the incidence-based method is needed in order to reveal the total possible gains from an implemented effort (or treatment). For instance, Heckman et al. (2010) use this approach to measure the potential gains from education efforts in early childhood. However, even their well-specified analysis needs to make use of imputed amounts.

PREVALENCE-BASED OR CROSS-SECTION METHOD

In contrast, the prevalence-based or cross-section method takes as its starting point the available population of individuals in a single year (or, more generally, over a fixed, shorter time period) (Drummond, 1992; World Health Organization, 2009).

This method of calculation determines the total cost of the entire population based on all available individuals. If certain age groups, or genders, are more dominant in the population in a given year, then the calculated costs will reflect this composition. Hence, the cross-section method can answer the question 'What is the (yearly) cost of the item under consideration for the current population?'

The calculated costs may be presented as either cost per individual or as a total cost for the entire population. If the individual cost is presented, then this cost reflects the *yearly cost* of the average person of the population and not—as in the case of the life-cycle-method—the cost during a lifespan.

There are two main advantages of the cross-section method. Firstly, the calculation can utilize the newest and most up-to-date data available. By using data from only a single year, the method enables the use of the latest data year. This means that the method can not only give the most up-to-date information, but it can also give the cost estimates calculated on the basis of the largest population possible, a fact that is particularly important in cases with an immature treatment-group population with relatively few observations, such as ours.

Secondly, the method yields an estimate of the actual yearly cost in the year of observation (Larg and Moss, 2011). This yearly cost may then be compared to conventional yearly measures, such as the average work income of individuals in the case of individual costs or the yearly health budget in the case of aggregate, macroeconomic costs.

The main weakness of the cross-section method is the fact that the estimates are based on a single population with all the characteristics of this particular population being part of the calculated costs (Larg and Moss, 2011; Tarricone, 2006). The estimates from a cross-section calculation thus represent a 'snapshot of a moment in time' and may not be a good estimate of costs in future years. This would, for example, be the case if costs are expected to change dramatically as a population ages.

CHOICE OF METHOD

When estimating the effects of ADHD, we used the population and the distribution of individuals with ADHD in Denmark in 2010 as the basis of our analysis.

Estimates of this form could in principle be used for both a COI calculation based on the life-cycle or incidence-based method where individuals are 'stacked' to form a full life-cycle perspective and for calculation using the prevalence-based or cross-section method.

Nevertheless, we have chosen to use the cross-section method, because this method makes the best use of data and because the group of adults with ADHD—with only a relatively small share of individuals older than 35—is simply not mature enough to make good life-cycle estimates. This choice of method is also the most common in cost-of-illness studies (Clabaugh and Ward, 2008).

It would be preferable to carry out the calculation on data that are more recent than 2010 in order to be able both to include more individuals in the calculation (namely, those that have been diagnosed in the period from 2010 onwards) and to reflect the current situation as well as possible. However, this has not been possible due to data constraints.

10.2.3 *Data Sources and Calculation Method*

The cost calculations below will be divided into the effects concerning the private sector (individuals) and the effects concerning the public sector (the state).

The effects measured for the **private sector** are the following:

WAGE INCOME
The wage income is often regarded as an indicator of the individual's productivity and the value of the work performed. If individuals with ADHD have lower productivity than others, then this lower productivity will on average be reflected in their wage income. Data from registers available from Statistics Denmark contain yearly wage incomes for all individuals in Denmark, and from Part III we have estimates for both yearly and hourly wage income. It should be noted that since the size of an individual's wage income is strongly influenced by his or her educational achievement, the impact of ADHD on education is partly measured here as the impact on wage income earned.

INCOME TAXES
Data from registers available from Statistics Denmark contains yearly income taxes for all individuals in Denmark. Individuals pay tax on their earned income. More taxes are paid on a high income than on a low income. Thus, any difference in income between individuals with ADHD and individuals who do not have ADHD will also be reflected in the amount of income taxes paid.

TRANSFER INCOME
If individuals with ADHD have lower work income on average than individuals who do not have ADHD, then in a welfare state, we would expect part of

this income loss (on average) to be covered by income transfers from the public sector. In our analysis we include information about the following income transfers:

- Social-security benefits. This is the basic income transfer that is available to all individuals with permanent Danish residency if they fulfil the criterion of having no other possible income source.

- Early-retirement benefit. This is a pension income given to individuals who have been assessed and been found to have lost the ability to work productively. The early-retirement benefit is in principle given for life (until reaching the normal retirement age), but may be revoked if an individual regains the ability to work.

- Sickness benefit. This is a benefit available to persons who are ill and who are employed or unemployed. It is therefore not available to persons who are not in the labour force (e.g. students).

- Education benefit. This is an income transfer available to individuals currently in education and is given to almost all students enrolled in further education in Denmark.

For all the included income transfers, individual yearly data is available in the registers from Statistics Denmark. However, for sickness benefit the numbers include only benefits paid by the public sector, which is only for long sick leaves of more than twenty-one days (in 2010). For illness periods shorter than twenty-one days, employers bear the full cost of the illness as they in most cases have to pay employees their full wage. This means that the cost estimates for sickness benefits clearly underestimates the total labour-market cost due to illness, since it is likely that individuals with ADHD are also more likely to have more short illness periods than the control groups. However, the total social cost will not be affected by this since the short illness periods for which sickness benefit cannot be refunded from the public sector involves only an internal transfer within the private sector. Also, while the register information contains the actual amount paid for social-security benefit, early-retirement benefit, and education benefit, this is not the case for sickness benefit, where only the number of days is recorded. Therefore the number of days has been multiplied by the maximum daily rate of 99 euros.

Unemployment benefit and labour-market activation schemes, which were part of the estimations in Chapters 7–9, are not included in the cost calculations. There are two reasons for this. First, since both the unemployment-benefit scheme and the labour-market activation system are (partly) financed by the unemployment insurance system, these two areas to a large extent involve only an internal transfer within the private sector. Second, the unemployment insurance system is financed in part by private premium payments and in part by a public subsidy. However, our data do not allow us to see how much has been paid by the two sides. Therefore, we are not able to separate the costs between the private and the public sector. All this notwithstanding, the omission of unemployment insurance and the labour-market activation system does not change the total social costs, since any subsidy paid by the public sector would be counterbalanced by a similar gain in the private sector.

MEDICINE EXPENSES

Since most individuals diagnosed with ADHD are offered a prescription for ADHD medication, one would expect individuals with ADHD to have higher medical expenses than individuals who do not have ADHD. The registers available from Statistics Denmark contain information about all sales of prescription medicine in Denmark with additional information about the price of the item sold and the share covered by the public-sector medicine subsidy.

VICTIMS OF CRIMES

It is hard to find precise estimates of the cost of being a victim of a crime. We use the cost calculated by the Cost-Benefit Knowledge Bank for Criminal Justice and multiply by the USD–EUR exchange rate to arrive at the cost measured in euros.[4] The costs measured at the knowledge bank are divided into various different categories depending on the type of crime of which an individual has been the victim. Using the aggregate Danish statistics for reported crimes we can calculate a weighted average of the costs to use as a unit cost for victims. This cost arrives at a total of 45,596 euros.

The effects measured for the **public sector** are the following:

INCOME TAXES

On the revenue side, the public sector will be affected through the difference in income taxes paid, as stated above. Note that since income tax is an expenditure for individuals and revenue for the public sector, the overall cost to society will be unaffected by the size of the income-tax effect. However, when looking at either the private sector or the public sector separately, income tax needs to be included and is therefore shown in the tables below.

In addition to this, any public sector activity is financed by distortionary income taxation, which imposes a deadweight loss on society as a whole. This deadweight loss arises because progressive income tax changes individuals' behaviour as the economic incentives change. For the calculation here, we do

---

[4] <http://cbkb.org/toolkit/victim-costs/>

not include any measure of the deadweight loss incurred by distortionary taxes as the precise value of the loss is hard to estimate.

TRANSFER EXPENDITURE
Income transfers as listed on the private-sector effects above are paid by the public sector. As was the case with income taxes, the income transfers are also neutral with respect to the overall cost to society, since they are income for the private sector but expenditure for the public sector.

HOSPITAL ADMISSIONS AND PRIMARY HEALTH-CARE SERVICES
Individuals with ADHD are being treated for a disorder within the hospital system or within the primary health-care system, and also have a large likelihood of having comorbid disorders. Therefore the number of hospital admissions, hospital treatments, and primary-care treatments are also higher than for individuals who do not have ADHD. In the data available from Statistics Denmark, precise cost estimates for treatment and admissions are available on an individual basis. These cost estimates are calculated on the basis of the rates paid by Danish Regions to the individual hospitals and primary-care facilities.

For costs related to services received in the primary health sector we have calculated unit costs for 2010 based on the total number of services provided and the total public costs incurred. This leads to costs of 24 euros for GP services, 79 euros for services from specialist practitioners, 64 euros for psychologist practitioners, and an average cost of 34 euros per service for all other areas.

MEDICAL EXPENSES
As stated previously, all prescription medicine is registered, including the share covered by the government subsidy.

TRAFFIC ACCIDENTS
From international studies it is well-known that individuals with ADHD are more likely to be involved in traffic accidents than other individuals. Data from Statistics Denmark allow us to measure the number of accidents with or without bodily harm. We use estimates from the Danish Road Directorate to measure the costs of these accidents.[5] The costs presented below are calculated as a weighted average of the costs of the two types of accident

---

[5] TERESA (The Ministry of Transports Model for Economic Analysis). We subtract the so-called 'welfare loss' from the cost of traffic accidents, as these losses will be covered by many of the other parts of our cost calculations. In addition, the amount is deflated to reflect the 2010 level. In total, this means that we arrive at a cost of 127,661 euros for accidents without bodily harm and a cost of 341,981 euros for accidents with bodily harm.

where the weights are determined by the actual prevalence of the two types of accident.

PLACEMENT OF CHILDREN AWAY FROM THEIR PARENTS AND PREVENTIVE MEASURES FOR CHILDREN AND ADOLESCENTS

Children may be placed in state-certified foster care when social services determine that parents are unable to care adequately for their child. Foster care may be permanent or time-limited. Also, families can gain access to so-called 'preventive measures' which include counselling, day-to-day help in the home and family, and shorter stays in respite care. The right of access to preventive measures is part of Danish welfare legislation (Law of Social Services), and is granted on the basis of a formal family-needs assessment by social services (§ 50 assessment) or if the child has chronic physical or mental functional impairment (including in some cases ADHD) (§ 48). The costs for these facilities are paid by local municipalities. As mentioned in Chapter 3, there is considerable variation between municipalities in how these services are administered and organized. The register data allow us to see how many children have accessed such measures, but not the exact cost thereof.

The cost included for placements away from home and for preventive measures is based only on the share of individuals who were actually in one of these measures in 2010, and not on the total number of individuals who have been in placement or in a preventive measure at some point. The reason for this is that the cost calculations here include costs in 2010 only and not any costs that might have been incurred when individuals were children.

The unit cost for placements and preventive measures is calculated by finding the total number of individuals in these measures in 2010. The number of individuals in placements is then divided into the municipalities' total operating expenses for 'foster care and places for children and young people', yielding a total unit cost of 56,457 euros, while the number of individuals in preventive measures is divided into the municipalities' total operating expenses for 'preventive arrangements for children and young people', yielding a total unit cost of 36,430 euros.

CRIME

Individuals with ADHD have a much higher probability of having committed a crime than individuals who do not have ADHD. These crimes give rise to a cost to society since crimes have to be investigated and criminals have to be prosecuted and sentenced. In the register data from Statistics Denmark, both the number and type of crimes committed are available. From other sources we have obtained measures for different types of crime in Denmark. These are:[6]

- Maximum fines and dropped charges: 461 euros.
- Suspended sentences and youth sanctions: 2,617 euros.
- At least one jail sentence: 19,258 euros.
- More than one jail sentence: 38,515 euros.

We use a weighted average of these cost measures, based on the share of individuals with ADHD who have been convicted of crimes according to these groups to calculate a unit cost for crimes. This leads to a unit cost for crimes of 5,727 euros.

EDUCATION

We have data on the individuals enrolled in secondary and further education in the data registers from Statistics Denmark. However, since we do not know the precise costs associated with the different types of education, we use a weighted average of the internal state transfer rate (based on a rate for a full year of student activity) for the different types of education to yield an overall yearly estimate for secondary and further education.

This leads to a weighted average yearly unit cost for education of 9,374 euros per person.

FAMILY SITUATION, ETC.

The calculations in the second part of this chapter do not include monetary estimates for all of the effects examined in Part III. For example, the difference in individuals' family situation, which is estimated in Part III, is not taken into account in the cost calculations. The main reason for this is that these effects are in essence non-pecuniary and should be treated as such. However all effects that could be allocated a monetary estimate have been included.

10.2.4 *Selection of Comparison Groups*

When calculating the cost of ADHD using the method described above, the cost is measured as the difference between the cost for the group of ADHD individuals and the cost for a comparison group. However, the choice of the comparison group will differ depending on the type of question we want to answer when calculating the cost.

---

[6] Estimates calculated by CEBR and the Danish Crime Prevention Council on the basis of time use stated by the Copenhagen Police and the State Prosecution. Details can be found in Jacobsen (2013).

Below, we shall present the private and social costs of ADHD by comparing the costs of individuals with ADHD to the cost for individuals from three other groups:

- The entire population (weighted to control for the age and gender composition as well as immigration status and region of residence of individuals with ADHD).

- The control group where we have matched demographic variables, parental-background variables, and the comorbidity background of individuals with ADHD (the C-Comor group from Part III).

- The control group where we have selected from the siblings of individuals in the treatment group where same-gender siblings as close in age as possible are selected (the Sib-Demo group from Part III).

This choice of comparison groups reflects a wish to answer the following three questions:

1. What is the cost of ADHD when comparing ADHD individuals to the average of the general population?

2. What is the cost of ADHD when comparing ADHD individuals to individuals who have the same opportunities in life, measured by the same background characteristics and mental illnesses? Specifically, the answer to this question enables us to assess the share of costs that are directly related to ADHD and the share of costs that are indirectly related to comorbid psychiatric diagnoses.

3. What is the cost of ADHD when comparing ADHD individuals to siblings who have had similar upbringing, but do not have an ADHD diagnosis?

10.3 Individual and Aggregate Costs of ADHD

The remainder of this chapter is divided into two subsections. The first contains cost calculations measured per individual per year. Such a calculation enables a comparison with other individual annual figures, such as average income, average income-tax payments, etc. The second subsection aggregates the values per person from the first part to find the total costs to society for the entire population of individuals with ADHD in 2010.

The figures calculated in the present chapter represent the private and social costs given the distribution of individuals with ADHD in 2010. Therefore, the calculated costs most accurately reflect the cost in that year. If the composition of the population of individuals with ADHD changes dramatically over time, then the costs may also change. However, the cost calculated in the present chapter will most likely be accurate for at least some years.

In each of the two subsections, the calculated costs will be compared to numbers of similar magnitude to provide illustrations of the size of the costs relative to well-known variables.

10.3.1 *Average Cost Per Individual*

In this subsection we present the results of the individual cost calculations for the DA and PA groups as well as for an average person with ADHD. The figures for the average individual with ADHD are calculated as a weighted average of the values for the DA and the PA groups, respectively. The weights used are the number of individuals in each of the two groups.

The figures presented here are given as averages per individual. That is, the amounts shown are the average yearly costs of a person with ADHD compared to an average person with the same characteristics.

Table 10.1 shows the average individual cost of ADHD for the DA group and the PA group when comparing these groups to the general population adjusted for gender, age, and immigration status and region. That is, the figures in Table 10.1 show the cost of ADHD when comparing the outcome of individuals with ADHD to the outcome of persons of similar gender, age, and immigration status living in the same region.

It is evident that the average individual total yearly cost is approximately 28,000 euros for the DA individuals and roughly 23,500 euros for the PA individuals when comparing to the general population. This is mainly due to the fact that individuals in the DA group have a greater loss of wage income and higher costs of placements and health costs. When looking at the private and public parts of the costs separately, we see that the private costs are 9,600 euros for the DA group and 8,600 euros for the PA group.

The private part of the cost calculation in general shows only small differences between the two groups, but the DA group has a slightly higher loss of disposable income and somewhat higher victim costs than the PA group.

Turning to the public part of the cost, we note that the taxes and income transfers listed under the private cost are repeated in this part of the table, albeit with opposite signs. The reason for this is that while income transfers are income for the private individuals they represent a cost of exactly the same magnitude to the public sector. Thus when aggregating, this transfer from one part of society to another cancels out and has no impact on the total social costs.

The composition of the public costs is such that more than half is due to loss of income taxes for both groups. For the DA group this loss amounts to almost 9,000 euros compared to a member of the general public, and for the PA group it is slightly higher than 8,000 euros. Also, both groups have public losses due to higher expenditures on income-replacement transfers. This means that the

Table 10.1. Cost difference between ADHD individuals and the general population, EUR per individual

Private costs		Diagnosed adults	Prescribed adults	Weighted average
Disposable income	Gross wage income	−21,614	−19,388	−20,013
	Social-security benefits	1,700	1,105	1,272
	Sickness benefits	170	147	153
	Early-retirement benefits	2,733	2,195	2,346
	Education benefits	−35	5	−6
	Income tax	8,951	8,083	8,327
Other private costs	Private expenditures on prescribed medication	−270	−255	−260
	Victim costs	−1,275	−544	−749
Total private costs		**−9,640**	**−8,653**	**−8,930**

Public costs		Diagnosed adults	Prescribed adults	Weighted average
Tax and transfers	Income tax	−8,951	−8,083	−8,327
	Social-security benefits	−1,700	−1,105	−1,272
	Sickness benefits	−170	−147	−153
	Early-retirement benefits	−2,733	−2,195	−2,346
Educational expenses	Education	81	37	50
	Education benefits	35	−5	6
Crime and traffic	Traffic accidents	−1,312	−733	−895
	Direct costs related to crimes	−598	−406	−460
Public expenses on placements	Placement	−1,175	−566	−737
	Preventive measures	−308	−178	−214
Medical expenses	Hospital admissions	−73	−70	−71
	General practitioners	−282	−187	−214
	Specialist practitioners	−61	−26	−36
	Psychologists	−126	−307	−256
	Other primary health-care services	−22	−55	−45
	Public expenditures on prescribed medication	−1,037	−782	−853
Total public costs		**−18,431**	**−14,805**	**−15,823**
TOTAL COSTS		**−28,071**	**−23,459**	**−24,753**

public sector has a large loss among the labour-market-related variables. The public sector actually saves a small amount on educational expenses, when comparing to an individual from the general population. Finally, the total health-related costs are roughly 1,600 euros higher for an individual of the DA group and roughly 1,400 euros higher for an individual from the PA group when compared to the average cost of the general population.

Table 10.2 shows a similar calculation as Table 10.1, but with the control groups changed, such that we control not only for gender, age, immigration status, and region, but also for other demographic variables, parental-background variables, and psychiatric comorbidity (the C-Comor control group). The estimates behind this cost calculation can be found in Chapter 7.

Table 10.2. Cost difference between ADHD individuals and the C-Comor group, EUR per individual

Private costs		Diagnosed adults	Prescribed adults	Weighted average
Disposable income	Gross wage income	−10,951	−11,966	−11,681
	Social-security benefits	1,321	903	1,020
	Sickness benefits	131	129	130
	Early-retirement benefits	419	1,027	857
	Education benefits	−57	2	−15
	Income tax	5,464	3,296	3,905
Other private costs	Private expenditures on prescribed medication	−219	−230	−227
	Victim costs	−474	−441	−451
Total private costs		**−4,367**	**−7,279**	**−6,462**

Public costs		Diagnosed adults	Prescribed adults	Weighted average
Tax and transfers	Income tax	−5,464	−3,296	−3,905
	Social-security benefits	−1,321	−903	−1,020
	Sickness benefits	−131	−129	−130
	Early-retirement benefits	−419	−1,027	−857
Educational expenses	Education	112	62	76
	Education benefits	57	−2	15
Crime and traffic	Traffic accidents	−466	−509	−497
	Direct costs related to crimes	−382	−253	−289
Public expenses on placements	Placement	−608	−378	−442
	Preventive measures	−153	−99	−114
Medical expenses	Hospital admissions	−29	−20	−23
	General practitioners	−187	−141	−154
	Specialist practitioners	−33	−43	−40
	Psychologists	−113	−327	−267
	Other primary health-care services	−6	−37	−29
	Public expenditures on prescribed medication	−773	−696	−718
Total public costs		**−9,918**	**−7,799**	**−8,394**
TOTAL COSTS		**−14,286**	**−15,078**	**−14,856**

As expected, controlling for more variables that are probably related to the outcome of the individuals reduces the measured costs. Thus, in Table 10.2 the total individual costs are just 14,300 euros for the DA group and 15,100 euros for the PA group, both significantly smaller than in Table 10.1.

When further comparing Tables 10.1 and 10.2, we can see that a large part of the smaller individual costs can be explained by a large decline in loss of disposable income. For instance, the loss of wage income is 10,900 euros and 12,000 euros for the two groups in Table 10.2, but 21,600 euros and 19,400 euros in Table 10.1. Thus, controlling for comorbidity (and the other background variables) has large implications on the labour-market outcome of the control group, as also seen in Chapter 7. Another point that is clear when looking at Tables 10.1 and 10.2 is that controlling for background variables changes the measured cost of ADHD somewhat more for the DA group than for the PA group. The main reason behind this is that individuals in the DA group have a high likelihood of more diagnosed comorbid disorders, and these disorders are clearly linked to poorer outcomes and hence to higher individual and social costs. The extent to which the members of the PA group also have comorbid disorders that are costly to society is not known if these disorders have been diagnosed in private practice. Hence, it is likely that there are unregistered background variables, such as comorbid psychiatric disorders, in the PA group for which we are just not able to control. While such variables may also exist for the DA group, they probably do so to a smaller extent.

A final point to mention is that although the measured private and social costs are smaller when controlling for background variables and comorbidity, large private and public costs remain. In fact, the total social costs as calculated in Table 10.2 are still more than half of the amount found when comparing to the general population.

Now, turning to the final cost calculation of this subsection, we look at Table 10.3. This table shows the private and social costs of ADHD when comparing individuals with ADHD to the Sib-Demo control group. The advantage of a sibling-based analysis is that siblings are similar with respect to many of the aspects that are difficult to observe. These aspects may influence characteristics concerning education and income, among others. For example, genetic differences and social-background factors during childhood and upbringing are similar across siblings. In this sense, we reduce the risk of unobserved differences between the treatment and control groups playing an important role in determining the differences between individuals with ADHD and individuals without. Thus, we attempt to explore possible biases that may influence the cost estimates in order to approximate the costs of ADHD as accurately as possible. More precisely, we select a control group of siblings of the same gender who have the same biological mother and father (see Chapter 8). In this analysis, we do not control for comorbid disorders.

The total individual yearly social costs of ADHD when comparing to non-ADHD siblings are 18,700 euros for the DA group and 17,400 euros for the PA group.

Compared to their siblings who are not diagnosed with ADHD, the loss of wage income is around 13–14,000 euros per year, and even when factoring in the savings in income-tax payments and the gains from higher income-replacement transfers, the loss of disposable income is still around 8,000 euros per year for both groups, or approximately 650 euros per month.

When we look at the public costs, we can see that the loss in terms of tax and transfers is only slightly higher for the DA group than for the PA group (in the order of 500 euros per year more for the DA group). For the other components of the public costs, the same is true, and both the cost of placements and the costs

Table 10.3. Cost difference between ADHD individuals and the Sib-Demo group, EUR per individual

Private costs		Diagnosed adults	Prescribed adults	Weighted average
Disposable income	Gross wage income	−14,693	−13,974	−14,176
	Social-security benefits	1,176	1,010	1,056
	Sickness benefits	108	112	111
	Early-retirement benefits	1,895	1,571	1,662
	Education benefits	−105	−17	−42
	Income tax	3,501	3,452	3,466
Other private costs	Private expenditures on prescribed medication	−279	−250	−258
	Victim costs	−197	−488	−406
Total private costs		**−8,593**	**−8,584**	**−8,587**

Public costs		Diagnosed adults	Prescribed adults	Weighted average
Tax and transfers	Income tax	−3,501	−3,452	−3,466
	Social-security benefits	−1,176	−1,010	−1,056
	Sickness benefits	−108	−112	−111
	Early-retirement benefits	−1,895	−1,571	−1,662
Educational expenses	Education	149	7	47
	Education benefits	105	17	42
Crime and traffic	Traffic accidents	−756	−537	−598
	Direct costs related to crimes	−409	−256	−299
Public expenses on placements	Placement	−683	−381	−466
	Preventive measures	−174	−84	−109
Medical expenses	Hospital admissions	−58	−30	−38
	General practitioners	−262	−184	−206
	Specialist practitioners	−119	−74	−86
	Psychologists	−127	−331	−274
	Other primary health-care services	−13	−42	−34
	Public expenditures on prescribed medication	−1,083	−781	−866
Total public costs		**−10,108**	**−8,821**	**−9,182**
TOTAL COSTS		**−18,701**	**−17,405**	**−17,769**

related to traffic and crime are slightly higher for the DA group. Finally, the total health costs are roughly 1,700 euros per year higher for the DA groups than for their non-ADHD siblings. For the PA group the health costs are 1,400 euros higher than for the control group.

Comparing to the earlier analyses in this chapter, we see that for both the DA group and the PA group (and hence also for the average individual with ADHD), the total costs in Table 10.3 are somewhere in between the costs calculated in Table 10.1 and the costs calculated in Table 10.2. This outcome most likely reflects the fact that using siblings as a control group is more accurate than using a random member of the general population (albeit one with similar age, gender, and immigrant status), but that failing to control for comorbidity results in an overestimation of the direct costs of ADHD.

Summing up this section, the cost calculations show that an average individual with ADHD has a total yearly social cost of approximately 18,000 euros when compared to his or her non-ADHD sibling.

When looking at the composition of the social costs of ADHD, all three tables in this section show that individuals with ADHD incur large costs due to their earnings ability in the labour market. This leads to a private loss, but also to a public loss, since the public sector loses tax income and compensates individuals with no or low labour income using a variety of income-replacement transfers. This compensation leads to a lower private cost and a higher public cost compared to a case where such welfare programmes were not in place, but it does not affect the total social cost per se. Finally, individuals with ADHD also have higher health-related costs, which are also mostly paid for by the public sector.

10.3.2 *Aggregate Costs to Society*

This subsection contains tables similar to Tables 10.1–10.3 above, where the numbers have been aggregated to reflect the total costs to society. Numbers in the tables below are measured in millions of euros. The numbers have been calculated by first multiplying the average cost per individual for the DA group by 5,331 (the total number of observations in the DA group), then multiplying the average cost per individual for the PA group by 13,662 (the total number of observations in the PA group), and finally adding together the two resulting numbers to reflect the total costs of ADHD diagnosed late in life. Since we do not include the individuals in the DC or the PC groups, we are thus not measuring the total cost for all adults with ADHD, but only the cost for those who have been undiagnosed when they were children. The numbers here are therefore a lower bound for the total costs to society of ADHD in adults.

Another reason why our aggregate estimates are underestimating the total costs is that there are adult individuals in the Danish population with undiagnosed ADHD. As we cannot find those individuals in the registers, they are not part of the cost calculations. We expect that the estimated average individual cost is upwards biased. The reason for this is that individuals diagnosed with or treated for ADHD are expected to generally represent severe ADHD cases compared to undiagnosed individuals in the population at large. This is because individuals who are affected by the condition sufficiently seriously for it to be an issue to themselves or to their surroundings will to a higher extent receive a diagnosis or be treated for the condition. The aggregate cost measures presented below on the other hand will be underestimated when only a certain percentage of adults with ADHD are diagnosed. In fact, Psykiatriudvalget (2013) shows that in 2011 almost 3,000 new adult individuals were diagnosed with ADHD (see also Table 3.3, which shows new adult individuals with an F90–98 diagnosis in 2011). As we base our estimates on 2010 numbers, these individuals are not part of the calculations here.[7] In this sense, we estimate the aggregate costs for the group of ADHD individuals who have been diagnosed later in life, and leave out the costs for those ADHD individuals who are undiagnosed.

Table 10.4 shows the total costs to society for individuals of similar age and gender and with same background with respect to immigrant status as the individuals with ADHD (Table 10.4 is thus similar to Table 10.1). In total, the overall yearly cost to society of ADHD among adults, when comparing to individuals of similar age and gender is 470 million euros, roughly equal to 0.2 per cent of GDP.

A little more than 300 million euros is paid by the public sector, and only 170 million euros constitute cost to the private sector. The private sector loss is partly due to a large loss of work income of 380 million euros, but a large share of this loss is covered by the fact that the individuals with ADHD pay 160 million euros less in taxes and receive roughly 72 million euros more in income transfers.

For the public sector, the loss of 160 million euros in income-tax revenue and the extra 72 million euros in income transfers obviously leads to a loss. This loss is made even larger by the fact that individuals with ADHD diagnosed as adults present extra health-care-related expenses of roughly 28 million euros compared to what would have been the case for a similar-sized group from the general population.

A final point to make regarding Table 10.4 is that although the individual costs of members of the DA group in Table 10.1 above are higher than for members of the PA group, the total cost is larger for the PA group, because the PA group is much larger in size.

Table 10.5 exhibits the total costs to society when comparing individuals with ADHD diagnosed as adults with individuals from the C-Comor control group, hence controlling for demographic background, parental variables, and comorbid psychiatric disorders.

In this case the total costs to society fall to 282 million euros, but compared to the numbers in Table 10.4 the change in the public costs is much larger than the change in the private costs. The private costs fall to 123 million euros, but the public costs fall to 159 million euros. The main reason for the large change in the public cost is that losses from income transfers and income

---

[7] Not all the 2011-diagnosed adult individuals with ADHD will be newcomers to the treatment groups. Some individuals, who in our data are part of the PA group, may have become diagnosed in the secondary health-care sector during 2011 and will thus now be in the DA group instead. Moreover, we only include individuals who were younger than 50 years old when diagnosed. For these reasons not all of the almost 3,000 new diagnosed adults can be added to the total.

Table 10.4. Aggregate cost difference between ADHD individuals and the general population, EUR millions

Private cost		Diagnosed adults	Prescribed adults	All
Disposable income	Gross wage income	−115.2	−264.9	−380.1
	Social-security benefits	9.1	15.1	24.2
	Sickness benefits	0.9	2.0	2.9
	Early-retirement benefits	14.6	30.0	44.6
	Education benefits	−0.2	0.1	−0.1
	Income tax	47.7	110.4	158.1
Other private costs	Private expenditures on prescribed medication	−1.4	−3.5	−4.9
	Victim costs	−6.8	−7.4	−14.2
Total private cost		**−51.4**	**−118.2**	**−169.6**

Public cost		Diagnosed adults	Prescribed adults	All
Tax and transfers	Income tax	−47.7	−110.4	−158.1
	Social-security benefits	−9.1	−15.1	−24.2
	Sickness benefits	−0.9	−2.0	−2.9
	Early-retirement benefits	−14.6	−30.0	−44.6
Educational expenses	Education	0.4	0.5	0.9
	Education benefits	0.2	−0.1	0.1
Crime and traffic	Traffic accidents	−7.0	−10.0	−17.0
	Direct costs related to crimes	−3.2	−5.5	−8.7
Public expenses on placements	Placement	−6.3	−7.7	−14.0
	Preventive measures	−1.6	−2.4	−4.1
Medical expenses	Hospital admissions	−0.4	−1.0	−1.3
	General practitioners	−1.5	−2.6	−4.1
	Specialist practitioners	−0.3	−0.4	−0.7
	Psychologists	−0.7	−4.2	−4.9
	Other primary health-care services	−0.1	−0.7	−0.9
	Public expenditures on prescribed medication	−5.5	−10.7	−16.2
Total public cost		**−98.3**	**−202.3**	**−300.5**
TOTAL COSTS		**−149.6**	**−320.5**	**−470.1**

taxes are much smaller. Also, the public costs of placements and health care are somewhat smaller in this case.

Table 10.6 shows the aggregate private and social costs for individuals with ADHD diagnosed as adults when compared to the Sib-Demo control group, hence using individuals' siblings as a control group. In this case, the total cost to society is measured at 338 million euros in 2010 and thus lies in between the levels measured in Tables 10.4 and 10.5. The total private costs are 163 million euros, roughly the same as in Table 10.4, but significantly larger than in Table 10.5. The main reason for the difference is the difference in the measured costs related to the labour market and income taxes. The measured loss of wage income is 222 million euros when comparing to non-ADHD siblings, but 380 million euros when comparing to the population at large.

Table 10.5. Aggregate cost difference between ADHD individuals and the C-Comor group, EUR millions

Private cost		Diagnosed adults	Prescribed adults	All
Disposable income	Gross wage income	−58.4	−163.5	−221.9
	Social-security benefits	7.0	12.3	19.4
	Sickness benefits	0.7	1.8	2.5
	Early-retirement benefits	2.2	14.0	16.3
	Education benefits	−0.3	0.0	−0.3
	Income tax	29.1	45.0	74.2
Other private costs	Private expenditures on prescribed medication	−1.2	−3.1	−4.3
	Victim costs	−2.5	−6.0	−8.6
Total private cost		**−23.3**	**−99.5**	**−122.7**

Public cost		Diagnosed adults	Prescribed adults	All
Tax and transfers	Income tax	−29.1	−45.0	−74.2
	Social-security benefits	−7.0	−12.3	−19.4
	Sickness benefits	−0.7	−1.8	−2.5
	Early-retirement benefits	−2.2	−14.0	−16.3
Educational expenses	Education	0.6	0.8	1.4
	Education benefits	0.3	−0.0	0.3
Crime and traffic	Traffic accidents	−2.5	−7.0	−9.4
	Direct costs related to crimes	−2.0	−3.5	−5.5
Public expenses on placements	Placement	−3.2	−5.2	−8.4
	Preventive measures	−0.8	−1.4	−2.2
Medical expenses	Hospital admissions	−0.2	−0.3	−0.4
	General practitioners	−1.0	−1.9	−2.9
	Specialist practitioners	−0.2	−0.6	−0.8
	Psychologists	−0.6	−4.5	−5.1
	Other primary health-care services	−0.0	−0.5	−0.5
	Public expenditures on prescribed medication	−4.1	−9.5	−13.6
Total public cost		**−52.9**	**−106.5**	**−159.4**
TOTAL COSTS		**−76.2**	**−206.0**	**−282.2**

The public costs total 174 million euros, of which 120 million euros are due to loss of income-tax revenue and higher payments of income-replacement transfers. Traffic accidents and crime costs add up to 17 million euros, and costs of placements and preventive measures total 11 million euros. Finally, the public-health costs are 28 million euros higher than for the control group when comparing to non-ADHD siblings.

10.4 Overall Conclusions

The overall conclusions based on the cost calculations in the present chapter are:

• There are large private and social costs of ADHD in Denmark. The overall yearly costs to society are estimated at around 340 million euros per year when using non-ADHD siblings as control group.

Table 10.6. Aggregate cost difference between ADHD individuals and the Sib-Demo group, EUR millions

Private cost		Diagnosed adults	Prescribed adults	All
Disposable income	Gross wage income	−78.3	−190.9	−269.2
	Social-security benefits	6.3	13.8	20.1
	Sickness benefits	0.6	1.5	2.1
	Early-retirement benefits	10.1	21.5	31.6
	Education benefits	−0.6	−0.2	−0.8
	Income tax	18.7	47.2	65.8
Other private costs	Private expenditures on prescribed medication	−1.5	−3.4	−4.9
	Victim costs	−1.0	−6.7	−7.7
Total private cost		**−45.8**	**−117.3**	**−163.1**

Public cost		Diagnosed adults	Prescribed adults	All
Tax and transfers	Income tax	−18.7	−47.2	−65.8
	Social-security benefits	−6.3	−13.8	−20.1
	Sickness benefits	−0.6	−1.5	−2.1
	Early-retirement benefits	−10.1	−21.5	−31.6
Educational expenses	Education	0.8	0.1	0.9
	Education benefits	0.6	0.2	0.8
Crime and traffic	Traffic accidents	−4.0	−7.3	−11.4
	Direct costs related to crimes	−2.2	−3.5	−5.7
Public expenses on placements	Placement	−3.6	−5.2	−8.8
	Preventive measures	−0.9	−1.1	−2.1
Medical expenses	Hospital admissions	−0.3	−0.4	−0.7
	General practitioners	−1.4	−2.5	−3.9
	Specialist practitioners	−0.6	−1.0	−1.6
	Psychologists	−0.7	−4.5	−5.2
	Other primary health-care services	−0.1	−0.6	−0.6
	Public expenditures on prescribed medication	−5.8	−10.7	−16.4
Total public cost		**−53.9**	**−120.5**	**−174.4**
TOTAL COSTS		**−99.7**	**−237.8**	**−337.5**

- The private costs of ADHD to individuals with ADHD are large in terms of loss of salary earnings. However, a part of this loss is covered by the receipt of income-replacement transfers and the fact that a lower income also results in lower tax payments, such that the total individual private costs are smaller. Nevertheless, compared to their non-ADHD siblings, individuals with ADHD still experience a loss of approximately 650 euros per month after taxes.

- The public costs of ADHD are also large. Not only does the public sector lose tax payments and pay out income-replacement benefits, but it also incurs large indirect costs for crime committed by individuals with ADHD and for traffic accidents involving persons with ADHD. There are also increased costs due to medical treatments and placements, but these are of a smaller magnitude. When compared to non-ADHD siblings, the average individual public costs of ADHD are thus 9,200 euros per year.

- Controlling for comorbidity leads to a significant reduction in the measured cost. This is particularly true for individuals in the DA group, but also to a smaller extent for individuals in the PA group. The main reason for this result is that the loss of work income in markedly smaller when controlling for comorbidity.

Appendix to Chapter 10: Robustness of Calculation of Private and Social Costs

In Part III it is found that individuals diagnosed with ADHD later in life have weaker attachment to the labour market than individuals in the control groups—i.e., a lower share of individuals with ADHD are employed, whereas a larger share receive welfare benefits and benefits from early-pension schemes.

A related question is whether the development of labour-market attachment has also been different for individuals with ADHD and non-ADHD individuals. As the Danish economy has been affected by the onset of the global financial crisis in 2008 and many workers have lost their jobs—especially unskilled jobs in industry—it is interesting to investigate the impact on individuals diagnosed with ADHD later in life to evaluate if they have had different development in their labour-market attachment than individuals in the control groups. In other words, it is interesting to ask whether individuals with ADHD to a higher extent have become marginalized during the financial crisis compared to groups of non-ADHD but otherwise similar individuals.

We have investigated this question and the overall impression is that individuals with ADHD have become more marginalized during the financial crisis than other 'vulnerable groups' in the labour market. This suggests that their labour-market attachment is especially weak in downturns.

Because of the weak attachment to the labour market, we perform a robustness analysis of the private and social costs of ADHD in this appendix. We are concerned about overestimating the private and social cost estimates when using 2009 data for occupational status since 2009 was an especially harsh year in the labour market for adult ADHD individuals.

Since relatively many ADHD individuals lost their jobs, the share of ADHD individuals in wage employment dropped faster than in the control groups. This dynamic may result in an overestimation of private and social costs of ADHD since an important cost contributor is lower wage income before taxes. The following tables are similar to the tables that were presented in the main text of this chapter. That is, we calculate costs as the difference between ADHD individuals and three different control groups at the individual level as well as the aggregate level. The control groups are the general adult population and the two groups labelled C-Comor and Sib-Demo, as in the main text of this chapter.

Table 10.A.1. Cost difference between ADHD individuals and the general population, EUR per individual

Private costs		Diagnosed adults	Prescribed adults	Weighted average
Disposable income	Gross wage income	−19,999	−16,647	−17,587
	Social-security benefits	718	530	583
	Sickness benefits	65	56	58
	Early-retirement benefits	1,316	1,170	1,211
	Education benefits	−85	8	−18
	Income tax	8,951	8,083	8,327
Other private costs	Private expenditures on prescribed medication	−270	−255	−260
	Victim costs	−1,275	−544	−749
Total private costs		**−10,579**	**−7,599**	**−8,435**

Public costs		Diagnosed adults	Prescribed adults	Weighted average
Tax and transfers	Income tax	−8,951	−8,083	−8,327
	Social-security benefits	−718	−530	−583
	Sickness benefits	−65	−56	−58
	Early-retirement benefits	−1,316	−1,170	−1,211
Educational expenses	Education	81	37	50
	Education benefits	85	−8	18
Crime and traffic	Traffic accidents	−1,312	−733	−895
	Direct costs related to crimes	−598	−406	−460
Public expenses on placements	Placement	−1,175	−566	−737
	Preventive measures	−308	−178	−214
Medical expenses	Hospital admissions	−73	−70	−71
	General practitioners	−282	−187	−214
	Specialist practitioners	−61	−26	−36
	Psychologists	−126	−307	−256
	Other primary health-care services	−22	−55	−45
	Public expenditures on prescribed medication	−1,037	−782	−853
Total public costs		**−15,877**	**−13,118**	**−13,892**
TOTAL COSTS		**−26,456**	**−20,717**	**−22,328**

Note: The calculation of cost differences in this table is based on employment and benefit shares in 2007, whereas the calculation in Table 10.1 is based on shares from 2009. In both cases difference estimates from Chapter 7 have been used.

The overall results established in this appendix are:

- When using results for occupational status for a boom year, there are still large private and social costs of ADHD in Denmark. The overall yearly costs to society are estimated to be slightly lower compared to the estimates presented the main text and are around 300 million euros per year when compared to the control group of non-ADHD siblings.

- The private costs of ADHD to individuals with ADHD are reduced somewhat but are still large in terms of loss of wage income. As in the baseline analysis of this chapter, a large share of this loss is covered by the receipt of income-replacement

Table 10.A.2. Cost difference between ADHD individuals and the C-Comor group, EUR per individual

Private costs		Diagnosed adults	Prescribed adults	Weighted average
Disposable income	Gross wage income	−10,569	−10,316	−10,387
	Social-security benefits	528	407	441
	Sickness benefits	51	44	46
	Early-retirement benefits	−45	541	377
	Education benefits	−70	−20	−34
	Income tax	5,464	3,296	3,905
Other private costs	Private expenditures on prescribed medication	−219	−230	−227
	Victim costs	−474	−441	−451
Total private costs		**−5,335**	**−6,718**	**− 6,330**

Public costs		Diagnosed adults	Prescribed adults	Weighted average
Tax and transfers	Income tax	−5,464	−3,296	−3,905
	Social-security benefits	−528	−407	−441
	Sickness benefits	−51	−44	−46
	Early-retirement benefits	45	−541	−377
Educational expenses	Education	112	62	76
	Education benefits	70	20	34
Crime and traffic	Traffic accidents	−466	−509	−497
	Direct costs related to crimes	−382	−253	−289
Public expenses on placements	Placement	−608	−378	−442
	Preventive measures	−153	−99	−114
Medical expenses	Hospital admissions	−29	−20	−23
	General practitioners	−187	−141	−154
	Specialist practitioners	−33	−43	−40
	Psychologists	−113	−327	−267
	Other primary health-care services	−6	−37	−29
	Public expenditures on prescribed medication	−773	−696	−718
Total public costs		**−8,569**	**−6,711**	**−7,232**
TOTAL COSTS		**−13,904**	**−13,429**	**−13,562**

Note: The calculation of cost differences is this table is based on employment and benefit shares in 2007, whereas the calculation in Table 10.2 is based on shares from 2009. In both cases difference estimates from Chapter 7 have been used.

benefit and the fact that a lower income also results in lower tax payments, such that the total individual private costs are relatively small.

• Controlling for comorbidity leads to a significant reduction in the measured cost, but the total cost estimates are robust to the choice of using the 2007 or 2009 distribution of occupational status.

Table 10.A.3. Cost difference between ADHD-individuals and the Sib-Demo group, EUR per individual

Private costs		Diagnosed adults	Prescribed adults	Weighted average
Disposable income	Gross wage income	−13,062	−11,879	−12,211
	Social-security benefits	584	502	525
	Sickness benefits	108	587	452
	Early-retirement benefits	926	971	959
	Education benefits	−162	−81	−104
	Income tax	3,501	3,452	3,466
Other private costs	Private expenditures on prescribed medication	−279	−250	−258
	Victim costs	−197	−488	−406
Total private costs		**−8,580**	**−7,186**	**−7,577**

Public costs		Diagnosed adults	Prescribed adults	Weighted average
Tax and transfers	Income tax	−3,501	−3,452	−3,466
	Social-security benefits	−584	−502	−525
	Sickness benefits	−108	−587	−452
	Early-retirement benefits	−926	−971	−959
Educational expenses	Education	149	7	47
	Education benefits	162	81	104
Crime and traffic	Traffic accidents	−756	−537	−598
	Direct costs related to crimes	−409	−256	−299
Public expenses on placements	Placement	−683	−381	−466
	Preventive measures	−174	−84	−109
Medical expenses	Hospital admissions	−58	−30	−38
	General practitioners	−262	−184	−206
	Specialist practitioners	−119	−74	−86
	Psychologists	−127	−331	−274
	Other primary health-care services	−13	−42	−34
	Public expenditures on prescribed medication	−1083	−781	−866
Total public costs		**−8,491**	**−8,125**	**−8,227**
TOTAL COSTS		**−17,071**	**−15,310**	**−15,804**

Note: The calculation of cost differences is this table is based on employment and benefit shares in 2007, whereas the calculation in Table 10.3 is based on shares from 2009. In both cases difference estimates from Chapter 8 have been used.

Table 10.A.4. Aggregate cost difference between ADHD individuals and the general population, EUR millions

Private cost		Diagnosed adults	Prescribed adults	All
Disposable income	Gross wage income	−106.6	−227.4	−334.0
	Social-security benefits	3.8	7.2	11.1
	Sickness benefits	0.3	0.8	1.1
	Early-retirement benefits	7.0	16.0	23.0
	Education benefits	−0.5	0.1	−0.3
	Income tax	47.7	110.4	158.1
Other private costs	Private expenditures on prescribed medication	−1.4	−3.5	−4.9
	Victim costs	−6.8	−7.4	−14.2
Total private cost		**−56.4**	**−103.8**	**−160.2**

Public cost		Diagnosed adults	Prescribed adults	All
Tax and transfers	Income tax	−47.7	−110.4	−158.1
	Social-security benefits	−3.8	−7.2	−11.1
	Sickness benefits	−0.3	−0.8	−1.1
	Early-retirement benefits	−7.0	−16.0	−23.0
Educational expenses	Education	0.4	0.5	0.9
	Education benefits	0.5	−0.1	0.3
Crime and traffic	Traffic accidents	−7.0	−10.0	−17.0
	Direct costs related to crimes	−3.2	−5.5	−8.7
Public expenses on placements	Placement	−6.3	−7.7	−14.0
	Preventive measures	−1.6	−2.4	−4.1
Medical expenses	Hospital admissions	−0.4	−1.0	−1.3
	General practitioners	−1.5	−2.6	−4.1
	Specialist practitioners	−0.3	−0.4	−0.7
	Psychologists	−0.7	−4.2	−4.9
	Other primary health-care services	−0.1	−0.7	−0.9
	Public expenditures on prescribed medication	−5.5	−10.7	−16.2
Total public cost		**−84.6**	**−179.2**	**−263.9**
TOTAL COSTS		**−141.0**	**−283.0**	**−424.1**

Note: The calculation of cost differences is this table is based on employment and benefit shares in 2007, whereas the calculation in Table 10.4 is based on shares from 2009. In both cases difference estimates from Chapter 7 have been used.

Table 10.A.5. Aggregate difference between ADHD individuals and the C-Comor group, EUR millions

Private cost		Diagnosed adults	Prescribed adults	All
Disposable income	Gross wage income	−56.3	−140.9	−197.3
	Social-security benefits	2.8	5.6	8.4
	Sickness benefits	0.3	0.6	0.9
	Early-retirement benefits	−0.2	7.4	7.2
	Education benefits	−0.4	−0.3	−0.6
	Income tax	29.1	45.0	74.2
Other private costs	Private expenditures on prescribed medication	−1.2	−3.1	−4.3
	Victim costs	−2.5	−6.0	−8.6
Total private cost		**−28.4**	**−91.8**	**−120.2**

Public cost		Diagnosed adults	Prescribed adults	All
Tax and transfers	Income tax	−29.1	−45.0	−74.2
	Social-security benefits	−2.8	−5.6	−8.4
	Sickness benefits	−0.3	−0.6	−0.9
	Early-retirement benefits	0.2	−7.4	−7.2
Educational expenses	Education	0.6	0.8	1.4
	Education benefits	0.4	0.3	0.6
Crime and traffic	Traffic accidents	−2.5	−7.0	−9.4
	Direct costs related to crimes	−2.0	−3.5	−5.5
Public expenses on placements	Placement	−3.2	−5.2	−8.4
	Preventive measures	−0.8	−1.4	−2.2
Medical expenses	Hospital admissions	−0.2	−0.3	−0.4
	General practitioners	−1.0	−1.9	−2.9
	Specialist practitioners	−0.2	−0.6	−0.8
	Psychologists	−0.6	−4.5	−5.1
	Other primary health-care services	−0.0	−0.5	−0.5
	Public expenditures on prescribed medication	−4.1	−9.5	−13.6
Total public cost		**−45.7**	**−91.7**	**−137.4**
TOTAL COSTS		**−74.1**	**−183.5**	**−257.6**

Note: The calculation of cost differences is this table is based on employment and benefit shares in 2007, whereas the calculation in Table 10.5 is based on shares from 2009. In both cases difference estimates from Chapter 7 have been used.

Table 10.A.6. Aggregate cost difference between ADHD individuals and the Sib-Demo group, EUR millions

Private cost		Diagnosed adults	Prescribed adults	All
Disposable income	Gross wage income	−69.6	−162.3	−231.9
	Social-security benefits	3.1	6.9	10.0
	Sickness benefits	0.6	8.0	8.6
	Early-retirement benefits	4.9	13.3	18.2
	Education benefits	−0.9	−1.1	−2.0
	Income tax	18.7	47.2	65.8
Other private costs	Private expenditures on prescribed medication	−1.5	−3.4	−4.9
	Victim costs	−1.0	−6.7	−7.7
Total private cost		**−45.7**	**−98.2**	**−143.9**

Public cost		Diagnosed adults	Prescribed adults	All
Tax and transfers	Income tax	−18.7	−47.2	−65.8
	Social-security benefits	−3.1	−6.9	−10.0
	Sickness benefits	−0.6	−8.0	−8.6
	Early-retirement benefits	−4.9	−13.3	−18.2
Educational expenses	Education	0.8	0.1	0.9
	Education benefits	0.9	1.1	2.0
Crime and traffic	Traffic accidents	−4.0	−7.3	−11.4
	Direct costs related to crimes	−2.2	−3.5	−5.7
Public expenses on placements	Placement	−3.6	−5.2	−8.8
	Preventive measures	−0.9	−1.1	−2.1
Medical expenses	Hospital admissions	−0.3	−0.4	−0.7
	General practitioners	−1.4	−2.5	−3.9
	Specialist practitioners	−0.6	−1.0	−1.6
	Psychologists	−0.7	−4.5	−5.2
	Other primary health-care services	−0.1	−0.6	−0.6
	Public expenditures on prescribed medication	−5.8	−10.7	−16.4
Total public cost		**−45.3**	**−111.0**	**−156.3**
TOTAL COSTS		**−91.0**	**−209.2**	**−300.2**

Note: The calculation of cost differences is this table is based on employment and benefit shares in 2007, whereas the calculation in Table 10.6 is based on shares from 2009. In both cases difference estimates from Chapter 8 have been used.

11

Discussion

In this final chapter we provide a summary of the key results presented in this book and outline key recommendations that may help to address the inequalities experienced by individuals with ADHD. The key results concerning the private and social costs of ADHD are discussed and put into a national and international context in Section 11.1. In addition, we discuss results from the literature on cost analyses performed for ADHD in more detail in Section 11.2. Moreover, we discuss generalizability of the established results beyond Denmark in Section 11.3., partly focusing on the psychiatric sector, partly on other sectors of the economy such as the labour market and the education sector. Finally, in Section 11.4 we discuss the limitations and strengths of the study.

11.1 Findings and Key Recommendations

The clear picture that has emerged from this study is that ADHD is associated with considerable private and social costs. It therefore seems appropriate to suggest an 'invest to save' framework that increases spending on early-intervention strategies that might mitigate the early impact of ADHD on academic attainment, family well-being, and early career productivity. The longer society waits to intervene in the life cycle of a disadvantaged child, the more costly it is to remedy the disadvantage (Heckman, 2008). It is possible to save resources later on by implementing effective strategies to reduce the negative impact of ADHD and reduce the associated private and social costs.

In this book, the impact of ADHD on private and social costs has been investigated using data from the Danish National Registers. Two clinical groups were explored: (i) a group of individuals who received a diagnosis of ADHD in adulthood within the secondary hospital-based health-care system in Denmark, but who had not received a diagnosis in childhood, referred to as **diagnosed adults** or DA, and (ii) a second group of individuals who were prescribed ADHD medications in adulthood in the primary health-care sector but had never been prescribed ADHD medications in childhood, referred to as **prescribed adults** or **PA**.

Previous chapters have explored these two clinical groups in detail. The two groups that focus on adults with ADHD have been compared to a number of different control groups, systematically testing and controlling for potential biases and extraneous effects resulting from demographic and familial factors. One control group consists of non-ADHD siblings, and the results obtained from a comparison of adults with ADHD and their non-ADHD siblings are the closest estimate to date of the true economic costs of ADHD on both the individual and the state.

The results demonstrate that with respect to a large group of performance measures grouped around occupational status, income and public transfers, crime and traffic accidents, childhood outcomes, family situation, and health measures, the group of diagnosed adults is associated with greater costs than prescribed adults. In turn, both groups of individuals with ADHD have considerably higher costs than non-ADHD controls even when extensive matching to control for demographic and family variables has been employed. We will here attempt to summarize each area of investigation in turn.

11.1.1 *Employment, Income, and Tax Contributions*

Our findings demonstrate the considerable impact of ADHD on employment, income, and therefore tax contributions. Compared to adults in the general population, adults with ADHD experience much lower levels of employment and considerably lower levels of wage income. Some income loss is compensated for through income transfers and lower tax contributions. However, income transfers and lower tax contributions lead to increased expenditures and less revenue for the public sector. The striking differences in employment levels, income, and tax contribution remain even when demographic and parental variables were controlled for, demonstrating that the low levels of employment and income experienced by adults with ADHD are not due entirely to demographic and familial variables.

When considering the absolute cost differences on employment, income, and tax compared to the general adult population, it can be seen that adults with ADHD in the DA group earned on average 21,600 euros less and that adults with ADHD in the PA group earned 19,400 less. This in turn leads to lower tax contributions of 9,000 euros for the DA group and 8,100 euros for the PA group. Looking at the findings from the sibling-control analysis, which controls for demographic and family influences, the cost differences are still considerable, with adults with ADHD earning roughly 14,200 euros less per year and paying 3,500 euros less in income taxes than their sibling controls.

In numeric terms, these numbers constitute a very large share of the total costs of ADHD, and the issue concerning employment and labour-market performance of individuals with ADHD are thus of high importance.

These findings are interesting but not unexpected. ADHD is associated with work-related problems in adulthood, such as lower occupational status (Mannuzza and Klein, 2000), less job stability (Murphy and Barkley, 1996), and an increased number of days absent from work in comparison to adults without ADHD (Secnik et al., 2005). A recent literature review on the impact of ADHD on occupational achievement by Adamou et al. (2013) concluded that adults with ADHD experience impairment in all aspects related to employment, from the initial job search, to the interview, and further on in employment. Adamou et al. (2013) highlight that some adults with ADHD find functional employment that masks organizational problems (e.g. where they have good secretarial or administrative support), or select jobs that complement their symptoms (e.g. highly creative work or sports). Nevertheless, most skilled and unskilled occupations (e.g. administration posts) will be hampered by symptoms of inattention, impulsivity, and hyperactivity.

While thirty years ago individuals with low levels of educational attainment could find a variety of low-skilled jobs involving outdoor working and low levels of concentration, now most low-skills jobs involve indoor working, sustained concentration, and interaction with the general public (for example, in call centres). Many of these low-skilled jobs may be unsuitable for some individuals with ADHD, which may help to explain the low level of employment in our study.

Both the results of our study and the wider scientific literature highlight the difficulties that adults with ADHD experience with gaining and maintaining employment (Adamou et al., 2013). There may indeed be many reasons for the barriers to employment for adults with ADHD, and it may be possible to develop effective training or retraining opportunities and employment schemes to prevent the early retirement of adults with ADHD. Such schemes could allow these individuals to become productive members of the workforce. However, research has not been carried out to investigate this area systematically. A recent consensus statement addressing occupational issues for adults with ADHD concluded that there is a lack of research on the topic of employment of adults with ADHD and, in general, a lack of understanding of how to address the occupational needs of adults with ADHD (Adamou et al., 2013).

RECOMMENDATIONS
- The occupational functioning of adults with ADHD should be explored. There is a need for an informed understanding of possible barriers to

employment for adults with ADHD, but also of the mediating factors that may lead to successful employment.

- The best ways to address the vocational needs of individuals with ADHD and so increase employability and improve occupational achievement should be investigated, in order to facilitate the development of effective employment schemes (see Adamou et al., 2013).

11.1.2 *Educational Attainment*

The very negative impact of ADHD on academic attainment in reality means that the majority of individuals with ADHD are going to be consigned to low incomes for their entire lifetime. Our results have highlighted the considerable impact of ADHD on educational attainment, both in terms of the highest level of education achieved and the grades achieved for core subjects, when compared with the average Danish citizen. The striking differences in educational attainment remain even when demographic and parental variables were controlled for, demonstrating that the lower levels of educational attainment experienced by adults with ADHD cannot be explained by differences in demographic and familial variables. Therefore, the impact of ADHD on educational attainment warrants considerable early investment. Regardless of the personal difficulties associated with poor school performance, or fewer years of education, studies have estimated that every additional year spent in education above the compulsory age of education provides 5–6 per cent in additional income per year (Hanushek et al., 2013; Harmon et al., 2003). Thus, the fewer years in education is presumably an important explanatory factor for the huge deficits in work income, and thus lower tax returns to society, that we observe.

The impact of adult ADHD on educational attainment is not surprising, but the magnitude of the difference demonstrated in this study is striking (see Chapters 7 and 8). Considerable evidence has demonstrated the impact of ADHD on educational attainment (DuPaul, 2007; Kuriyan et al., 2013). The first issue is school-readiness. Most children with ADHD do not enter school with the core skills necessary for their education. They lack the concentration skills necessary to engage successfully in lessons, and have levels of impulsivity and hyperactivity that make managing the child in the classroom difficult (Daley, 2006; Tarver, Daley, and Sayal, 2014). School-related difficulties in the primary school years include disruptive classroom behaviour and academic underperformance, including poor scores on standardized tests of achievement (Frazier et al., 2007). These difficulties continue into adulthood and have been demonstrated on both estimates of academic achievement as well as actual exam performance (Birchwood and Daley, 2012). Longitudinal studies have demonstrated that the association between ADHD and academic achievement is mediated by performance in the classroom, homework achievement, as well as behavioural difficulties (Langberg et al., 2011; Rapport et al., 1999).

The serious consequences of ADHD in childhood and adulthood in terms of educational attainment and functional outcomes have led researchers to suggest that early recognition and intervention for ADHD and comorbid mental disorders are of importance to improve the long-term outcome for individuals with ADHD (Fredriksen et al., 2014). Given the considerable evidence demonstrating the impact of ADHD on education (Daley and Birchwood, 2010) and the direct and indirect costs that can be attributed to the impact of ADHD on educational attainment, consideration of the impact of ADHD in Danish schools and colleges is of paramount importance.

RECOMMENDATIONS
- Ways to ensure school-readiness are important to secure a positive developmental pathway for children with early symptoms of ADHD.
- There is a lack of research that evaluates the efficacy of specific teacher-led intervention techniques and evidence-based school intervention programmes that can help support students with ADHD. Informed strategies to support and develop students with ADHD to increase educational attainment and educational performance should be investigated.

11.1.3 *Crime and Driving*

Results from this study have demonstrated that adults with ADHD commit more crimes and driving offences than the Danish average, and also commit more crimes and driving offences than their sibling controls. When we consider the absolute cost differences, we see that these crimes and driving offences cost considerably more than the Danish average, with estimated victim cost differences of 14 million euros, crime cost differences of 9 million euros, and traffic-accident cost differences of 17 million euros per year. When we consider the cost differences for adults with ADHD against their sibling controls, the cost differences are estimated to be as follows: victim costs of 8 million euros; crime costs of 6 million euros; and traffic-accident costs of 11 million euros per year. Again, these results are not surprising. A recent Danish study (Dalsgaard et al., 2013) followed a cohort of children who received a diagnosis of ADHD and reported that 47 per cent of the sample had received a criminal conviction in adulthood. A recent Swedish study of adults with ADHD found that treatment with methylphenidate significantly reduced the risk of criminality (Lichtenstein et al., 2012). In the present study it was found that individuals with ADHD were also more likely to be the victims of crime. Whilst ADHD symptoms including impulsive behaviour and inattention may contribute to becoming the victim of impulsive crimes committed by others, it is also likely that the relationship between ADHD symptoms and offending may well be explained indirectly by comorbid factors (Gudjonsson et al., 2014), including comorbid substance abuse. This is supported by results in Chapter 7, which show that differences in crime rates are reduced by approximately one-third, but still remain high, when comorbidity is controlled for.

The finding that adults with ADHD also commit more traffic crimes is equally unsurprising, as studies have shown that adults with ADHD are more likely to have traffic accidents (Vaa, 2005; Jerome et al., 2006). These risks are then compounded by the fact that adults with ADHD drive more frequently than adults without ADHD, which means that their poor driving skills represent a greater road-safety threat (Vaa, 2014).

RECOMMENDATIONS
- The impact of ADHD on crime is not fully understood. The best ways to identify and treat ADHD symptoms in the prison population and in young offenders to reduce crime should be explored in order to prevent the cycle of reoffending and the high costs attributed to the judicial and prison systems.
- In order to reduce traffic offences, adults with ADHD should be made more aware of the potential impact of their ADHD symptoms on driving performance.

11.1.4 *Health-Care Utilization*

This book has demonstrated that adults with ADHD use more health-care services than the Danish average, and also use more health-care services than their sibling controls. When we examine the yearly cost differences for health-care utilization and prescription medicine, adults with ADHD cost approximately 1,500 euros per person per year more than the Danish average, and a similar amount more than their sibling controls.

Again our findings are in line with previous research showing high levels of health-care utilization among individuals with ADHD. Pelham et al. (2007) estimated the economic burden of ADHD within the US and described costs for health-care utilization as large and comparable in magnitude to other serious medical and mental-health problems in both children and adults. Less is known about what determines the health-care utilization differences. Some of these differences can be attributed to assessment and treatments related to ADHD (Doshi et al., 2012) and some from accidents that result from inattention and impulsivity (Lange et al., 2014); other health-care usage may arise from common health-care problems associated with ADHD, as well as for other mental-health difficulties that may arise as a result of ADHD. It is not clear whether the extra health-care utilization of these individuals is higher or lower than the optimal. It may, in fact, be that further health-care utilization can lead to improvements in other areas.

RECOMMENDATIONS

- Early intervention (i.e., the identification and treatment of mental-health problems as early as possible) is currently a focus of international concern (McGorry, 2013; Collins, 2010; Patel et al., 2013). The potential value of early intervention as a way of optimizing development and outcomes in ADHD is not fully understood and needs further investigation. The benefits of early identification and intervention for ADHD should be investigated in order to improve the developmental trajectories in ADHD (Sonuga-Barke and Halperin, 2010; Halperin, Bédard, and Curchack-Lichtin, 2012).

- The relationship between ADHD and increased health-care utilization is not fully understood and warrants further research. Research should inform the development of management approaches to improve health-care outcomes for individuals with ADHD and reduce the burden of care (see also Kawatkar et al., 2014).

- The role of impulsivity and inattention in the aetiology of other serious psychiatric difficulties (e.g. adolescent self-harm) is not understood. It may be useful to investigate how the alleviation of core ADHD symptoms may improve co-occuring psychiatric conditions of ADHD in order to improve health-care outcomes and reduce the burden of care.

11.1.5 *Impact on the Family*

ADHD is a disorder that impacts not only the individual but also their family. This is evident from the findings of this study, which demonstrate considerable expenditures on preventive measures and respite/foster care for adults with ADHD, compared to both the Danish average and their sibling controls. When we examine the cost differences for family-related expenditure, adults with ADHD cost about 1000 euros more per year than the Danish average, and about 600 euros per year more than their sibling controls. However, as we examine an adult only population, this rather low level of direct costs is to be expected. Yet our findings also show that individuals with ADHD are more likely to have been placed away from home or been in receipt of preventive measures as a child.

ADHD is a complex neurodevelopmental disorder with a social context. It is associated with social disadvantage (Russell et al., 2014; Nigg and Craver, 2014). Children with ADHD have an impact on their parents and families, and vice versa. Parents of children with ADHD experience more parenting stress—and severity of ADHD symptoms is associated with parenting stress (Theule et al., 2013). Adverse family environments and parenting practices are commonly observed in families of children with ADHD (Hinshaw 2002; Johnston and Mash 2001). However, the extent to which such parenting practices are causal factors in the development of ADHD, or rather responses to negative child behaviour remains unclear. Longitudinal evidence exploring the temporal relationship between parenting and ADHD is beginning to emerge but thus far has produced relatively mixed findings (Lifford et al., 2008; Keown, 2012). It is most likely that the relationship between parenting and child behaviour is bidirectional, and parents respond to genetically determined negative child behaviour in a way that serves to maintain or exacerbate the child's behaviour (Johnston and Jassy, 2007). Supporting and encouraging parents to engage in supportive and proactive parenting therefore has the potential to interrupt risk pathways (Sonuga-Barke et al., 2005). Additionally, parenting may also be an important factor contributing to other areas of functioning that are commonly suboptimal in ADHD, including oppositional behaviour and academic, social, and cognitive functioning (Deault, 2010; Hughes and Ensor, 2009).

RECOMMENDATIONS
- The best ways to support families of children and young people with ADHD should be identified in order to support family stability and help reduce expenditure on preventive measures and respite/foster care.
- The provision of psycho-education and parent and teacher-based interventions should be considered. International evidence highlights the relative effectiveness of self-help and online interventions (Daley and O'Brien, 2013), and these may provide acceptable cost-effective solutions.

11.1.6 *Comorbidity*

This study found a considerable degree of comorbidity associated with a diagnosis of ADHD. Adults in the DA group were found to have an average of 4.3 different psychiatric diagnoses compared with an average of 1.8 diagnoses for the PA group and 0.3 diagnoses for the rest of the population. Secondly, the number of comorbid diagnoses related to substance abuse is particularly large for the DA group (see Chapter 4). At the same time, negative life events (e.g. offending, unemployment, low educational attainment, family break-up) were considerably more prominent for adults with ADHD.

These results are supported by existing findings in the literature, showing that approximately 70–80 per cent of adult patients with ADHD have at least one comorbid disorder (Kessler et al., 2006). Thus, individuals with ADHD suffer significantly more often from other psychiatric disorders and are, furthermore, impaired in several areas of psychosocial functioning (Sobanski, 2006). Together, increased comorbidity, functional impairment, and negative life events significantly burden the life of adults with ADHD (Garcia et al., 2012), a conclusion that is supported by the findings outlined in this book.

RECOMMENDATIONS
- The best ways to identify and manage ADHD in the context of substance-abuse disorders should be investigated to ensure that effective treatment approaches are available for this group of individuals. The benefits of recently published guidelines for the diagnosis and treatment of ADHD in adults with substance-abuse disorders can be explored (Matthys et al., 2014).
- Ways to increase access to mental-health care for children and adolescents with or at risk of ADHD should be investigated to help prevent the development of associated negative conditions and life events for individuals with ADHD.
- Professionals working in adult mental health, and health services generally, often remain unaware about the clinical presentation and the consequences of ADHD in adults (Kooij et al., 2010; Kawatkar, 2014). This includes the recognition of ADHD in the context of substance abuse and as a comorbid disorder associated with other mental-health disorders (e.g. depression and anxiety). Increasing awareness of ADHD among adult clinicians will therefore be important.

11.2 Comparison of Results to Related Literature

In this section we discuss the current status of cost analyses of ADHD and compare these to the findings of the present study. First, we will discuss the current status of cost analyses of ADHD. Most studies have investigated the cost of ADHD based on child and adolescent cases, but a few have been conducted on the basis of ADHD in adults. Two recent reviews have summarized findings in the US and Europe, respectively. Doshi et al. (2012) include a systematic review of US-based cost studies of ADHD, and found that adult costs are significantly higher than childhood costs, since income and productivity losses are large for adults. The Doshi review reports a total cost of ADHD in the US of USD 143–266 billion (in 2010 prices), which is roughly 1–2 per cent of GDP. These costs are somewhat higher than the costs presented in the current study. However, total costs have been calculated by multiplying individual costs of ADHD by estimated prevalence rates in *the full population*. The present study, however, calculates costs based on the observed prevalence rate in the adult population, which is much lower. This difference implies that the reported adult costs in the Doshi review do not distinguish between individuals diagnosed as children and individuals diagnosed as adults. Looking closer at the adult costs, Doshi et al. (2012) report productivity losses of USD 87–138 billion out of total adult cost of USD 105–194 billion. Consistent with the findings from our study, these results indicate that productivity and income losses are the main contributing factors to the total cost of ADHD.

Le et al. (2014) conducted a systematic review of cost-of-illness studies for ADHD in childhood and adolescence in Europe. Using a similar methodology to that of Doshi et al. (2012), individual costs were collected from seven studies and used to calculate total annual costs of ADHD. The study used the Netherlands as a reference point, and the total national costs of ADHD were estimated. However, this analysis was limited to ADHD in children and adolescents and did not identify the productivity losses related to adult ADHD. The total estimated costs for the Netherlands were 1041–1529 million euros.

Hodgkins et al. (2011), conducted a cost-of-illness study for adult ADHD using health-care and employment-related costs. They compared adults with ADHD to two control groups. The first control group consisted of adults without ADHD and the second control group consisted of individuals diagnosed with depression. Using health-care claim databases they found that ADHD was associated with higher health-care costs than the non-ADHD control group, but smaller costs than the depression control group. With respect to labour-market losses they found no difference in the total costs between individuals with ADHD and non-ADHD individuals, which may be explained by the study's use of health insurance databases, which contain mainly individuals who are employed.

Kotsopoulos et al. (2013) estimated the fiscal consequences of ADHD in Germany, using differences in educational attainment between individuals with and without to link to labour-market earnings and income-tax payments. It was found that the lifetime net tax revenue for a non-ADHD individual was approximately 80,000 euros higher compared to an individual with untreated ADHD. However, as the Kotsopoulos study did not estimate yearly costs, these results are not directly comparable to the findings of the present study.

Finally, Fletcher (2014) explored the impact of childhood ADHD on adult labour-market outcomes using a school-based, longitudinal study of the health-related behaviours of adolescents and their outcomes in young adulthood. The findings showed that childhood ADHD reduced adult employment by approximately 10 percentage points, reduced earnings by 33 per cent, and increased social-assistance receipts by 15 points.

11.2.1 Comparison of Present Study Results and Findings in the Literature

In this subsection, we perform back-of-the-envelope calculations to investigate the aggregate costs of ADHD diagnosed in adulthood across countries. In Table 11.1, we have calculated the aggregate costs of ADHD for five countries in addition to Denmark. These are Canada, France, the Netherlands, the US, and the UK. The calculations are carried out by simply taking the individual cost of ADHD and multiplying this by the prevalence rate of ADHD and by the country's population in the age group between 18 and 50 years.

The aggregate costs presented in Table 11.1 vary for three reasons. First, the costs vary across countries due to different magnitude of the adult population. Second, the costs vary across applied prevalence rates. Third, the costs vary across applied individual costs. These results are presented to put the findings from the literature outlined above into perspective.

It was reported above that Doshi et al. (2012) calculated total costs on the basis of individual costs and estimated prevalence rates which resulted in an estimated total cost of ADHD at a magnitude of USD 105–194 billion. Using the estimated prevalence rate of Simon et al. (2009), i.e. 2.5% we estimate a total cost of almost 84 billion euros. Using an average USD/EUR exchange rate of 1.27, this aggregate cost amounts to USD 107 billion, which is within the same range reported in Doshi et al. (2012).

Table 11.1. Aggregate social cost for ADHD individuals for different countries, EUR millions

		Canada	Denmark	France	Netherlands	United Kingdom	United States
Prevalence rate from:		Cost estimates from sibling analysis					
Present study	0.8%	2,183	337	3,959	1,044	4,033	19,796
Simon et al. (2009)	2.5%	6,643	1,027	12,045	3,175	12,270	60,233
		Cost estimates from analysis using general population					
Present study	0.8%	3,041	470	5,515	1,454	5,618	27,577
Simon et al. (2009)	2.5%	9,254	1,431	16,780	4,424	17,093	83,909
Population (18–49 years)		14,953,601	2,311,645	27,114,916	7,148,383	27,621,979	135,592,181

Source: Based on cost estimates from Table 10.1 and Table 10.3; the prevalence rate found in this study from 18,993 individuals with ADHD diagnosed in adulthood—corresponding to 0.8%—and country-specific population in the age group 18–50 years. The latter data stem from US Census, international database. In addition to our own calculated prevalence rate, the rate from Simon et al. (2009) of 2.5% is applied.

Another observation is that the total costs calculated for the Netherlands in Le et al. (2014) are low compared to our measure of 4.4 billion euros determined using the prevalence rate estimate of Simon et al. (2009) and the general population as the control group. However, it should be kept in mind that the study by Le et al. (2014) was based on children and adolescents with ADHD. As a consequence, it did not identify productivity losses related to adult ADHD.

The results in Table 11.1 are of interest because the presented total cost estimates across different countries may provide a better impression of the magnitude of the obtained results for Denmark. Even though these are back-of-an-envelope calculations, they are of interest because they fit well with cost estimates presented in the ADHD literature.

Although the results presented in Table 11.1 are interesting, it is of course courageous—some might say preposterous—to base cost calculations for many countries on Danish cost estimates only. We will discuss this issue of generalizability in Section 11.3 and highlight the extent to which results can indeed be applied to contexts outside Denmark by providing a qualitative discussion of the robustness of the results in Table 11.1. But, for now, we maintain that even though the results are uncertain, they nevertheless present interesting information.

11.2.2 Comparing Costs of ADHD to Other Illnesses

A brief illustration of cost-of-illness analyses for certain other illnesses may offer an impression of the relative costs of ADHD. The studies mentioned below are highlighted for the purpose of comparison only.

The total social cost of arthritis in Denmark was estimated at 900 million euros in a recent calculation, but arthritis is estimated to affect 17 per cent of the population, whereas the prevalence rate for ADHD is much smaller (Johnsen et al., 2014; Polanczyk et al., 2007). Specifically, the present study estimated the total cost of adult ADHD to be 340–470 million euros for an observed prevalence rate of 0.8 per cent.

Luppa et al. (2007) conducted a systematic review of costs associated with depression. A total of twenty-four studies from different countries were included, and it was found that the total direct and indirect costs of depression were in the range of USD 3000–6200 per individual per year. When mortality costs were included (an aspect that has not been included in the present study), the total costs per individual increased by USD 200–400. The costs for depression are thereby much lower than the costs of ADHD estimated by the present study of 18,000–25,000 euros per individual—equivalent to 23,000–32,000 USD using an average USD/EUR exchange rate of 1.27.

Other relevant studies include those of Sado et al. (2013) and Ng et al. (2014). Sado et al. (2013) estimated the total costs of schizophrenia in Japan at USD 23.8 billion in 2008, which corresponded to 0.5 per cent of GDP. Their analysis included health care, medication, productivity losses, and mortality costs. They did not, however, include costs of crime or traffic accidents. Ng et al. (2014) conducted a systematic review of cost-of-illness studies of diabetes mellitus, including a total of thirty studies from different countries. Average annual direct costs ranged from USD 130 to USD 14,000 per patient, and the indirect costs exhibited a similarly wide range. The highest costs were found for the US.

In light of these studies, our estimates of the costs of adult ADHD appear large compared to other cost-of-illness studies that have looked at individual data. Also, the total costs are small in our study, primarily because of the relatively low observed prevalence rate. However, due to different methods and different data sources, direct comparison of the studies is difficult and should be done with caution.

11.3 Generalizability Beyond Denmark

This study is based on analyses of data from identified groups of the Danish population with or without ADHD. It therefore seems reasonable to question whether the results outlined in this book are specific to Denmark, or whether it is indeed possible to generalize the results to other countries. The present section attempts to answer these very important questions by extending the quantitative evaluation in the previous section with some more qualitative answers. More precisely, we provide a brief overview of the Danish welfare system and highlight some of the methodological difficulties involved in generalizing cost analyses performed in one country across to different countries. The extent to which this study has managed these methodological challenges is then discussed.

11.3.1 *Denmark as a Welfare State: Some Basic Facts*

Denmark is a small, high-income country. It has a high population density and demographic development similar to other western European countries. Denmark has a parliamentary democracy and a long tradition of social welfare (Olejaz et al., 2012). For example, legislation provides residents with the right to equal access to health care and education. Finances for public services are derived through state incomes from a number of different sources, including personal income tax payable on wages and almost all other forms of income (Olejaz et al., 2012).

Danish welfare legislation is based on the principle that all residents are guaranteed rights and support in the event of unemployment, sickness, or dependency. Social-security benefits and social services are available to residents in need, regardless of their attachment to the labour market. Areas such as health and education have traditionally received high priority in Denmark. Danish health-care expenditure both as a percentage of gross domestic product (GDP) and per capita is higher than the average for EU15 countries.[1] By way of comparison, the health-care expenditure in Denmark is 9.9 per cent of GDP or USD 3630 per capita, whereas health-care expenditure in the UK is 9.0 per cent of GPD or USD 3230 per capita according to 2011 figures from the WHO Regional Office for Europe (Olejaz et al., 2012). In terms of education, the OECD report 'Education at a Glance: 2014' shows that education expenditure is a high public priority in Denmark. On average OECD countries use 6.1 per cent of their GDP on education, whereas in Denmark the figure is 7.9 per cent (OECD, 2014). In terms of investment at the elementary education level, Denmark ranks eighth on expenditure out of the thirty-three OECD countries involved in the OECD analysis.

11.3.2 *General Methodological Challenges in Comparing Public-Service Systems*

The above description of the welfare state gives a few examples of how Denmark differs from other countries in terms of public expenditure and how it spends more on areas such as health care and education. This may lead to the obvious conclusion that the measures of outcomes in the present study cannot easily be generalized to other countries, as the outcomes used are clearly different compared to other countries. This is a fair point. The present analysis has indeed evaluated a vast range of social and private outcomes for adults with ADHD in the same study, including health, education, income transfers, crime, prison services, and so on. The range of outcomes assessed is in itself unprecedented in the current economic literature on ADHD. Yet, this broad range of outcomes clearly also complicates comparisons of overall findings to other countries, as health-care systems, prison systems, education systems, and what defines them vary considerably.

It is beyond the scope of this book to provide a comprehensive comparison of social and private outcomes between countries. And while it is not our aim to present an extensive review of the complexities involved in comparing

---

[1] EU15 countries consist of Austria, Belgium, Denmark, Finland, France, Germany, Greece, Ireland, Italy, Luxembourg, the Netherlands, Portugal, Spain, Sweden, and the United Kingdom.

such outcomes, this discussion does warrant a brief summary of some of the methodological challenges involved in generalizing the present findings to other countries. These are:

Differences in definitions of systems between countries: There is considerable variation in the definition of health care between countries. A service that is classified as health care in one country may constitute social services in another. For example, occupational-health services may be financed by health services in some countries, whereas in other countries the same services may be provided by social services (Schoitz et al., 2010). And in the US, health-care costs and services do not include psychiatry, whereas in Denmark and the UK psychiatry is embedded in the classification of health care (Søgaard, Frølich, and Krasnik, 2011). Thus, the cost of health care for adults with ADHD, who utilize psychiatric services more frequently, will be different across countries depending on whether psychiatric services are part of the overall definition of health care or not.

Availability of data: The Danish registers contain a plethora of different data. But the data is not entered according to a priori research hypotheses. Rather, researchers form hypotheses and are able to access existing data in the registers to confirm or refute their hypotheses. Thus, there may be outcomes crucial to calculating the costs of ADHD that are simply not available. One such example is outcomes related to certain aspects of community mental-health care. Yet, reliable registers containing community-care services from local municipalities are currently not available. Not only may this lead to an underestimate in costings, but it may also lead to a minor misrepresentation of service use in Denmark. This example illustrates that the cost estimates presented in this book may be underestimated for areas where data availability has inadequate coverage. Such underestimates will of course also carry over to other countries when Danish estimates are applied to other countries.

11.3.3 *Managing the Challenges*

We are confident that the rigorous approach that we have applied to the very detailed data available from the Danish national registers has provided results that apply not only in a Danish context but also internationally. To some degree this has been documented in Table 11.1. In addition to this, the use of sibling data to create cost differences helps to control for many differences between the Danish systems of health, social care, education, employment, and social services and those of other countries.

We argue that the remaining differences between Denmark and other countries will not lead to higher social costs. However, there will most likely be different allocation of costs to the private and public cost categories. In the following paragraphs we discuss these differences:

- **Labour market**: The Danish labour market is characterized by relatively high earnings at the bottom of the income distribution and a relatively compressed wage distribution, such that the difference between the top earners and bottom earners is smaller in Denmark than in most other Western countries. Also, a relatively large share of the labour force is employed in the public sector, as education and health care constitute public-sector services. In relation to the labour-market performance of individuals with ADHD, this means that it is probably harder to gain entry into the labour market, since very few low-wage jobs exist. If individuals with an ADHD diagnosis have lower productivity than other individuals (with the same formal qualifications) then that may lead to difficulties in finding ordinary employment in a labour market with inflexible wage rates. Combined with generous welfare-state income transfers, the implications for our study are most likely that the difference in employment rates between individuals with ADHD and the various control groups may be larger in Denmark than would be expected in other countries. These Danish labour-market characteristics may well have two opposite effects on costs. On the one hand, a lower employment rate of individuals with ADHD will increase the costs of ADHD. On the other hand, individuals with ADHD in employment will receive a higher wage income in Denmark compared to other countries—an effect that reduces costs on ADHD in Denmark. Although the net effect of an inflexible wage on ADHD costs is unclear, we expect the effect of the employment rate to dominate, implying that the labour market will have higher costs of ADHD in Denmark.

- **Education**: In Denmark, education is free and on top of this education grants are the highest in the world. Hence, even though the educational attainment of individuals with ADHD is poor, it may be even poorer in countries where students have to pay tuition fees and take out loans to finance their studies. In addition to this, Denmark has a well-developed apprenticeship system embedded in the state education system. These elements may well imply that individuals with ADHD are relatively well-educated and supported in education compared to other countries, which thereby leads to relatively low private costs of ADHD in Denmark.

- **Income transfers**: One important difference between Denmark and other countries is that income transfers from the state to individuals are relatively generous. This may well imply that the Danish state has to cover a larger share of total social costs compared to other countries. The flip side is, of course, that individuals with ADHD have to cover a lower cost share.

As a consequence, the private costs of ADHD may well be higher in other countries, whereas the public costs may be lower.

- **Differences in diagnostic systems and practices**: There are some differences in the practices of psychiatric clinics in Denmark that may impact on costs. For example, in Denmark, in line with the majority of European countries, the ICD-10 protocol is used for the diagnosis of mental-health disorders, including ADHD. The ICD-10 criteria for ADHD represent a more stringent set of symptoms than the DSM-5, which is widely used in the US and South America, for example. The groups of individuals identified through the Danish registers may as a consequence be expected to represent a group of individuals carrying more severe ADHD symptoms than a group of individuals with ADHD identified in a country where the DSM-5 is employed (see Polanczyk et al., 2007; Polanczyk et al., 2014). More severe ADHD symptomatology may result in greater functional impairment. Hence, a group of individuals diagnosed with ADHD using the ICD-10 may carry higher private and social costs per individual. However, the number of individuals with an ADHD diagnosis will be lower, which implies that the aggregate costs will be lower than if DSM-5 were used.

- **Costs and financing of prescription medication**: Prescriptions in Denmark are not part of the free Danish health-care system, and citizens pay a certain part of medication costs. Individuals with ADHD may be eligible for subsidies for their ADHD medication by way of application through the Danish Department of Health or social services. However, the extent to which prescriptions are actually purchased may depend on personal finances. In countries where medication costs are fully covered, individuals may pick up prescriptions more regularly. Differences in public health-care coverage and subsidies between countries will create different estimates in terms of health-care costs. In the present application for Denmark, an effect from not fully covered medication costs is expected to result in a lower number of individuals with ADHD identified through their purchase of ADHD medication, and thereby an underestimation of aggregate costs for ADHD.

The Danish welfare state is in many respects different from other countries. Yet, we have attempted to estimate the costs of ADHD for other countries, including the UK and the US, based on the results of the present study. The quantitative findings were presented in Table 11.1 in the previous section, whereas a more qualitative-based approach has been taken to discuss generalizability beyond Denmark in this section. While robust cost estimation on ADHD patient samples exists especially for the US (Doshi et al., 2012), no studies to date have controlled for family and environmental influences on costs in the form of the robust controls applied in this study. Even so, when we apply our Danish costs in the calculations of back-of-the-envelope estimates we find aggregate ADHD costs for the US to be of the same magnitude as those found in Doshi et al. (2012). Consequently, we believe that our cost estimates for Denmark—especially total social costs per individual—can be used for calculating conservative estimates of aggregate social costs of ADHD for other countries.

11.4 Limitations and Strengths of the Study

In this final section, we stress that there are important limitations to the analysis that readers should keep in mind. The most important ones are:

The applied cost measure: This measure only includes measurable financial costs in terms of lower income, transfer income, costs to medication, etc. The measure does *not* include *indirect* costs related to ADHD such as the financial costs for the impact on spouse, children, and parents of an adult with ADHD, for example costs of a relative's or carer's sick leave, or the costs of being the victim of a crime committed by an adult with ADHD. Nor does the cost measure include an estimate of any emotional costs related to ADHD.

The applied cross-sectional cost analysis: The measure does not give a full picture of costs over time. As described in Section 10.2, we have chosen to use a cross-sectional method, because this method makes the best use of data and because the group of adults with ADHD is simply not mature enough to make good life-cycle estimates. This choice implies that the obtained estimates represent a 'snapshot of a moment in time' and may not be a good estimate of costs in future years. This would, for example, be the case if costs are expected to change dramatically as a population ages. Moreover, the costs cannot be attributed to a representative individual over the course of their life and do not answer the question 'What will be the total cost for an average individual over the entire lifespan?' Instead the question that is answered is 'What is the (yearly) ADHD cost for the current population?'

Limitations of register data analysis: A final comment to the analysis performed in this book should be mentioned: Danish registers have limitations which are important to note. These include the following: data collected are not research-led, which means that essential information for specific analyses may be missing; variation in coding between clinicians and institutions (discussed in Chapter 3) may led to variation in data quality; it is often difficult to understand and manage missing information. (See Thygesen and Ersbøll, 2014 for comprehensive discussion of the strengths and limitations of register-based research.)

On the other hand, there is also considerable strengths in register-based studies including the following: the data are already collected and provide a very large sample size; there is limited/no selection bias; the available information of exposures and outcomes for a whole population is unique; the data are collected independently of research questions (see Thygesen and Ersbøll, 2014). Together, these methodological strengths make register-based studies extremely useful for a robust study of the social and private costs of ADHD.

References

Aboraya, A., Rankin, E., France, C., El-Missiry, A., and John, C. 2006, 'The reliability of psychiatric diagnosis revisited: The clinician's guide to improve the reliability of psychiatric diagnosis', *Psychiatry (Edgmont)*, vol. 3, no. 1, p. 41.

Adamou, M., Arif, M., Asherson, P., Aw, T.-C., Bolea, B., Coghill, D., Gudjónsson, G., Halmøy, A., Hodgkins, P., Müller, U., Pitts, M., Trakoli, A., Williams, N., and Young, S. 2013, 'Occupational issues of adults with ADHD', *BMC Psychiatry*, vol. 13, no. 1, p. 59.

American Psychiatric Association 1994, *Diagnostic and Statistical Manual of Mental Disorders*, 4th edn, Washington, DC, American Psychiatric Association.

American Psychiatric Association 2013, *Diagnostic and Statistical Manual of Mental Disorders*, 5th edn, Washington, DC, American Psychiatric Association.

Anastopoulos, A.D., Shelton, T.L., DuPaul, G.J., and Guevremont, D.C. 1993, 'Parent training for attention-deficit hyperactivity disorder: Its impact on parent functioning', *Journal of Abnormal Child Psychology*, vol. 21, no. 5, pp. 581–96.

Angrist, J.D. and Pischke, J. 2009, *Mostly Harmless Econometrics: An Empiricist's Companion*, Princeton, NJ, Princeton University Press.

Arngrim, T., Brødsgaard, M., Christiansen, P.B., Dalsgaard, S., Geoffroy, M.B., Jacobsen, T.B., Jørgensen, M.B., Warrer, T., Toft, T., and Warrer, T. 2013, *Retningslinjer for diagnostik og behandling af ADHD hos voksne*, Copenhagen, Dansk Psykiatrisk Selskab.

Baadsgaard, M. and Quitzau, J. 2011, 'Danish registers on personal income and transfer payments', *Scandinavian Journal of Public Health*, vol. 39, no. 7 Suppl, pp. 103–5.

Banaschewski, T., Brandeis, D., Heinrich, H., Albrecht, B., Brunner, E., and Rothenberger, A. 2003, 'Association of ADHD and conduct disorder—brain electrical evidence for the existence of a distinct subtype', *Journal of Child Psychology and Psychiatry*, vol. 44, no. 3, pp. 356–76.

Banerjee, T.D., Middleton, F., and Faraone, S.V. 2007, 'Environmental risk factors for attention-deficit hyperactivity disorder', *Acta Paediatrica*, vol. 96, no. 9, pp. 1269–74.

Barkley, R.A. 2002, 'Major life activity and health outcomes associated with attention-deficit/hyperactivity disorder', *Journal of Clinical Psychiatry*, vol. 63, suppl. 12, pp. 10–15.

Barkley, R.A., Fischer, M., Smallish, L., and Fletcher, K. 2002, 'The persistence of attention-deficit/hyperactivity disorder into young adulthood as a function of reporting source and definition of disorder', *Journal of Abnormal Psychology*, vol. 111, no. 2, pp. 279–89.

Barkley, R.A., Fischer, M., Smallish, L., and Fletcher, K. 2006, 'Young adult outcome of hyperactive children: adaptive functioning in major life activities', *Journal of the American Academy of Child and Adolescent Psychiatry*, vol. 45, no. 2, pp. 192–202.

Barry, T.D., Lyman, R.D., and Klinger, L.G. 2002, 'Academic underachievement and attention-deficit/hyperactivity disorder: The negative impact of symptom severity on school performance', *Journal of School Psychology*, vol. 40, no. 3, pp. 259–83.

Bateman, B., Warner, J.O., Hutchinson, E., Dean, T., Rowlandson, P., Gant, C., Grundy, J., Fitzgerald, C., and Stevenson, J. 2004, 'The effects of a double blind, placebo controlled, artificial food colourings and benzoate preservative challenge on hyperactivity in a general population sample of preschool children', *Archives of Disease in Childhood*, vol. 89, no. 6, pp. 506–11.

Biederman, J. 2005, 'Attention-deficit/hyperactivity disorder: a selective overview', *Biological Psychiatry*, vol. 57, no. 11, pp. 1215–20.

Biederman, J., Newcorn, J., and Sprich, S. 1991, 'Comorbidity of attention deficit hyperactivity disorder', *American Journal of Psychiatry*, vol. 148, no. 5, pp. 564–77.

Birchwood, J. and Daley, D. 2012, 'Brief report: The impact of Attention Deficit Hyperactivity Disorder (ADHD) symptoms on academic performance in an adolescent community sample', *Journal of Adolescence*, vol. 35, no. 1, pp. 225–31.

Bor, W., Sanders, M.R., and Markie-Dadds, C. 2002, 'The effects of the Triple P-Positive Parenting Program on preschool children with co-occurring disruptive behavior and attentional/hyperactive difficulties'. *Journal of Abnormal Child Psychology*, vol. 30, no. 6, pp. 571–87.

Børne- og Ungdomspsykiatrisk Selskab i Danmark (Society for Child and Adolescent Psychiatry) 2008, *Referenceprogram for udredning og behandling af børn og unge med ADHD*, Copenhagen, Børne- og Ungdomspsykiatrisk Selskab i Danmark.

Brookes, K., Xu, X., Chen, W., Zhou, K., Neale, B., Lowe, N., Anney, R., Franke, B., Gill, M., and Ebstein, R. 2006, 'The analysis of 51 genes in DSM-IV combined type attention deficit hyperactivity disorder: Association signals in DRD4, DAT1 and 16 other genes', *Molecular Psychiatry*, vol. 11, no. 10, pp. 934–53.

Busch, B., Biederman, J., Cohen, L.G., Sayer, J.M., Monuteaux, M.C., Mick, E., Zallen, B., and Faraone, S.V. 2002, 'Correlates of ADHD among children in pediatric and psychiatric clinics', *Psychiatric Services*, vol. 53, no. 9, pp. 1103–11.

Cartwright, K.L., Bitsakou, P., Daley, D., Gramzow, R.H., Psychogiou, L., Simonoff, E., Thompson, M.J., and Sonuga-Barke, E.J. 2011, 'Disentangling child and family influences on maternal expressed emotion toward children with attention-deficit/hyperactivity disorder', *Journal of the American Academy of Child and Adolescent Psychiatry*, vol. 50, no. 10, pp. 1042–53.

Chronis, A.M., Jones, H.A., and Raggi, V.L. 2006, 'Evidence-based psychosocial treatments for children and adolescents with attention-deficit/hyperactivity disorder', *Clinical Psychology Review*, vol. 26, no. 4, pp. 486–502.

Clabaugh, G. and Ward, M.M. 2008, 'Cost-of-illness studies in the United States: A systematic review of methodologies used for direct cost', *Value in Health*, vol. 11, no. 1, pp. 13–21.

Clark, M.L., Cheyne, J.A., Cunningham, C.E., and Siegel, L.S. 1988, 'Dyadic peer interaction and task orientation in attention-deficit-disordered children', *Journal of Abnormal Child Psychology*, vol. 16, no. 1, pp. 1–15.

Collins, F.S. 2010, 'Opportunities for research and NIH'. *Science*, vol. 327, no. 5961, pp. 36–7.

Connor, D.F., Steeber, J., and McBurnett, K. 2010, 'A review of attention-deficit/hyper-activity disorder complicated by symptoms of oppositional defiant disorder or conduct disorder', *Journal of Developmental and Behavioral Pediatrics*, vol. 31, no. 5, pp. 427–40.

Conners, C.K., March, J.S., Frances, A., Wells, K.C., and Ross, R. 2001, 'Treatment of attention deficit hyperactivity disorder: Expert consensus guidelines'. *Journal of Attention Disorders*, vol. 4, pp. 7–128.

Cook, E.H. Jr, Stein, M.A., Krasowski, M.D., Cox, N.J., Olkon, D.M., Kieffer, J.E., and Leventhal, B.L. 1995, 'Association of attention-deficit disorder and the dopamine transporter gene', *American Journal of Human Genetics*, vol. 56, no. 4, pp. 993–8.

Copeland, W.E., Adair, C.E., Smetanin, P., Stiff, D., Briante, C., Colman, I., Fergusson, D., Horwood, J., Poulton, R., and Costello, E.J. 2013, 'Diagnostic transitions from childhood to adolescence to early adulthood', *Journal of Child Psychology and Psychiatry*, vol. 54, no. 7, pp. 791–9.

Corkum, P., Moldofsky, H., Hogg-Johnson, S., Humphries, T., and Tannock, R. 1999, 'Sleep problems in children with Attention-Deficit/Hyperactivity Disorder: Impact of subtype, comorbidity, and stimulant medication', *Journal of the American Academy of Child and Adolescent Psychiatry*, vol. 38, no. 10, pp. 1285–93.

Costa, N., Derumeaux, H., Rapp, T., Garnault, V., Ferlicoq, L., Gillette, S., Andrieu, S., Vellas, B., Lamure, M., and Grand, A. 2012, 'Methodological considerations in cost of illness studies on Alzheimer disease', *Health Economics Review*, vol. 2, no. 1, pp. 1–12.

Cunningham, C.E., Bremner, R., and Boyle, M. 1995, 'Large group community-based parenting programs for families of preschoolers at risk for disruptive behaviour disorders: Utilization, cost effectiveness, and outcome', *Journal of Child Psychology and Psychiatry*, vol. 36, no. 7, pp. 1141–59.

Daley, D. 2006, 'Attention deficit hyperactivity disorder: A review of the essential facts', *Child: Care, Health and Development*, vol. 32, no. 2, pp. 193–204.

Daley, D. and Birchwood, J. 2010, 'ADHD and academic performance: Why does ADHD impact on academic performance and what can be done to support ADHD children in the classroom?', *Child: Care, Health and Development*, vol. 36, no. 4, pp. 455–64.

Daley, D., Jones, K., Hutchings, J., and Thompson, M. 2009, 'Attention deficit hyper-activity disorder in pre-school children: Current findings, recommended interventions and future directions', *Child: Care, Health and Development*, vol. 35, no. 6, pp. 754–66.

Daley, D. and O'Brien, M. 2013, 'A small-scale randomized controlled trial of the self-help version of the New Forest Parent Training Programme for children with ADHD symptoms', *European Child and Adolescent Psychiatry*, vol. 22, no. 9, pp. 543–52.

Daley, D., Sonuga-Barke, E.J., and Thompson, M. 2003, 'Assessing expressed emotion in mothers of preschool AD/HD children: Psychometric properties of a modified speech sample', *British Journal of Clinical Psychology*, vol. 42, no. 1, pp. 53–67.

Daley, D. and Thompson, M. 2007, 'Parent training for ADHD in preschool children', *Advances in ADHD*, vol. 2, no. 1, pp. 11–16.

Daley, D., Van der Oord, S., Ferrin, M., Danckaerts, M., Doepfner, M., Cortese, S., and Sonuga-Barke, E.J. (European ADHD Guidelines Group) 2014, 'Behavioral interventions in attention-deficit/hyperactivity disorder: A meta-analysis of randomized controlled trials across multiple outcome domains', *Journal of the American Academy of Child and Adolescent Psychiatry*, vol. 53, no. 8, pp. 835–47. e5.

Dalsgaard, S., Mortensen, P.B., Frydenberg, M., and Thomsen, P.H. 2013, 'Long-term criminal outcome of children with attention deficit hyperactivity disorder', *Criminal Behaviour and Mental Health*, vol. 23, no. 2, pp. 86–98.

Damm, O., Hodek, J.-M., and Greiner, W. 2009, 'Methodological standards for cost-of-illness studies using breast cancer, prostate cancer and colon cancer as an example', *Zeitschrift fur Evidenz, Fortbildung und Qualitat im Gesundheitswesen*, vol. 103, no. 6, pp. 305–18.

Danish Regions 2011, *The Regions—In brief*. Copenhagen, Danish Regions. Available as download at: <http://www.regioner.dk/~/media/Filer/Om%20regionerne/Regionerne%20-%20kort%20fortalt%202011%20-%20engelsk.ashx>.

Davé, S., Nazareth, I., Senior, R., and Sherr, L. 2008, 'A comparison of father and mother report of child behaviour on the strengths and difficulties questionnaire', *Child Psychiatry and Human Development*, vol. 39, no. 4, pp. 399–413.

Deault, L.C. 2010, 'A systematic review of parenting in relation to the development of comorbidities and functional impairments in children with attention-deficit/hyperactivity disorder (ADHD)', *Child Psychiatry and Human Development*, vol. 41, no. 2, pp. 168–92.

Deloitte 2012, *Analyse af kapaciteten i psykiatrien*, Copenhagen, Deloitte Consulting.

Diamantopoulou, S., Rydell, A., Thorell, L.B., and Bohlin, G. 2007, 'Impact of executive functioning and symptoms of attention deficit hyperactivity disorder on children's peer relations and school performance', *Developmental Neuropsychology*, vol. 32, no. 1, pp. 521–42.

Dinn, W.M., Robbins, N.C., and Harris, C.L. 2001, 'Adult attention-deficit/hyperactivity disorder: Neuropsychological correlates and clinical presentation', *Brain and Cognition*, vol. 46, no. 1, pp. 114–21.

Doshi, J.A., Hodgkins, P., Kahle, J., Sikirica, V., Cangelosi, M.J., Setyawan, J., Erder, M.H., and Neumann, P.J. 2012, 'Economic impact of childhood and adult attention-deficit/hyperactivity disorder in the United States', *Journal of the American Academy of Child and Adolescent Psychiatry*, vol. 51, no. 10, pp. 990–1002. e2.

Drummond, M. 1992, 'Cost-of-illness studies', *PharmacoEconomics*, vol. 2, no. 1, pp. 1–4.

DuPaul, G.J. 2007, 'School-based interventions for students with Attention Deficit Hyperactivity Disorder: Current status and future directions', *School Psychology Review*, vol. 36, no. 2, pp. 183–94.

DuPaul, G.J., McGoey, K.E., Eckert, T.L., and VanBrakle, J. 2001, 'Preschool children with attention-deficit/hyperactivity disorder: Impairments in behavioral, social, and school functioning', *Journal of the American Academy of Child and Adolescent Psychiatry*, vol. 40, no. 5, pp. 508–15.

DuPaul, G.J., Weyandt, L.L., and Janusis, G.M. 2011, 'ADHD in the classroom: Effective intervention strategies', *Theory into Practice*, vol. 50, no. 1, pp. 35–42.

Erhardt, D. and Baker, B.L. 1990, 'The effects of behavioral parent training on families with young hyperactive children', *Journal of Behavior Therapy and Experimental Psychiatry*, vol. 21, no. 2, pp. 121–32.

Faraone, S.V. 2000, 'Attention Deficit Hyperactivity Disorder in adults: Implications for theories of diagnosis', *Current Directions in Psychological Science*, vol. 9, no. 1, pp. 33–6.

Faraone, S.V., Doyle, A.E., Mick, E., and Biederman, J. 2001, 'Meta-analysis of the association between the 7-repeat allele of the dopamine D4 receptor gene and attention deficit hyperactivity disorder', *American Journal of Psychiatry*, vol. 158, no. 7, pp. 1052–7.

Faraone, S.V., Perlis, R.H., Doyle, A.E., Smoller, J.W., Goralnick, J.J., Holmgren, M.A., and Sklar, P. 2005, 'Molecular genetics of Attention-Deficit/Hyperactivity Disorder', *Biological Psychiatry*, vol. 57, no. 11, pp. 1313–23.

Faraone, S.V., Sergeant, J., Gillberg, C., and Biederman, J. 2003, 'The worldwide prevalence of ADHD: Is it an American condition?', *World Psychiatry: Official Journal of the World Psychiatric Association (WPA)*, vol. 2, no. 2, pp. 104–13.

Farrington, D.P., Loeber, R., and Van Kammen, W.B. 1990, 'Long-term criminal outcomes of hyperactivity-impulsivity-attention deficit and conduct problems in childhood', in Robins, L.N. and Rutter, M. (eds), *Straight and Devious Pathways from Childhood to Adulthood*, New York, Cambridge University Press, pp. 62–81.

Feingold, B.F. 1982, 'The role of diet in behaviour', *Ecology of Disease*, vol. 1, no. 2–3, pp. 153–65.

Fergusson, D.M., Horwood, L.J., and Lynskey, M.T. 1993, 'The effects of conduct disorder and attention deficit in middle childhood on offending and scholastic ability at age 13', *Journal of Child Psychology and Psychiatry*, vol. 34, no. 6, pp. 899–916.

Fischer, M., Barkley, R.A., Fletcher, K.E., and Smallish, L. 1993, 'The adolescent outcome of hyperactive children: Predictors of psychiatric, academic, social, and emotional adjustment', *Journal of the American Academy of Child and Adolescent Psychiatry*, vol. 32, no. 2, pp. 324–32.

Fletcher, J.M. 2014, 'The effects of childhood ADHD on adult labor market outcomes', *Health Economics*, vol. 23, no. 2, pp. 159–81.

Ford, T., Goodman, R., and Meltzer, H. 2003, 'The British Child and Adolescent Mental Health Survey 1999: The prevalence of DSM-IV disorders', *Journal of the American Academy of Child and Adolescent Psychiatry*, vol. 42, no. 10, pp. 1203–11.

Frazier, T.W., Youngstrom, E.A., Glutting, J.J., and Watkins, M.W. 2007, 'ADHD and achievement: Meta-analysis of the child, adolescent, and adult literatures and a concomitant study with college students', *Journal of Learning Disabilities*, vol. 40, no. 1, pp. 49–65.

Fredriksen, M., Dahl, A.A., Martinsen, E.W., Klungsoyr, O., Faraone, S.V., and Peleikis, D.E. 2014, 'Childhood and persistent ADHD symptoms associated with educational failure and long-term occupational disability in adult ADHD', *ADHD Attention Deficit and Hyperactivity Disorders*, vol. 6, no. 2, pp. 87–99.

Frick, P.J., Kamphaus, R.W., Lahey, B.B., Loeber, R., Christ, M.A.G., Hart, E.L., and Tannenbaum, L.E. 1991, 'Academic underachievement and the disruptive behavior disorders', *Journal of Consulting and Clinical Psychology*, vol. 59, no. 2, pp. 289–94.

Gadow, K.D. and Nolan, E.E. 2002, 'Differences between preschool children with ODD, ADHD, and ODD ADHD symptoms', *Journal of Child Psychology and Psychiatry*, vol. 43, no. 2, pp. 191–201.

Garcia, C.R., Bau, C.H.D., Silva, K.L., Callegari-Jacques, S.M., Salgado, C.A.I., Fischer, A.G., Victor, M.M., Sousa, N.O., Karam, R.G., Rohde, L.A., Belmonte-de-Abreu, P., and Grevet, E.H. 2012, 'The burdened life of adults with ADHD: Impairment beyond comorbidity', *European Psychiatry*, vol. 27, no. 5, pp. 309–13.

Geissler, J. and Lesch, K. 2011, 'A lifetime of attention-deficit/hyperactivity disorder: diagnostic challenges, treatment and neurobiological mechanisms', *Expert Review of Neurotherapeutics*, vol. 11, no. 10, pp. 1467–84.

Ghuman, J.K., Ginsburg, G.S., Subramaniam, G., Ghuman, H.S., Kau, A.S., and Riddle, M.A. 2001, 'Psychostimulants in preschool children with attention-deficit/hyperactivity disorder: Clinical evidence from a developmental disorders institution', *Journal of the American Academy of Child and Adolescent Psychiatry*, vol. 40, no. 5, pp. 516–24.

Gillberg, C., Gillberg, I.C., Rasmussen, P., Kadesjö, B., Söderström, H., Råstam, M., Johnson, M., Rothenberger, A., and Niklasson, L. 2004, 'Co-existing disorders in ADHD—implications for diagnosis and intervention', *European Child and Adolescent Psychiatry*, vol. 13, no. 1, pp. i80–i92.

Glutting, J.J., Youngstrom, E.A., and Watkins, M.W. 2005, 'ADHD and college students: Exploratory and confirmatory factor structures with student and parent data', *Psychological Assessment*, vol. 17, no. 1, p. 44.

Greene, R.W. and Ablon, J.S. 2001, 'What does the MTA study tell us about effective psychosocial treatment for ADHD?', *Journal of Clinical Child Psychology*, vol. 30, no. 1, pp. 114–21.

Greene, R.W., Biederman, J., Faraone, S.V., Sienna, M., and Garcia-Jetton, J. 1997, 'Adolescent outcome of boys with attention-deficit/hyperactivity disorder and social disability: Results from a 4-year longitudinal follow-up study', *Journal of Consulting and Clinical Psychology*, vol. 65, no. 5, p. 758.

Greenhill, L., Kollins, S., Abikoff, H., McCracken, J., Riddle, M., Swanson, J., McGough, J., Wigal, S., Wigal, T., Vitiello, B., Skrobala, A., Posner, K., Ghuman, J., Cunningham, C., Davies, M., Chuang, S., and Cooper, T. 2006, 'Efficacy and safety of immediate-release methylphenidate treatment for preschoolers with ADHD', *Journal of the American Academy of Child and Adolescent Psychiatry*, vol. 45, no. 11, pp. 1284–93.

Gruber, R., Sadeh, A., and Raviv, A. 2000, 'Instability of sleep patterns in children with Attention-Deficit/Hyperactivity Disorder', *Journal of the American Academy of Child and Adolescent Psychiatry*, vol. 39, no. 4, pp. 495–501.

Gudjonsson, G.H., Sigurdsson, J.F., Sigfusdottir, I.D., and Young, S. 2014, 'A national epidemiological study of offending and its relationship with ADHD symptoms and associated risk factors', *Journal of Attention Disorders*, vol. 18, no. 1, pp. 3–13.

Hakkaart-van Roijen, L., Zwirs, B., Bouwmans, C., Tan, S.S., Schulpen, T., Vlasveld, L., and Buitelaar, J. 2007, 'Societal costs and quality of life of children suffering from attention deficit hyperactivity disorder (ADHD)', *European Child and Adolescent Psychiatry*, vol. 16, no. 5, pp. 316–26.

Halperin, J.M., Bédard, A.V., and Curchack-Lichtin, J.T. 2012, 'Preventive interventions for ADHD: A neurodevelopmental perspective', *Neurotherapeutics*, vol. 9, no. 3, pp. 531–41.

Hanushek, E.A., Schwerdt, G., Wiederhold, S., and Woessmann, L. 2013, *Returns to skills around the world: Evidence from PIAAC*, Cambridge, MA, NBER Working Paper No. 19762.

Harmon, C., Oosterbeek, H., and Walker, I. 2003, 'The returns to education: Microeconomics', *Journal of Economic Surveys*, vol. 17, no. 2, pp. 115–56.

Hartman, R.R., Stage, S.A., and Webster-Stratton, C. 2003, 'A growth curve analysis of parent training outcomes: Examining the influence of child risk factors (inattention, impulsivity, and hyperactivity problems), parental and family risk factors', *Journal of Child Psychology and Psychiatry*, vol. 44, no. 3, pp. 388–98.

Heckman, J.J. 2008, 'The case for investing in disadvantaged young children', in *Big Ideas for Children: Investing in our Nation's Future*, Washington, DC, First Focus, pp. 49–58.

Heckman, J.J., Ichimura, H., Smith, J., and Todd, P. 1998, 'Characterizing selection bias using experimental data', Econometrica, vol. 66, no. 5, pp. 1017–98.

Heckman, J.J., Ichimura, H., and Todd, P. 1998, 'Matching as an econometric evaluation estimator', *The Review of Economic Studies*, vol. 65, no. 2, pp. 261–94.

Heckman, J.J., Moon, S.H., Pinto, R., Savelyev, P., and Yavitz, A. 2010, *A new cost-benefit and rate of return analysis for the Perry Preschool Program: A summary*, Bonn, IZA Policy Paper No. 17.

Hesslinger, B., Thiel, T., Tebartz van Elst, L., Hennig, J., and Ebert, D. 2001, 'Attention-deficit disorder in adults with or without hyperactivity: Where is the difference? A study in humans using short echo ^{1}H-magnetic resonance spectroscopy', *Neuroscience Letters*, vol. 304, no. 1, pp. 117–19.

Hinnenthal, J.A., Perwien, A.R., and Sterling, K.L. 2005, 'A comparison of service use and costs among adults with ADHD and adults with other chronic diseases', *Psychiatric Services*, vol. 56, no. 12, pp. 1593–9.

Hinshaw, S.P. 2002, 'Preadolescent girls with attention-deficit/hyperactivity disorder: I. Background characteristics, comorbidity, cognitive and social functioning, and parenting practices', *Journal of Consulting and Clinical Psychology*, vol. 70, no. 5, pp. 1086–98.

Hinshaw, S.P. 2007, 'Moderators and mediators of treatment outcome for youth with ADHD: Understanding for whom and how interventions work', *Ambulatory Pediatrics*, vol. 7, no. 1, pp. 91–100.

Hinshaw, S.P. and Melnick, S.M. 1995, 'Peer relationships in boys with attention-deficit hyperactivity disorder with and without comorbid aggression', *Development and Psychopathology*, vol. 7, no. 4, pp. 627–47.

Hodgkins, P., Montejano, L., Sasane, R., and Huse, D. 2011, 'Cost of illness and comorbidities in adults diagnosed with attention-deficit/hyperactivity disorder: A retrospective analysis', *The Primary Care Companion to CNS Disorders*, vol. 13, no. 2, doi 10.4088/PCC.10m01030.

Hodgson, T.A. and Meiners, M.R. 1982, 'Cost-of-illness methodology: A guide to current practices and procedures', *The Milbank Memorial Fund Quarterly. Health and Society*, vol. 60, no. 3, pp. 429–62.

Hughes, C.H. and Ensor, R.A. 2009, 'How do families help or hinder the emergence of early executive function?', *New Directions for Child and Adolescent Development*, vol. 2009, no. 123, pp. 35–50.

Inoue, K., Nadaoka, T., Oiji, A., Morioka, Y., Totsuka, S., Kanbayashi, Y., and Hukui, T. 1998, 'Clinical evaluation of attention-deficit hyperactivity disorder by objective quantitative measures', *Child Psychiatry and Human Development*, vol. 28, no. 3, pp. 179–88.

Jacobsen, R.H. 2013, *Samfundsøkonomisk cost-benefit-analyse af kriminalpræventive indsatser*, Copenhagen, Centre for Economic and Business Research.

James, W. 1880, 'Great men, great thoughts, and the environment', Lecture delivered before the Harvard Natural History Society (published in *Atlantic Monthly*, October, 1880).

Jensen, V.M. and Rasmussen, A.W. 2011, 'Danish education registers', *Scandinavian Journal of Public Health*, vol. 39, no. 7 Suppl, pp. 91–4.

Jerome, L., Segal, A., and Habinski, L. 2006, 'What we know about ADHD and driving risk: A literature review, meta-analysis and critique', *Journal of the Canadian Academy of Child and Adolescent Psychiatry = Journal de l'Academie canadienne de psychiatrie de l'enfant et de l'adolescent*, vol. 15, no. 3, pp. 105–25.

Johnsen, N.F., Koch, M.B., Davidsen, M., and Juel, K. 2014, *De samfundsøkonomiske omkostninger ved artrose*, Odense, Danish National Institute of Public Health.

Johnston, C. and Jassy, J.S. 2007, 'Attention-deficit/hyperactivity disorder and oppositional/conduct problems: Links to parent–child interactions', *Journal of the Canadian Academy of Child and Adolescent Psychiatry = Journal de l'Academie canadienne de psychiatrie de l'enfant et de l'adolescent*, vol. 16, no. 2, pp. 74–9.

Johnston, C. and Mash, E.J. 2001, 'Families of children with attention-deficit/hyperactivity disorder: Review and recommendations for future research', *Clinical Child and Family Psychology Review*, vol. 4, no. 3, pp. 183–207.

Johnston, C., Mash, E.J., Miller, N., and Ninowski, J.E. 2012, 'Parenting in adults with attention-deficit/hyperactivity disorder (ADHD)', *Clinical Psychology Review*, vol. 32, no. 4, pp. 215–28.

Jones, K., Daley, D., Hutchings, J., Bywater, T., and Eames, C. 2007, 'Efficacy of the Incredible Years Basic parent training programme as an early intervention for children with conduct problems and ADHD', *Child: Care, Health and Development*, vol. 33, no. 6, pp. 749–56.

Jones, K., Daley, D., Hutchings, J., Bywater, T., and Eames, C. 2008, 'Efficacy of the Incredible Years Programme as an early intervention for children with conduct problems and ADHD: Long-term follow-up', *Child: Care, Health and Development*, vol. 34, no. 3, pp. 380–90.

Kadesjö, C., Kadesjö, B., Hägglöf, B., and Gillberg, C. 2001, 'ADHD in Swedish 3- to 7-year-old children', *Journal of the American Academy of Child and Adolescent Psychiatry*, vol. 40, no. 9, pp. 1021–8.

Kawatkar, A.A., Knight, T.K., Moss, R.A., Sikirica, V., Chu, L., Hodgkins, P., Erder, M.H., and Nichol, M.B. 2014, 'Impact of mental health comorbidities on health care utilization and expenditure in a large US managed care adult population with ADHD', *Value in Health*, vol. 17, no. 6, pp. 661–8.

Keown, L.J. 2012, 'Predictors of boys' ADHD symptoms from early to middle child-hood: The role of father–child and mother–child interactions', *Journal of Abnormal Child Psychology*, vol. 40, no. 4, pp. 569–81.

Kessler, R., Adler, L., Barkley, R., Biederman, J., Conners, C., Demler, O., Faraone, S., Greenhill, L., Howes, M., and Secnik, K. 2006, 'The prevalence and correlates of adult ADHD in the United States: Results from the National Comorbidity Survey Replication', *American Journal of Psychiatry*, vol. 163, no. 4, pp. 716–23.

Kildemoes, H.W., Sorensen, H.T., and Hallas, J. 2011, 'The Danish National Prescription Registry', *Scandinavian Journal of Public Health*, vol. 39, no. 7 Suppl, pp. 38–41.

Kollins, S., Greenhill, L., Swanson, J., Wigal, S., Abikoff, H., McCracken, J., Riddle, M., McGough, J., Vitiello, B., Wigal, T., Skrobala, A., Posner, K., Ghuman, J., Davies, M., Cunningham, C., and Bauzo, A. 2006, 'Rationale, design, and methods of the Preschool ADHD Treatment Study (PATS)', *Journal of the American Academy of Child and Adolescent Psychiatry*, vol. 45, no. 11, pp. 1275–83.

Konrad, K., Neufang, S., Thiel, C.M., Specht, K., Hanisch, C., Fan, J., Herpertz-Dahlmann, B., and Fink, G.R. 2005, 'Development of attentional networks: An fMRI study with children and adults', *NeuroImage*, vol. 28, no. 2, pp. 429–39.

Kooij, S.J., Bejerot, S., Blackwell, A., Caci, H., Casas-Brugue, M., Carpentier, P.J., Edvinsson, D., Fayyad, J., Foeken, K., Fitzgerald, M., Gaillac, V., Ginsberg, Y., Henry, C., Krause, J., Lensing, M.B., Manor, I., Niederhofer, H., Nunes-Filipe, C., Ohlmeier, M.D., Oswald, P., Pallanti, S., Pehlivanidis, A., Ramos-Quiroga, J.A., Rastam, M., Ryffel-Rawak, D., Stes, S., and Asherson, P. 2010, 'European consensus statement on diagnosis and treatment of adult ADHD: The European Network Adult ADHD', *BMC Psychiatry*, vol. 10, no. 67, doi 10.1186/1471-244X-10-67.

Kotsopoulos, N., Connolly, M.P., Sobanski, E., and Postma, M.J. 2013, 'The fiscal consequences of ADHD in Germany: A quantitative analysis based on differences in educational attainment and lifetime earnings', *The Journal of Mental Health Policy and Economics*, vol. 16, no. 1, pp. 27–33.

Krummel, D.A., Seligson, F.H., Guthrie, H.A., and Gans, D.A. 1996, 'Hyperactivity: Is candy causal?', *Critical Reviews in Food Science and Nutrition*, vol. 36, no. 1–2, pp. 31–47.

Kuriyan, A.B., Pelham, W.E. Jr, Molina, B.S., Waschbusch, D.A., Gnagy, E.M., Sibley, M.H., Babinski, D.E., Walther, C., Cheong, J., and Yu, J. 2013, 'Young adult educational and vocational outcomes of children diagnosed with ADHD', *Journal of Abnormal Child Psychology*, vol. 41, no. 1, pp. 27–41.

Kustanovich, V., Merriman, B., McGough, J., McCracken, J., Smalley, S., and Nelson, S. 2003, 'Biased paternal transmission of SNAP-25 risk alleles in attention-deficit hyperactivity disorder', *Molecular Psychiatry*, vol. 8, no. 3, pp. 309–15.

Kvist, A.P., Nielsen, H.S., and Simonsen, M. 2013, 'The importance of children's ADHD for parents' relationship stability and labor supply', *Social Science and Medicine*, vol. 88, pp. 30–8.

Lahey, B.B., Pelham, W.E., Loney, J., Kipp, H., Ehrhardt, A., Lee, S.S., Willcutt, E.G., Hartung, C.M., Chronis, A., and Massetti, G. 2004, 'Three-year predictive validity of DSM-IV attention deficit hyperactivity disorder in children diagnosed at 4–6 years of age', *American Journal of Psychiatry*, vol. 161, no. 11, pp. 2014–20.

Lahey, B.B., Pelham, W.E., Stein, M.A., Loney, J., Trapani, C., Nugent, K., Kipp, H., Schmidt, E., Lee, S., and Cale, M. 1998, 'Validity of DSM-IV Attention-Deficit/Hyperactivity Disorder for younger children', *Journal of the American Academy of Child and Adolescent Psychiatry*, vol. 37, no. 7, pp. 695–702.

Langberg, J.M., Molina, B.S., Arnold, L.E., Epstein, J.N., Altaye, M., Hinshaw, S.P., Swanson, J.M., Wigal, T., and Hechtman, L. 2011, 'Patterns and predictors of adolescent academic achievement and performance in a sample of children with attention-deficit/hyperactivity disorder', *Journal of Clinical Child and Adolescent Psychology*, vol. 40, no. 4, pp. 519–31.

Lange, H., Buse, J., Bender, S., Siegert, J., Knopf, H., and Roessner, V. 2014, 'Accident proneness in children and adolescents affected by ADHD and the impact of medication', *Journal of Attention Disorders*, published online, doi 10.1177/1087054713518237.

Larg, A. and Moss, J.R. 2011, 'Cost-of-illness studies', *PharmacoEconomics*, vol. 29, no. 8, pp. 653–71.

Lavigne, J.V., Gibbons, R.D., Christoffel, K.K., Arend, R., Rosenbaum, D., Binns, H., Dawson, N., Sobel, H., and Isaacs, C. 1996, 'Prevalence rates and correlates of psychiatric disorders among preschool children', *Journal of the American Academy of Child and Adolescent Psychiatry*, vol. 35, no. 2, pp. 204–14.

Le, H.H., Hodgkins, P., Postma, M.J., Kahle, J., Sikirica, V., Setyawan, J., Erder, M.H., and Doshi, J.A. 2014, 'Economic impact of childhood/adolescent ADHD in a European setting: The Netherlands as a reference case', *European Child and Adolescent Psychiatry*, vol. 23, no. 7, pp. 587–98.

Lee, S.S., Humphreys, K.L., Flory, K., Liu, R., and Glass, K. 2011, 'Prospective association of childhood attention-deficit/hyperactivity disorder (ADHD) and substance use and abuse/dependence: A meta-analytic review', *Clinical Psychology Review*, vol. 31, no. 3, pp. 328–41.

Leibson, C.L., Katusic, S.K., Barbaresi, W.J., Ransom, J., and O'Brien, P.C. 2001, 'Use and costs of medical care for children and adolescents with and without attention-deficit/hyperactivity disorder', *JAMA*, vol. 285, no. 1, pp. 60–6.

Lichtenstein, P., Halldner, L., Zetterqvist, J., Sjölander, A., Serlachius, E., Fazel, S., Långström, N., and Larsson, H. 2012, 'Medication for attention deficit–hyperactivity disorder and criminality', *New England Journal of Medicine*, vol. 367, no. 21, pp. 2006–14.

Lifford, K.J., Harold, G.T., and Thapar, A. 2008, 'Parent–child relationships and ADHD symptoms: A longitudinal analysis', *Journal of Abnormal Child Psychology*, vol. 36, no. 2, pp. 285–96.

Loe, I.M. and Feldman, H.M. 2007, 'Academic and educational outcomes of children with ADHD', *Journal of Pediatric Psychology*, vol. 32, no. 6, pp. 643–54.

Luppa, M., Heinrich, S., Angermeyer, M.C., König, H., and Riedel-Heller, S.G. 2007, 'Cost-of-illness studies of depression: A systematic review', *Journal of Affective Disorders*, vol. 98, no. 1, pp. 29–43.

Lynge, E., Sandegaard, J.L., and Rebolj, M. 2011, 'The Danish National Patient Register', *Scandinavian Journal of Public Health*, vol. 39, no. 7 Suppl, pp. 30–3.

Madsen, H.B. 2007, *Sundhedsret*, 1st edn, Copenhagen, Jurist- og Økonomforbundets Forlag.

Mannuzza, S. and Klein, R.G. 2000, 'Long-term prognosis in attention-deficit/hyperactivity disorder', *Child and Adolescent Psychiatric Clinics of North America*, vol. 9, no. 3, pp. 711–26.

Mannuzza, S., Klein, R.G., Bessler, A., Malloy, P., and LaPadula, M. 1993, 'Adult outcome of hyperactive boys: Educational achievement, occupational rank, and psychiatric status', *Archives of General Psychiatry*, vol. 50, no. 7, pp. 565–76.

Mariani, M.A. and Barkley, R.A. 1997, 'Neuropsychological and academic functioning in preschool boys with attention deficit hyperactivity disorder', *Developmental Neuropsychology*, vol. 13, no. 1, pp. 111–29.

Martinussen, R., Hayden, J., Hogg-Johnson, S., and Tannock, R. 2005, 'A meta-analysis of working memory impairments in children with attention-deficit/hyperactivity disorder', *Journal of the American Academy of Child and Adolescent Psychiatry*, vol. 44, no. 4, pp. 377–84.

Matthys, F., Stes, S., van den Brink, W., Joostens, P., Möbius, D., Tremmery, S., and Sabbe, B. 2014, 'Guideline for screening, diagnosis and treatment of ADHD in adults with substance use disorders', *International Journal of Mental Health and Addiction*, vol. 12, no. 5, pp. 629–47.

Matza, L.S., Paramore, C., and Prasad, M. 2005, 'A review of the economic burden of ADHD', *Cost Effectiveness and Resource Allocation*, vol. 3, no. 1, pp. 1–9.

McCann, D., Barrett, A., Cooper, A., Crumpler, D., Dalen, L., Grimshaw, K., Kitchin, E., Lok, K., Porteous, L., Prince, E., Sonuga-Barke, E., Stevenson, J., and Warner, J.O. 2007, 'Food additives and hyperactive behaviour in 3-year-old and 8/9-year-old children in the community: A randomised, double-blinded, placebo-controlled trial', *The Lancet*, vol. 370, no. 9598, pp. 1560–7.

McGee, R., Williams, S., and Feehan, M. 1992, 'Attention deficit disorder and age of onset of problem behaviors', *Journal of Abnormal Child Psychology*, vol. 20, no. 5, pp. 487–502.

McGorry, P. 2013, 'Prevention, innovation and implementation science in mental health: The next wave of reform', *The British Journal of Psychiatry. Supplement*, vol. 202, no. s54, pp. 3–4.

Michelson, D., Faries, D., Wernicke, J., Kelsey, D., Kendrick, K., Sallee, F.R., and Spencer, T. (Atomoxetine ADHD Study Group). 2001, 'Atomoxetine in the treatment of children and adolescents with attention-deficit/hyperactivity disorder: A randomized, placebo-controlled, dose-response study', *Pediatrics*, vol. 108, no. 5, p. E83.

Ministeriet for Sundhed og Forebyggelse 2012, *Lov om udrednings- og behandlingsgaranti* (Law of assessment and treatment guarantee, Law no. 1401, 23rd December, 2012).

Moncrieff, J. and Timimi, S. 2010, 'Is ADHD a valid diagnosis in adults? No', *British Medical Journal (Clinical Research Edition)*, vol. 340, p. c547.

Monitoreringsgruppen 2013. Available at: <http://www.monitoreringsgruppen.dk/>.

Mori, L. and Peterson, L. 1995, 'Knowledge of safety of high and low active-impulsive boys: Implications for child injury prevention', *Journal of Clinical Child Psychology*, vol. 24, no. 4, pp. 370–6.

Morrell, J. and Murray, L. 2003, 'Parenting and the development of conduct disorder and hyperactive symptoms in childhood: A prospective longitudinal study from

2 months to 8 years', *Journal of Child Psychology and Psychiatry*, vol. 44, no. 4, pp. 489–508.

Mors, O., Perto, G.P., and Mortensen, P.B. 2011, 'The Danish psychiatric central research register', *Scandinavian Journal of Public Health*, vol. 39, no. 7, pp. 54–7.

MTA Group: Jensen, P. S., Arnold, L. E., Richter, J. E., Severe, J. B., Vereen, D., Vitiello, B., and Conners, C.K. 1999, 'Moderators and mediators of treatment response for children with attention-deficit/hyperactivity disorder: The multimodal treatment study of children with Attention-Deficit/Hyperactivity Disorder', *Archives of General Psychiatry*, vol. 56, no. 12, pp. 1088–96.

Munk-Jørgensen, P. and Andersen, B. 2009, 'Diagnoses and dropout among patients of Danish psychiatrists in private practice', *Psychiatric Services*, vol. 60, no. 12, pp. 1680–2.

Murphy, K. and Barkley, R.A. 1996, 'Attention deficit hyperactivity disorder adults: Comorbidities and adaptive impairments', *Comprehensive Psychiatry*, vol. 37, no. 6, pp. 393–401.

National Institute for Clinical Excellence 2000, *Guidance on the use of methylphenidate (Ritalin, Equasym) for attention deficit/hyperactivity disorder (ADHD) in childhood*, London, National Institute for Clinical Excellence.

National Institute for Clinical Excellence 2008, *Attention Deficit/Hyperactivity Disorder: Diagnosis and Management of ADHD in Children, Young People and Adults*. CG72. London, National Institute for Clinical Excellence.

Ng, C.S., Lee, J.Y., Toh, M.P., and Ko, Y. 2014, 'Cost-of-illness studies of diabetes mellitus: A systematic review', *Diabetes Research and Clinical Practice*, vol. 105. no. 2, pp. 151–63.

Nigg, J.T. 2001, 'Is ADHD a disinhibitory disorder?', *Psychological Bulletin*, vol. 127, no. 5, pp. 571–98.

Nigg, J.T. and Craver, L. 2014, 'Commentary: ADHD and social disadvantage: An inconvenient truth?—A reflection on Russell et al. (2014) and Larsson et al. (2014)', *Journal of Child Psychology and Psychiatry*, vol. 55, no. 5, pp. 446–7.

Nijmeijer, J.S., Minderaa, R.B., Buitelaar, J.K., Mulligan, A., Hartman, C.A., and Hoekstra, P.J. 2008, 'Attention-deficit/hyperactivity disorder and social dysfunctioning', *Clinical Psychology Review*, vol. 28, no. 4, pp. 692–708.

OECD 2014, *Education at a Glance 2014: OECD Indicators*, Paris, OECD Publishing.

Olejaz, M., Juul, A., Rudkjøbing, A., Birk, H.O., and Krasnik, A. 2012. 'Denmark: Health System Review' *Health Systems in Transition*, vol. 14, no. 2, pp. 1–192.

Parnas, J., Mors, O., and Kragh-Sørensen, P. 2009, 'Psykiatriens teoretiske fundament: Sygdomsbegreb, klassifikation og diagnostik', in *Klinisk Psykiatri*, 3rd edn, Copenhagen, Munksgård, pp. 29–76.

Patel, V., Belkin, G.S., Chockalingam, A., Cooper, J., Saxena, S., and Unützer, J. 2013, 'Grand challenges: Integrating mental health services into priority health care platforms'. *PLoS Medicine*, vol. 10, no. 5, doi e1001448.

Pelham, W.E., Foster, E.M., and Robb, J.A. 2007, 'The economic impact of attention-deficit/hyperactivity disorder in children and adolescents', *Ambulatory Pediatrics*, vol. 7, no. 1, pp. 121–31.

Pelham, W.E. Jr, Wheeler, T., and Chronis, A. 1998, 'Empirically supported psycho-social treatments for attention deficit hyperactivity disorder', *Journal of Clinical Child Psychology*, vol. 27, no. 2, pp. 190–205.

Perring, C. 1997, 'Medicating children: The case of Ritalin', *Bioethics*, vol. 11, no. 3–4, pp. 228–40.

Peterson, B.S., Pine, D.S., Cohen, P., and Brook, J.S. 2001, 'Prospective, longitudinal study of tic, obsessive-compulsive, and attention-deficit/hyperactivity disorders in an epidemiological sample', *Journal of the American Academy of Child and Adolescent Psychiatry*, vol. 40, no. 6, pp. 685–95.

Pierce, E.W., Ewing, L.J., and Campbell, S.B. 1999, 'Diagnostic status and symptomatic behavior of hard-to-manage preschool children in middle childhood and early adolescence', *Journal of Clinical Child Psychology*, vol. 28, no. 1, pp. 44–57.

Pisterman, S., McGrath, P., Firestone, P., Goodman, J.T., Webster, I., and Mallory, R. 1989, 'Outcome of parent-mediated treatment of preschoolers with attention deficit disorder with hyperactivity', *Journal of Consulting and Clinical Psychology*, vol. 57, no. 5, pp. 628–35.

Polanczyk, G., de Lima, M., Horta, B., Biederman, J., and Rohde, L. 2007, 'The worldwide prevalence of ADHD: A systematic review and metaregression analysis', *American Journal of Psychiatry*, vol. 164, no. 6, pp. 942–8.

Polanczyk, G.V., Willcutt, E.G., Salum, G.A., Kieling, C., and Rohde, L.A. 2014, 'ADHD prevalence estimates across three decades: An updated systematic review and meta-regression analysis', *International Journal of Epidemiology*, vol. 43, no. 2, pp. 434–42.

Pollard, S., Ward, E.M., and Barkley, R.A. 1984, 'The effects of parent training and Ritalin on the parent–child interactions of hyperactive boys', *Child and Family Behavior Therapy*, vol. 5, no. 4, pp. 51–70.

Psykiatriudvalget 2013, *Indsatsen for mennesker med psykiske lidelser—udvikling i diagnoser og behandling, Bilagsrapport 2*. Available at: <http://www.sum.dk/Aktuelt/Nyheder/Psykiatri/2013/Oktober/~/media/Filer%20-%20Publikationer_i_pdf/2013/Rapport-psykiatriudvalg-okt-2013/21-10-2013/21102013Indsatsenformenneskermedpsylisk elidelserbilag2web.ashx>.

Rapport, M.D., Scanlan, S.W., and Denney, C.B. 1999, 'Attention-deficit/hyperactivity disorder and scholastic achievement: A model of dual developmental pathways', *Journal of Child Psychology and Psychiatry*, vol. 40, no. 8, pp. 1169–83.

Rosenbaum, P.R. and Rubin, D.B. 1983, 'The central role of the propensity score in observational studies for causal effects'. *Biometrika*, vol. 70, no. 1, pp. 41–55.

Rubia, K., Smith, A.B., Taylor, E., and Brammer, M. 2007, 'Linear age-correlated functional development of right inferior fronto-striato-cerebellar networks during response inhibition and anterior cingulate during error-related processes', *Human Brain Mapping*, vol. 28, no. 11, pp. 1163–77.

Rubin, D.B. 1974, 'Estimating causal effects of treatments in randomized and nonrandomized studies', *Journal of Educational Psychology*, vol. 66, no. 5, pp. 688–701.

Russell, G., Ford, T., Rosenberg, R., and Kelly, S. 2014, 'The association of attention deficit hyperactivity disorder with socioeconomic disadvantage: Alternative explanations and evidence', *Journal of Child Psychology and Psychiatry*, vol. 55, no. 5, pp. 436–45.

Sachdev, P. 1999, 'Attention deficit hyperactivity disorder in adults', *Psychological Medicine*, vol. 29, no. 3, pp. 507–14.

Sado, M., Inagaki, A., Koreki, A., Knapp, M., Kissane, L.A., Mimura, M., and Yoshimura, K. 2013, 'The cost of schizophrenia in Japan', *Neuropsychiatric Disease and Treatment*, vol. 9, pp. 787–98.

Schachar, R., Mota, V.L., Logan, G.D., Tannock, R., and Klim, P. 2000, 'Confirmation of an inhibitory control deficit in attention-deficit/hyperactivity disorder', *Journal of Abnormal Child Psychology*, vol. 28, no. 3, pp. 227–35.

Schiötz, M.L., Søgaard, J., Vallgårda, S., and Krasnik, A. 2010, 'Internationale sammenligninger af sundhedssystemer', *Ugeskrift for Laeger*, vol. 172, no. 10, pp. 771–4.

Secnik, K., Swensen, A., and Lage, M.J. 2005, 'Comorbidities and costs of adult patients diagnosed with attention-deficit hyperactivity disorder', *PharmacoEconomics*, vol. 23, no. 1, pp. 93–102.

Seidler, F., Levin, E., Lappi, S., and Slotkin, T. 1992, 'Fetal nicotine exposure ablates the ability of postnatal nicotine challenge to release norepinephrine from rat brain regions', *Developmental Brain Research*, vol. 69, no. 2, pp. 288–91.

Seipp, C.M. and Johnston, C. 2005, 'Mother–son interactions in families of boys with attention-deficit/hyperactivity disorder with and without oppositional behavior', *Journal of Abnormal Child Psychology*, vol. 33, no. 1, pp. 87–98.

Simon, V., Czobor, P., Balint, S., Meszaros, A., and Bitter, I. 2009, 'Prevalence and correlates of adult attention-deficit hyperactivity disorder: Meta-analysis', *The British Journal of Psychiatry: The Journal of Mental Science*, vol. 194, no. 3, pp. 204–11.

Smith, A., Taylor, E., Warner Rogers, J., Newman, S., and Rubia, K. 2002, 'Evidence for a pure time perception deficit in children with ADHD', *Journal of Child Psychology and Psychiatry*, vol. 43, no. 4, pp. 529–42.

Sobanski, E. 2006, 'Psychiatric comorbidity in adults with attention-deficit/hyperactivity disorder (ADHD)', *European Archives of Psychiatry and Clinical Neuroscience*, vol. 256, no. 1, pp. i26–i31.

Søgaard, J., Frølich, A., and Krasnik, A. 2011, 'Sundhedsudgifter i USA, Kaiser Permanente, Danmark, Storbritannien og andre lande', in A. Frølich (ed.), *Hvad kan det danske sundhedsvæsen lære af Kaiser Permanente? En sammenligning mellem den amerikanske forsikringsorganisation Kaiser Permanente og det danske sundhedsvaesen*, Odense, Syddansk Universitetsforlag, pp. 61–75.

Solanto, M.V., Abikoff, H., Sonuga-Barke, E., Schachar, R., Logan, G.D., Wigal, T., Hechtman, L., Hinshaw, S., and Turkel, E. 2001, 'The ecological validity of delay aversion and response inhibition as measures of impulsivity in AD/HD: A supplement to the NIMH multimodal treatment study of AD/HD', *Journal of Abnormal Child Psychology*, vol. 29, no. 3, pp. 215–28.

Sonuga-Barke, E.J. 2002, 'Psychological heterogeneity in AD/HD—a dual pathway model of behaviour and cognition', *Behavioural Brain Research*, vol. 130, no. 1, pp. 29–36.

Sonuga-Barke, E.J. 2004, 'On the reorganization of incentive structure to promote delay tolerance: A therapeutic possibility for AD/HD?', *Neural Plasticity*, vol. 11, no. 1–2, pp. 23–8.

Sonuga-Barke, E.J., Auerbach, J., Campbell, S.B., Daley, D., and Thompson, M. 2005, 'Varieties of preschool hyperactivity: Multiple pathways from risk to disorder', *Developmental Science*, vol. 8, no. 2, pp. 141–50.

Sonuga-Barke, E.J., Brandeis, D., Cortese, S., Daley, D., Ferrin, M., Holtmann, M., Stevenson, J., Danckaerts, M., Van der Oord, S., Döpfner, M., Dittmann, R., Simonoff, E., Zuddas, A., Banaschewski, T., Buitelaar, J., Coghill, D., Hollis, C., Konofal, E., Lecendreux, M., Wong, I., and Sergeant, J. 2013, 'Nonpharmacological interventions for ADHD: Systematic review and meta-analyses of randomized controlled trials of dietary and psychological treatments', *American Journal of Psychiatry*, vol. 170, no. 3, pp. 275–89.

Sonuga-Barke, E.J., Dalen, L., and Remington, B. 2003, 'Do executive deficits and delay aversion make independent contributions to preschool attention-deficit/hyperactivity disorder symptoms?', *Journal of the American Academy of Child and Adolescent Psychiatry*, vol. 42, no. 11, pp. 1335–42.

Sonuga-Barke, E.J., Daley, D., Thompson, M., Laver-Bradbury, C., and Weeks, A. 2001, 'Parent-based therapies for preschool attention-deficit/hyperactivity disorder: A randomized, controlled trial with a community sample', *Journal of the American Academy of Child and Adolescent Psychiatry*, vol. 40, no. 4, pp. 402–8.

Sonuga-Barke, E. J. and Halperin, J. M. 2010, 'Developmental phenotypes and causal pathways in attention deficit/hyperactivity disorder: Potential targets for early intervention?', *Journal of Child Psychology and Psychiatry*, vol. 51, no. 4, pp. 368–89.

Sonuga-Barke, E.J., Houlberg, K., and Hall, M. 1994, 'When is 'impulsiveness' not impulsive? The case of hyperactive children's cognitive style', *Journal of Child Psychology and Psychiatry*, vol. 35, no. 7, pp. 1247–53.

Sonuga-Barke, E.J., Lamparelli, M., Stevenson, J., Thompson, M., and Henry, A. 1994, 'Behaviour problems and pre-school intellectual attainment: The associations of hyperactivity and conduct problems', *Journal of Child Psychology and Psychiatry*, vol. 35, no. 5, pp. 949–60.

Sonuga-Barke, E.J., Lasky-Su, J., Neale, B.M., Oades, R., Chen, W., Franke, B., Buitelaar, J., Banaschewski, T., Ebstein, R., and Gill, M. 2008, 'Does parental expressed emotion moderate genetic effects in ADHD? An exploration using a genome wide association scan', *American Journal of Medical Genetics Part B: Neuropsychiatric Genetics*, vol. 147, no. 8, pp. 1359–68.

Sonuga-Barke, E.J., Minocha, K., Taylor, E.A., and Sandberg, S. 1993, 'Inter-ethnic bias in teachers' ratings of childhood hyperactivity', *British Journal of Developmental Psychology*, vol. 11, no. 2, pp. 187–200.

Sonuga-Barke, E.J., Williams, E., Hall, M., and Saxton, T. 1996, 'Hyperactivity and delay aversion III: The effect on cognitive style of imposing delay after errors', *Journal of Child Psychology and Psychiatry*, vol. 37, no. 2, pp. 189–94.

Span, S.A., Earleywine, M., and Strybel, T.Z. 2002, 'Confirming the factor structure of attention deficit hyperactivity disorder symptoms in adult, nonclinical samples', *Journal of Psychopathology and Behavioral Assessment*, vol. 24, no. 2, pp. 129–36.

Speltz, M.L., McClellan, J., DeKlyen, M., and Jones, K. 1999, 'Preschool boys with oppositional defiant disorder: Clinical presentation and diagnostic change', *Journal of the American Academy of Child and Adolescent Psychiatry*, vol. 38, no. 7, pp. 838–45.

Spira, E.G. and Fischel, J.E. 2005, 'The impact of preschool inattention, hyperactivity, and impulsivity on social and academic development: A review', *Journal of Child Psychology and Psychiatry*, vol. 46, no. 7, pp. 755–73.

Sprich, S., Biederman, J., Crawford, M.H., Mundy, E., and Faraone, S.V. 2000, 'Adoptive and biological families of children and adolescents with ADHD', *Journal of the American Academy of Child and Adolescent Psychiatry*, vol. 39, no. 11, pp. 1432–7.

Sprich-Buckminster, S., Biederman, J., Milberger, S., Faraone, S.V., and Lehman, B.K. 1993, 'Are perinatal complications relevant to the manifestation of ADD? Issues of comorbidity and familiality', *Journal of the American Academy of Child and Adolescent Psychiatry*, vol. 32, no. 5, pp. 1032–7.

Statens Serum Institut 2012, *Salget af ADHD-medicin fra 2002–2011*, Copenhagen, Statens Serum Institut.

Statistics Denmark 2012, *Indkomster 2010*, Copenhagen, Danmarks Statistik.

Stevens, S.E., Sonuga-Barke, E.J., Kreppner, J.M., Beckett, C., Castle, J., Colvert, E., Groothues, C., Hawkins, A., and Rutter, M. 2008, 'Inattention/overactivity following early severe institutional deprivation: Presentation and associations in early adolescence', *Journal of Abnormal Child Psychology*, vol. 36, no. 3, pp. 385–98.

Sundhedsstyrelsen 2008, *Vejledning om ordination af afhængighedsskabende lægemidler Vejledning nr. 38 af 18. juni 2008*, Copenhagen, Sundhedsstyrelsen.

Sundhedsstyrelsen 2010, *Fokusrapport—vurdering af sikkerheden ved brug af methylphenidat*, Copenhagen, Sundhedsstyrelsen.

Sundhedsstyrelsen 2012, *Faglige retningslinjer for henvisning til psykolog for patienter med let til moderat depression eller let til moderat angst*, Copenhagen, Sundhedsstyrelsen.

Sundhedsstyrelsen 2013, *Specialevejledning børne- og ungdomspsykiatri*, Copenhagen, Sundhedsstyrelsen.

Sundhedsstyrelsen 2014, *National klinisk retningslinje for udredning og behandling af ADHD hos børn og unge—med fokus på diagnoserne 'forstyrrelse af aktivitet og opmærksomhed' og 'Opmærksomhedsforstyrrelse uden hyperaktivitet' i henhold til ICD-10*, Copenhagen, Sundhedsstyrelsen. Available at <http://www.sst.dk>.

Sundhedsstyrelsen 2015, *National klinisk retingslinje for udredning og behandling af ADHD hos voksne–med forstyrrelse af aktivitet og opmaerksomhed samt opmaerksomhedsforstyrrelse uden hyperaktivitet*. Copenhagen, Sundhedsstyrelsen.

Swanson, J.M., Arnold, L.E., Vitiello, B., Abikoff, H.B., Wells, K.C., Pelham, W.E., March, J.S., Hinshaw, S.P., Hoza, B., Epstein, J.N., Elliott, G.R., Greenhill, L.L., Hechtman, L., Jensen, P.S., Kraemer, H.C., Kotkin, R., Molina, B., Newcorn, J.H., Owens, J.H., Severe, J., Hoagwood, K., Simpson, S., Wigal, T., and Hanley, T. 2002, 'Response to commentary on the multimodal treatment study of ADHD (MTA): Mining the meaning of the MTA', *Journal of Abnormal Child Psychology*, vol. 30, no. 4, pp. 327–32.

Swanson, J.M., Greenhill, L., Wigal, T., Kollins, S., Stehli, A., Davies, M., Chuang, S., Vitiello, B., Skrobala, A., Posner, K., Abikoff, H., Oatis, M., McCracken, J., McGough, J., Riddle, M., Ghuman, J., Cunningham, C., and Wigal, S. 2006, 'Stimulant-related reductions of growth rates in the PATS', *Journal of the American Academy of Child and Adolescent Psychiatry*, vol. 45, no. 11, pp. 1304–13.

Swanson, J.M., Kraemer, H.C., Hinshaw, S.P., Arnold, L.E., Conners, C.K., Abikoff, H.B., Clevenger, W., Davies, M., Elliott, G.R., Greenhill, L.L., Hechtman, L., Hoza, B.,

Jensen, P.S., March, J.S., Newcorn, J.H., Owens, E.B., Pelham, W.E., Schiller, E., Severe, J.B., Simpson, S., Vitiello, B., Wells, K., Wigal, T., and Wu, M. 2001, 'Clinical relevance of the primary findings of the MTA: Success rates based on severity of ADHD and ODD symptoms at the end of treatment', *Journal of the American Academy of Child and Adolescent Psychiatry*, vol. 40, no. 2, pp. 168–79.

Szobot, C.M., Rohde, L.A., Bukstein, O., Molina, B.S., Martins, C., Ruaro, P., and Pechansky, F. 2007, 'Is attention-deficit/hyperactivity disorder associated with illicit substance use disorders in male adolescents? A community-based case-control study', *Addiction*, vol. 102, no. 7, pp. 1122–30.

Tarricone, R. 2006, 'Cost-of-illness analysis: What room in health economics?', *Health Policy*, vol. 77, no. 1, pp. 51–63.

Tarver, J., Daley, D., and Sayal, K. 2014, 'Attention-deficit hyperactivity disorder (ADHD): An updated review of the essential facts', *Child: Care, Health and Development*, vol. 40, no. 6, pp. 762–74.

Taylor, N., Fauset, A., and Harpin, V. 2010, 'Young adults with ADHD: An analysis of their service needs on transfer to adult services', *Archives of Disease in Childhood*, vol. 95, no. 7, pp. 513–17.

Thapar, A., Cooper, M., Eyre, O., and Langley, K. 2013, 'Practitioner Review: What have we learnt about the causes of ADHD?', *Journal of Child Psychology and Psychiatry*, vol. 54, no. 1, pp. 3–16.

Thapar, A., Holmes, J., Poulton, K., and Harrington, R. 1999, 'Genetic basis of attention deficit and hyperactivity', *The British Journal of Psychiatry: The Journal of Mental Science*, vol. 174, no. 2, pp. 105–11.

Thapar, A., Langley, K., Asherson, P., and Gill, M. 2007, 'Gene–environment interplay in attention-deficit hyperactivity disorder and the importance of a developmental perspective'. *The British Journal of Psychiatry*, vol. 190, no. 1, pp. 1–3.

Theule, J., Wiener, J., Tannock, R., and Jenkins, J.M. 2013, 'Parenting stress in families of children with ADHD: A meta-analysis', *Journal of Emotional and Behavioral Disorders*, vol. 21, no. 1, pp. 3–17.

Thomsen, P.H. 2011, *Hvordan diagnostiseres og behandles ADHD?* Copenhagen, Institut for Rationel Farmakoterapi. Available at: <http://www.irf.dk/dk/publikationer/rationel_farmakoterapi/maanedsblad/2011/hvordan_diagnostiseres_og_behandles_adhd.htm>.

Thygesen, L.C. and Ersbøll, A.K. 2014, 'When the entire population is the sample: Strengths and limitations in register-based epidemiology', *European Journal of Epidemiology*, vol. 29, no. 8, pp. 551–8.

Vaa, T. 2005, *Impairments, diseases, age and their relative risks of accident involvement: Results from meta-analysis*, Oslo, TØI Report 690.

Vaa, T. 2014, 'ADHD and relative risk of accidents in road traffic: A meta-analysis', *Accident Analysis and Prevention*, vol. 62, pp. 415–25.

van Emmerik-van Oortmerssen, K., van de Glind, G., van Den Brink, W., Smit, F., Crunelle, C.L., Swets, M., and Schoevers, R.A. 2012, 'Prevalence of attention-deficit hyperactivity disorder in substance use disorder patients: A meta-analysis and meta-regression analysis', *Drug and Alcohol Dependence*, vol. 122, no. 1, pp. 11–19.

Watkins, M.W., Lei, P., and Canivez, G.L. 2007, 'Psychometric intelligence and achievement: A cross-lagged panel analysis', *Intelligence*, vol. 35, no. 1, pp. 59–68.

Wigal, T., Greenhill, L., Chuang, S., McGough, J., Vitiello, B., Skrobala, A., Swanson, J., Wigal, S., Abikoff, H., Kollins, S., McCracken, J., Riddle, M., Posner, K., Ghuman, J., Davies, M., Thorp, B., and Stehli, A. 2006, 'Safety and tolerability of methylphenidate in preschool children with ADHD', *Journal of the American Academy of Child and Adolescent Psychiatry*, vol. 45, no. 11, pp. 1294–303.

Wilens, T.E., Biederman, J., and Spencer, T. 1994, 'Clonidine for sleep disturbances associated with attention-deficit hyperactivity disorder', *Journal of the American Academy of Child and Adolescent Psychiatry*, vol. 33, no. 3, pp. 424–6.

Willoughby, M.T. 2003, 'Developmental course of ADHD symptomatology during the transition from childhood to adolescence: A review with recommendations', *Journal of Child Psychology and Psychiatry*, vol. 44, no. 1, pp. 88–106.

Wolraich, M.L., Wibbelsman, C.J., Brown, T.E., Evans, S.W., Gotlieb, E.M., Knight, J.R., Ross, E.C., Shubiner, H.H., Wender, E.H., and Wilens, T. 2005, 'Attention-deficit/ hyperactivity disorder among adolescents: A review of the diagnosis, treatment, and clinical implications', *Pediatrics*, vol. 115, no. 6, pp. 1734–46.

World Health Organization 1992, *The ICD-10 classification of mental and behavioural disorders: Clinical descriptions and diagnostic guidelines*, Geneva, World Health Organization.

World Health Organization 2009, *WHO guide to identifying the economic consequences of disease and injury*, Geneva, World Health Organization.

Zito, J.M., Safer, D.J., Gardner, J.F., Boles, M., and Lynch, F. 2000, 'Trends in the prescribing of psychotropic medications to preschoolers', *JAMA*, vol. 283, no. 8, pp. 1025–30.

Index

Printed and bound by CPI Group (UK) Ltd, Croydon, CR0 4YY